The Significance of
the Ark Narrative

Studies in Biblical Literature

Hemchand Gossai
General Editor

Vol. 129

PETER LANG
New York • Washington, D.C./Baltimore • Bern
Frankfurt am Main • Berlin • Brussels • Vienna • Oxford

James M. Street

The Significance of
the Ark Narrative

Literary Formation and Artistry
in the Book of Chronicles

PETER LANG
New York • Washington, D.C./Baltimore • Bern
Frankfurt am Main • Berlin • Brussels • Vienna • Oxford

Library of Congress Cataloging-in-Publication Data

Street, James M.
The significance of the ark narrative: literary formation and
artistry in the book of Chronicles / James M. Street.
p. cm. — (Studies in biblical literature; v. 129)
Includes bibliographical references and index.
1. Bible. O.T. Chronicles, 1st, XV–XVI—Criticism, Narrative.
2. Ark of the Covenant—Biblical teaching. I. Title.
BS1345.52.S77   222'.63066—dc22   2009013785
ISBN 978-1-4331-0663-7
ISSN 1089-0645

Bibliographic information published by **Die Deutsche Bibliothek**.
Die Deutsche Bibliothek lists this publication in the "Deutsche
Nationalbibliografie"; detailed bibliographic data is available
on the Internet at http://dnb.ddb.de/.

© 2009 Peter Lang Publishing, Inc., New York
29 Broadway, 18th floor, New York, NY 10006
www.peterlang.com

Table of Contents

Editor's Preface

More than ever the horizons in biblical literature are being expanded beyond that which is immediately imagined; important new methodological, theological, and hermeneutical directions are being explored, often resulting in significant contributions to the world of biblical scholarship. It is an exciting time for the academy as engagement in biblical studies continues to be heightened.

This series seeks to make available to scholars and institutions, scholarship of a high order, and which will make a significant contribution to the ongoing biblical discourse. This series includes established and innovative directions, covering general and particular areas in biblical study. For every volume considered for this series, we explore the question as to whether the study will push the horizons of biblical scholarship. The answer must be yes for inclusion.

In this volume, Jim Street examines the centrality of the ark narrative in Chronicles, arguing that it is the theological hub for the Davidic narrative. Discussing the works of Japhet and Williamson, the author notes that while these scholars have broached thematic issues in their respective studies, and have forged new directions, much has been left undone. This study adds significantly to the new theological direction that is being shaped by attention to various themes in Chronicles. Noting that the Chronicler has material that is unique to him, Street argues that it is incumbent upon scholars to discern the theological trajectory that is developed by the Chronicler. Scholars who are engaged in this area of scholarship will find much here to examine, reflect on, challenge and I believe above all allow for a serious expansion of the discourse beyond historical matters.

The horizon has been expanded.

Hemchand Gossai
Series Editor

Acknowledgments

This book is the climax of a long process. The study began as my Dissertation during my time at Dallas Theological Seminary, entitled: *The Significance of the Ark Narrative in 1 Chronicles to the History of Israel's Religion.* I wish to thank Eugene H. Merrill, Richard A. Taylor, and Gary N. Knoppers for their comments and insights which made the dissertation better than it would otherwise have been. I also wish to thank my wife, Kim. Her constant encouragement to finish and granting me freedom to study allowed the project to move forward more quickly than planned.

Abbreviations

AB	Anchor Bible
ABD	*Anchor Bible Dictionary*. Edited by David Noel Freedman. 6 vols. New York: Doubleday, 1992
AH	Achaemenid History
AJSL	*American Journal of Semitic Languages and Literatures*
AJT	*American Journal of Theology*
AnBib	Analecta biblica
ANE	Ancient Near East
AOTC	Abingdon Old Testament Commentaries
ARAB	*Ancient Records of Assyria and Babylonia*. Daniel David Luckenbill. 2 vols. Chicago: Chicago University Press, 1926–1927
ARI	*Assyrian Royal Inscriptions*. A. K. Grayson. 2 vols. Records of the Ancient Near East. Wiesbaden: Harrassowitz, 1972–1976
ATD	Das Alte Testament Deutsch
ATSAT	Arbeiten zu Text und Sprache im Alten Testament
AUSS	*Andrews University Seminary Studies*
BASOR	*Bulletin of the American Schools of Oriental Research*
BBB	Bonner biblische Beiträge
BBET	Beiträge zur biblischen Exegese und Theologie
BCOT	Biblical Commentary on the Old Testament
BDB	Brown, F., S. R. Driver, and C. A. Briggs. *A Hebrew and English Lexicon of the Old Testament*. Oxford: Clarendon Press, 1907
BEATAJ	Beiträge zur Erforschung des Alten Testaments und des antiken Judentums
BHS	*Biblia Hebraica Stuttgartensia*. Edited by K. Elliger and W. Rudolph. Stuttgart: Deutsche Bibelgesellschaft, 1983
Bib	*Biblica*
BIS	Biblical Interpretation Series
BJS	Brown Judaic Studies
BJSUC	Biblical and Judaic Studies from the University of California
BKAT	Biblischer Kommentar: Altes Testament
BRS	Biblical Resource Series
BSac	*Bibliotheca sacra*

BTB	*Biblical Theology Bulletin*
BWA(N)T	Beiträge zur Wissenschaft vom Alten (und Neuen) Testament
BZAW	Beihefte zur Zeitschrift für die alttestamentliche Wissenschaft
CANE	*Civilizations of the Ancient Near East.* Edited by J. Sasson. 4 vols. New York: Scribner's Sons, 1995
CAT	Commentaire de l'Ancien Testament
CBC	Cambridge Bible Commentary
CBQ	*Catholic Biblical Quarterly*
CBQMS	Catholic Biblical Quarterly Monograph Series
CCS	Communicator's Commentary Series
ConBOT	Coniectanea biblica: Old Testament Series
CRINT	Compendia rerum iudaicarum ad Novum Testamentum
CTM	*Concordia Theological Monthly*
CurBS	*Currents in Research: Biblical Studies*
Dtr	the Deuteronomist
EdF	Erträge der Forschung
EgT	*Église et théologie*
EH	Europäische Hochschulschriften
ErIsr	*Eretz-Israel*
EvQ	*Evangelical Quarterly*
EvT	*Evangelische Theologie*
FAS	Freiburger altorientalische Studien
FAT	Forschungen zum Alten Testament
FCBS	Fortress Classics in Biblical Studies
FOTL	Forms of the Old Testament Literature
FRLANT	Forschungen zur Religion und Literatur des Alten und Neuen Testaments
FTS	Freiburger theologische Studien
GHAT	Göttinger Handkommentar zum Alten Testament
GKC	*Gesenius' Hebrew Grammar.* Edited by E. Kautzsch. Translated by A. E. Cowley. 2d ed. Oxford: Clarendon Press, 1910
GTS	Grazer theologische Studien
HALOT	Koehler, L., W. Baumgartner, and J. J. Stamm, *The Hebrew and Aramaic Lexicon of the Old Testament.* Translated and edited under the supervision of M. E. J. Richardson. 5 vols. Leiden: Brill, 1994–1999
HAT	Handbuch zum Alten Testament

HB	Hebrew Bible
HBT	*Horizons in Biblical Theology*
Hen	*Henoch*
HeyJ	*Heythrop Journal*
Hok	*Hokhma*
HSM	Harvard Semitic Monographs
HTR	*Harvard Theological Review*
HTKAT	Herders theologischer Kommentar zum Alten Testament
ICC	International Critical Commentary
Int	*Interpretation*
JANESCU	*Journal of the Ancient Near Eastern Society of Columbia University*
JAOS	*Journal of the American Oriental Society*
JBL	*Journal of Biblical Literature*
JEA	*Journal of Egyptian Archaeology*
JETS	*Journal of the Evangelical Theological Society*
JHNES	Johns Hopkins Near Eastern Studies
JNSL	*Journal of Northwest Semitic Languages*
JSJ	*Journal for the Study of Judaism in the Persian, Hellenistic, and Roman Periods*
JSNTSup	Journal for the Study of the New Testament: Supplement Series
JSOT	*Journal for the Study of the Old Testament*
JSOTSup	Journal for the Study of the Old Testament: Supplement Series
JSS	*Journal of Semitic Studies*
JTS	*Journal of Theological Studies*
KAI	*Kanaanäische und aramäische Inschriften.* Herbert R. Donner and W. Röllig. 5th ed. Wiesbaden: Harrassowitz, 2002–
KAT	Kommentar zum Alten Testament
LAI	Library of Ancient Israel
Levant	*Levant*
LS	*Louvain Studies*
LSTS	Library of Second Temple Studies
LTQ	*Lexington Theological Quarterly*
LXX	Septuagint
MT	Masoretic Text
mp	masculine plural
NAC	New American Commentary

NCBC	New Century Bible Commentary
NEchtBAT	Neue Echter Bible Altes Testament
NES	Near Eastern Studies
NIDOTTE	*New International Dictionary of Old Testament Theology and Exegesis.* Edited by Willem A. VanGemeren. 5 vols. Grand Rapids: Zondervan, 1997
NJBC	*New Jerome Biblical Commentary.* Edited by R. E. Brown et al. Englewood Cliffs, N.J.: Prentice Hall, 1990
ÖBS	Österreichische biblische Studien
OBT	Overtures to Biblical Theology
OEANE	*The Oxford Encyclopedia of Archaeology in the Near East.* Edited by E. M. Meyers. New York: Oxford University Press, 1997
Or	*Orientalia*
OTL	Old Testament Library
OTM	Oxford Theological Monographs
OTS	Oudtestamentische Studiën
OTWSAOTE	Ou-Testamentiese Werkgemeenskap in Suid-Africa: Old Testament Essays
P	Priestly source
PEGLMBS	*Proceedings, Eastern Great Lakes and Midwest Biblical Societies*
PFES	Publications of the Finnish Exegetical Society
RANE	Records of the Ancient Near East
RB	*Revue biblique*
ResQ	*Restoration Quarterly*
RTP	*Revue de théologie et de philosophie*
RTS	Reprints and Translations Series
SBL	Studies in Biblical Literature
SBLDS	Society of Biblical Literature Dissertation Series
SBLEJL	Society of Biblical Literature Early Judaism and Its Literature
SBLSS	Society of Biblical Literature Symposium Series
SBTS	Sources for Biblical and Theological Study
Schol	*Scholastik*
SHANE	Studies in the History of the Ancient Near East
SHCANE	Studies in the History and Culture of the Ancient Near East
SNTSMS	Society for New Testament Studies Monograph Series
SOTSMS	Society for Old Testament Study Monograph Series
STDJ	Studies on the Texts of the Desert of Judah

TA	*Tel Aviv*
TBC	Torch Bible Commentaries, ed. John Marsh and Alan Richardson
TBT	*The Bible Today*
TDOT	*Theological Dictionary of the Old Testament*. Edited by G. J. Botterweck and H. Ringgren. Translated by J. T. Willis et al. 14 vols. Grand Rapids: Eerdmans, 1974–
Text	*Textus*
TLOT	*Theological Lexicon of the Old Testament*. Edited by E. Jenni, with assistance from C. Westermann. Translated by M. E. Biddle. 3 vols. Peabody, Mass.: Hendrickson, 1997
TOTC	Tyndale Old Testament Commentaries
TQ	*Theologische Quartalschrift*
Transeu	*Transeuphratène*
TRE	*Theologische Realenzyklopädie*. Edited by G. Krause and G. Müller. Berlin. 1977–
TT	*The Theologian*
TynBul	*Tyndale Bulletin*
VT	Supplements to Vetus Testamentum
VTSup	Vetus Testamentum Supplements
WBC	Word Biblical Commentary
WMANT	Wissenschaftliche Monographien zum Alten und Neuen Testament
WUNT	Wissenschaftliche Untersuchungen zum Neuen Testament
YNER	Yale Near Eastern Researches
ZAW	*Zeitschrift für alttestamentliche Wissenschaft*
ZDPV	*Zeitschrift des deutschen Palästina-Vereins*

CHAPTER ONE

Introduction

Need for the Study

The study of Chronicles has become a matter of renewed interest in the past twenty years. This interest can be attributed to many factors; most notable among them is an emphasis on literary analysis treating the Chronicler on his own terms.[1] Literary analysis has caused writing on the subject of historical criticism and the debate about the reliability of the Chronicler's history to focus on the development of these literary issues, although this historical debate also continues. Canonical criticism also proves to be a fruitful avenue of research and marks for some scholars a major move away from redaction criticism. Finally, the desire to arrive at some theological synthesis of the book, since the Chronicler interpreted his sources in accordance with his theological purpose, has created much research interest in recent years. This change in the way scholars view Chronicles places the book among the major areas of study in the Hebrew Bible.

The results of these changes have caused some scholars to look at the final form of Chronicles as the most important aspect of the text itself. Nevertheless, others still argue for revisions and additions to the text. Scholars have recently changed the way they view source material in Chronicles. Previously it was used to analyze the Chronicler's interest and bias. Now it is used to discover his method of composition and the purpose of the narrative. Moreover, the attempt to develop a theological synthesis of the Chronicler has surfaced in recent years; however, this attempt is still in its beginning stages. Scholars in the field such as Williamson and Japhet have suggested major themes, but the treatment has been anything but a systematic analysis.

Several of these themes have implications for this work. One of the more complete treatments is by Japhet, who addresses worship in two parallel ways. First, she argues that idolatry is not compatible with the exclusive worship of Yahweh. Second, she argues that the correct performance of cultic ritual involves a proper attitude toward Yahweh.[2] Another theme, one addressed by Williamson, is the temple and its significance. He states that the temple served as "a focus for the reunification of the divided and scattered people of Israel."[3] The use of song in cultic ritual also serves as a key theological idea throughout the book. Two recent attempts at understanding this material have been made. First, Kleinig argues that the use of song announces Yahweh's presence with his people showing his acceptance of them. Thus, music and song were a central part of the cultic ritual.[4] A second attempt by Leithart is based mainly on

Kleinig's previous research. He argues that the cultic use of song functioned to highlight the atoning values of worship. Thus, for Leithart worship in the Second Temple period had redemptive value.[5] As early as 1984, Barker addressed these themes and attempted a theological analysis of the ark narrative in Chronicles.[6] His analysis dealt with the Chronicler's purpose and used the synoptic portions of this narrative as a template for the major themes. Barker used only the themes from this passage which supported his overarching theme of continuity and legitimacy. Hence, work in this area has begun, but the task remains to complete the theological analysis.

The above outline has been incorporated to show the present field of study of Chronicles in the past two decades and to provide direction for this current study. It serves as a general outline to express fully the need for a study of the ark narrative in Chronicles. In this writer's opinion the ark narrative in Chronicles acts as a theological hub around which everything else moves not only within the Davidic narrative but also within the book as a whole. Fretheim supports this theory when he states, "the Chronicler uses this event, which has to do with the ark, as a focal point around which to set forth his special concerns."[7] He goes on to list these concerns as (1) the Levites, (2) David, (3) things of the sanctuary.[8]

The thesis is supported by three main issues. First, this hypothesis is based on the continuance of these themes found elsewhere in the book. Second, the Chronicler gives a great deal of attention to developing this narrative, and much of the material he includes is unique to his book, hence it speaks directly to his purposes. Third, the movement of the ark into Jerusalem plays a major role in the way the Chronicler develops the cult under David. While some scholars have argued that the central emphasis on the cult is in 1 Chr 23—27 and that from there everything else is framed within the Davidic narrative, this writer views the ark narrative as laying an essential foundation for this later narrative.[9]

This thesis is also based on the premise that the movement of the ark, the structuring of the city of Jerusalem, and David's development of the institutions of the priests and Levites were determinative factors for the nation, both politically and religiously. Thus, David's reorganization of the cult in chapters 23–27 is secondary to this narrative, although it too plays a major role in the development of the cult, especially since it orders the permanent temple's cultic division. One element needs to be clarified at this point. The Chronicler was writing during the postexilic period about the preexilic period. In following the Samuel narrative the Chronicler also portrays the ark narrative as the critical portion of David's reign. Although, the First Temple had an ark, there was no ark present in the Second Temple. Thus, the Chronicler by highlighting the movement of the ark provided a clear tie to his theology. It illustrates his purpose of showing a continuation between the First Temple, which also had links to Sinai, with that of the Second Temple. The Chronicler was not merely a historian recasting events from the past; he was a theologian who interpreted those events for his postexilic readers.[10]

The difference between these two narratives (chapters 15–16 and 23–27) is that within the section of the ark narrative treated in chapters15–16, David had both established himself in the city of Jerusalem and built houses for himself (15:1); he then established the ark in Jerusalem (15–16). While one could certainly argue that the central point is the temple and its services that were instituted by Solomon, this writer sees David's organization as primary. Thus, the subsequent completion of the task by Solomon is in line with David's desire in this present passage. This desire becomes explicit in 1 Chr 17:1 when David tells Nathan that he wants to build a temple to house the ark. If one can agree, at least for the moment, that this is the central point of the nation's political and religious ordering, then this passage is also essential for establishing unity.[11] At the time of this writing, no full treatment of this narrative addresses these issues in detail. Therefore, the need exists for further research in the book of Chronicles as a whole.

Additional research in Chronicles is of paramount importance. Auld's comment regarding the Deuteronomistic history, adds to the importance of this research. He states, "What I am arguing here is that we should begin much nearer to the end and move successively earlier. At first, this may appear counterintuitive. However, it is clear that early postbiblical tradition greatly elaborated the previously unexplored 'lives' of early figures such as Adam, Enoch, and Noah. Hence, the idea that the history of Israel was gradually written backward from Kings via Deuteronomy to Genesis may not be so strange after all."[12] Although Auld is referring to the Deuteronomistic history, it seems logical that one should start at the end in order to understand the beginning. This could be illustrated in any number of ways. Perhaps one example that finds broad scholarly agreement will be sufficient. Virtually all scholars contend that the Hebrew Bible went through some form of editing during this period. For the conservative Jewish and Christian community, that editing was largely done under Ezra.[13] For the critical scholar, the entire Pentateuch would have gone through its final redaction at this time. This means that the Persian period affected the entire Hebrew Bible.

The Dead Sea Scrolls include several non-canonical texts. Although these works are not of the same authority as the canonical literature, they do represent postexilic thought in Judea and aid in understanding this period. One clear example of the changes that took place during this time is found in the Temple Scroll. In this document one finds certain changes in the law of

Deuteronomy. For example, the king's authority is limited by a council of thirty-six members. It also contains laws concerning the temple and festival sacrifice, but these issues are not clearly mentioned in Deuteronomy. Therefore, they must be a later development based on Deuteronomistic laws and other traditions.[14]

Purpose of the Study

Many scholars view Chronicles as having a general unity regarding authorship. However, several scholars have followed Noth's literary hypothesis by arguing for pro-Levitical or pro-priestly additions to the text. This may not necessarily be the better hypothesis.

The purpose of this monograph is to look into the issue of the various literary hypotheses in order to determine if they can be sustained in this narrative. If they fail to account adequately for the data in this narrative, then the Levitical and priestly material found in this passage is primary material for the Chronicler. The importance of this premise needs to be addressed because it results in the arrangement of the priests and Levites having a more central role within the work of the Chronicler. This means that David's organization of the clergy portrays Israel as a cultic community. The worship planned by David and carried out under the authority of the Levites and priests is consistently emphasized throughout the book. Selman states, "The main aim of chapter 15 is not to describe the Levites' history and organization. The two central themes seem to be David's role *vis-à-vis* the Levites and the priority of worship in Israel. David is the person chiefly responsible for the Levites' transformed role (vv. 3, 11, 16)....This theme, however, is subsidiary to the primary aim of giving specific encouragement about the activities and personnel of Israel's worship."[15] Therefore, related but secondary to the role of the clergy in worship are the roles of David and his dynasty in the organization and the subsequent reorganizations of the cult. David is portrayed as a cult founder, and several of the kings reorganize the cult during times of religious renewal. The king's activities need to be examined as well to discover why the Chronicler included them within his narrative.

The thesis itself goes beyond addressing the supposition of later priestly and Levitical editors. Noth changed the understanding of the central purpose of the Chronicler to that of the temple and worship, but he linked this directly to the monarchy.[16] Prior to Noth, von Rad argued that the temple and Israel's history did not form the center of the Chronicler's work. He believed that it was the throne of David under the law and grace of God.[17] Recently, some scholars have questioned Noth's change of purpose.[18] This questioning must be addressed in order to discover the Chronicler's reason for writing.

Arriving at a conclusion of the Chronicler's reason for writing will hopefully lead to a clearer understanding of the arrangement and significance of worship in Chronicles and by implication the Second Temple period as well. Most of the preliminary work has been done in several journal articles and in monographs. These data need to be organized into a complete synthesis in order to understand fully and appreciate the Chronicler's work. Since most of the material that addresses worship is in the unique sections of the Chronicler's presentation, the primary focus of this work will be on that material; however, the synoptic material will not be ignored. Because the Chronicler was writing so far from the events himself, it goes without saying that he utilized sources of one type or another.

Hopefully, future scholars will find further inroads into the author's reasons for writing this book. He was, without doubt, an accomplished exegete and theologian who had much to say about his own social-political and religious environment, the community's interest in tradition, and where true authority was to be found.

Organization of the Study

The major chapters of this work will address the role that the ark narrative (1 Chr 15–16) plays in the development of Israel's religion. Chapters two and three will address the various literary-critical hypotheses. Chapter two will include a literary analysis of the respective units in this narrative in order to show how the Chronicler elegantly constructed his work. This analysis will help develop the point of unity throughout the narrative, although caution is important because improper use of literary analysis can lead to the assumption of unity. Therefore, careful analysis of the evidence will insure that there is indeed proof for such an assumption.[19] A translation of each unit of material will begin each section. This translation will also require text-critical issues to be addressed at this point. This text-critical analysis will reflect only those cases where the sense of the text is affected by the variant. It will reflect the translation given and the reason for the choice made in the translation. Further, there will be some basic discussion about the source of the material.

After this initial inquiry into the unity of the work, an examination of these literary-critical hypotheses will open the discussion of chapter three. Following this examination, arguments that support the need to reconsider the literary-critical issue will develop from recent research. These arguments will address the genealogies (1 Chr 1–9) and David's final organization of the cult and national polity (1 Chr 23–27). Then a discussion of the implications of this reexamination will take place. The thesis will develop out of the Chronicler's purpose for writing the book and the Chronicler's delineation and support of the narrative themes throughout the book. These themes find their most significant development in the narratives of the various kings.

Examining the Chronicler's use of the narrative records of Israel's kings, the reader is immediately confronted with the fact that the Chronicler idealized the reigns of David and Solomon.[20] One can clearly see that David was the standard by which other kings were judged in the Deuteronomistic History.[21] This Davidic idealization shows that one of the major functions of David, and to a lesser extent of Solomon, is found in the cult.[22] How David's successors measure up to his faithfulness to Yahweh will determine if they experience blessing or rejection during their reigns. This seems quite similar to many ancient Near Eastern royal inscriptions regarding the founding of dynasties and the formation of cults. Therefore, an examination of this ancient Near Eastern background will be developed.

The remaining two chapters will be the heart of the work. The concerns of the previous chapters all help to illuminate both the direction of scholarship in the field and the various background issues that pertain to the text. These two chapters will address the text with the implications of the findings of these previous chapters. Chapters four and five will delve into exegetical and theological matters. Within the exegetical portion, the author will develop a detailed analysis of the text. As a result of the interest of this work, the main emphasis will be on the material unique to the Chronicler. Additionally, the way the Chronicler integrated this unique material into his known sources will play a role in discovering the various emphases of the Chronicler. The parallel material in 2 Samuel and that of the various Psalms will also be discussed. The ark narrative in Samuel will aid in the development of the discussion of the parallel texts.[23] General conclusions regarding these sources will indicate the reason the Chronicler varied from them. The conclusions for the differences between the Samuel narrative and this one should be in line with the purpose discovered in the unique material.

This examination must be done with a close eye on the Chronicler's own time period. He may be writing about the monarchy but his audience is clearly postexilic. This fact must always remain the focus for understanding the Chronicler's reason for writing. The purpose of Chronicles will show how the book spoke directly to the postexilic community and how the postexilic community was to understand these various themes.

The fifth chapter addresses the theological significance of the ark narrative. A discussion of the larger narrative (1 Chr 10–29) will precede the major discussion. Then the second part of the ark narrative (1 Chr 15–16) will be analyzed. The author will attempt to derive the theological framework and content directly from the exegetical arguments that have come from the analysis of the passage in the preceding chapters. This will allow one to avoid superimposing an outline or system upon the content of this narrative. Finally, this writer will note the major theological themes that stem from the exegetical analysis of the narrative. These themes include the following: (1) the ark, (2) the city of Jerusalem, and (3) the Chronicler's theology of worship. As a result of this inquiry, the reason for the Chronicler's inclusion of this unique material within his work will become evident. This should lead the reader into a better understanding of Israel's worship system in the postexilic period.

Notes

1. The term Chronicler, for this writer, means the author of Chronicles. He is more than a mere compiler of sources; he is an ingenious creator who is able to take the sources in their various forms at his disposal and create a unique theological point of view.
2. Sara Japhet, *The Ideology of the Book of Chronicles and Its Place in Biblical Thought*, trans. Anna Barber, 2d ed., BEATAJ 9 (Frankfurt am Main: Lang, 1997), 199–265. Also see Isaac Kalimi, *The Reshaping of Ancient Israelite History in Chronicles* (Winona Lake, Ind.: Eisenbrauns, 2005).
3. H. G. M. Williamson, "The Temple in the Books of Chronicles," in *Templum Amicitae: Essays on the Second Temple Presented to Ernst Bammel*, ed. W. Horbury, JSNTSup 48 (Sheffield: JSOT Press, 1991), 29.
4. John W. Kleinig, *The LORD's Song: The Basis, Function and Significance of Choral Music in Chronicles*, JSOTSup 156 (Sheffield: JSOT Press, 1993), 187–89.
5. Peter J. Leithart, *From Silence to Song: The Davidic Liturgical Revolution* (Moscow, Idaho: Canon, 2003).
6. David G. Barker, "The Theology of the Chronicler: A Synoptic Investigation of 1 Chronicles 13, 15–17 and 2 Samuel 6–7" (Th.D. diss., Grace Theological Seminary, 1984), microfiche.
7. Terence E. Fretheim, "The Cultic Use of the Ark of the Covenant in the Monarchial Period" (Ph.D. diss., Princeton Theological Seminary, 1967), 205.
8. Ibid., 206.
9. John Wesley Wright, "The Origin and Function of 1 Chronicles 23–27" (Ph.D. diss., University of Notre Dame, 1989); and John W. Wright, "From Center to Periphery: 1 Chronicles 23–27 and the Interpretation of Chronicles in the Nineteenth Century," in *Priests, Prophets, and Scribes: Essays on the Formation and Heritage of Second Temple Judaism in Honour of Joseph Blenkinsopp*, ed. Eugene C. Ulrich et al., JSOTSup 149 (Sheffield: JSOT Press, 1992), 20–42.
10. This issue must be developed fully in chapter five. At this point it should be noted that the Chronicler is using this major event in the life of David to show that the symbol of Yahweh's presence was allowed to be transported to Jerusalem by Yahweh. Although the symbol of his presence is no longer in the temple, his presence remains. Therefore, Yahweh is to be worshiped properly in Jerusalem at the temple because it is the place where he caused his presence to dwell (Deut 12:5–7). This proper worship is the means by which the nation is able to maintain a proper covenant relation with Yahweh. Thus, proper worship leads to the hope that Yahweh will once again act on behalf of the nation. It also gives the postexilic readers a feeling of continuity with the past. The ark and the tabernacle were both present in Solomon's temple. Thus the Chronicler is attempting to show continuity with both the Mosaic traditions and the Davidic institutions with the worship that took place in his own day.

11. Mosis, although not addressing the same issues as this work, makes a strong argument for the central role of the ark narrative within the book as a whole (Rudolf Mosis, *Untersuchungen zur Theologie des chronistischen Geschichtswerkes*, FTS 92 [Freiburg: Herder, 1973], 45–80).

12. Graeme A. Auld, "The Former Prophets (Joshua, Judges, 1–2 Samuel, 1–2 Kings)," in *The Hebrew Bible Today: An Introduction to Critical Issues*, ed. Steven L. McKenzie and M. Patrick Graham (Louisville, Ky.: Westminster/Knox, 1998), 67.

13. According to several Jewish sources the traditional view is that Ezra and the elders under him edited several books and closed the canon. See 2 Esdr 14:44-50; *b. B. Bat* 14b-15a. Further, according to 2 Macc 2:13, Nehemiah founded a library and collected books written by the prophets, the kings, and David.

14. Regarding the Temple Scroll in general, see Dwight D. Swanson, *The Temple Scroll and the Bible: The Methodology of 11QT*, STDJ 14 (Leiden: Brill), 1995.

15. Martin J. Selman, *1 Chronicles: An Introduction and Commentary*, TOTC 10a (Downers Grove, Ill.: Inter-Varsity, 1994), 161.

16. Martin Noth, *The Chronicler's History*, trans. H. G. M. Williamson, JSOTSup 50 (Sheffield: JSOT Press, 1987), 34, 100–2.

17. Gerhard von Rad, *Das Geschichtsbild des chronistischen Werkes*, BWA(N)T 54 (Stuttgart: Kohlhammer, 1930), 120.

18. John W. Wright, "The Founding Father: the Structure of the Chronicler's David Narrative," *JBL* 117 (1998): 45–49.

19. One may raise the point that De Vries and others have attempted this, but De Vries has attempted to find the purpose of the book in its arrangement of material, although it is admitted that he addresses this issue as well (Simon J. De Vries, *1 and 2 Chronicles*, FOTL 11 [Grand Rapids: Eerdmans, 1989]). The works of Allen and Duke have been the two most notable attempts at a literary composition in this regard (Leslie C. Allen, "Kerygmatic Units in 1 and 2 Chronicles," *JSOT* 41 [1988]: 21–36; and Rodney K. Duke, *The Persuasive Appeal of the Chronicler: A Rhetorical Analysis*, JSOTSup 88 [Sheffield: Almond Press, 1990]).

20. The major idealization in Chronicles is of David. However, the Chronicler also omitted the faults of Solomon as well. Throntveit sees the reigns of David and Solomon being idealized, although he does not use this term. He clearly shows that the various changes from the parallel text in Samuel and Kings display a *tendenz* that sets both kings up as ideal monarchs. See Mark A. Throntveit, *When Kings Speak: Royal Speech and Royal Prayer in Chronicles*, SBLDS 93 (Atlanta: Scholars Press, 1987), 17–23; 26–30; 32–36. Further, he argues that the Chronicler omits all the events of the so-called 'Succession Narrative' in Dtr in order to justify Solomon as Yahweh's chosen temple-builder and to solidify the unity of his reign with that of his father" (ibid., 47 and see also the broader discussion 42–47).

21. For example, 1 Kgs 9:4; 11:4, 6, 33, 38; 14:8; 15:3, 11; 2 Kgs 14:3; 16:2; 18:3; 22:2.

22. Examples of kings being judged in light of their father David include: 2 Chr 7:17; 17:3; 28:1; 29:2; and 34:2. The majority of these direct references of kings being compared to David have parallels in the Deuteronomistic History. The way the Chronicler has shaped his picture of David allows his reader to see this comparison in his own work which seems to be different from that of Kings.

23. There are several works that address the ark narrative in Samuel. These may be touched on throughout the work as significant parallels come up. However, the major discussion will be in this fourth chapter. One of the key aspects that needs to be discussed is the differences between the parallel accounts. On the ark narrative in Samuel see P. Kyle McCarter, *2 Samuel*, AB 9 (Garden City, N.Y.: Doubleday, 1984), 173–84; Patrick D. Miller, and J. J. M. Roberts, *The Hand of the Lord: A Reassessment of the "Ark Narrative" of 1 Samuel*, JHNES (Baltimore:

Johns Hopkins University Press, 1977); C. L. Seow, *Myth, Drama, and the Politics of David's Dance*, HSM 44 (Atlanta: Scholars Press, 1989); and Antony F. Campbell, *The Ark Narrative (1 Sam 4–6; 2 Sam 6): A Form-Critical and Traditio-Historical Study* (Missoula, Mont.: Scholars Press, 1975). In addition to these works there are several dissertations that have addressed this area as well. See Fretheim, "The Cultic Use of the Ark of the Covenant,"108–26; Jared Judd Jackson, "The Ark Narratives: An Historical, Textual, and Form-Critical Study of 1 Samuel 4–6 and 2 Samuel 6" (Th.D. diss., Union Theological Seminary, N.Y., 1962); Gert Floris Snyman, "Biblical Hermeneutics and Reception Theory: The Authority of Biblical Texts and the Chronicler's Interpretation of the Sacred Story of the Ark" (Th.D. diss., University of South Africa, 1991). Snyman's work falls outside of this work but his work on reception theory is comprehensive and his text critical work is atypical of most text critics as he is trying to find traces of texts behind the Chronicles text. His point of concern then is in the construction of a text and not its reconstruction into the *Ur* text.

CHAPTER TWO

Literary-Critical Issues

Introduction

Allen's article influenced scholarly thought regarding the Chronicler's great literary skill. He developed the Chronicler's use of chiasm, inclusion, and keywords within the various structural units of the book. He states that key terms do appear to be used as rhetorical unit markers. Their role falls into three categories: *inclusio*, recurring motifs, and contrasting motifs.[1] He touches briefly on 1 Chr 15, but does not comment on chapter 16. This seems odd as the discussion of chapter 15 comes within the broader unit of the ark narrative for him (1 Chr 13–15).[2] Further, he does not treat chapter 15 in detail.

A general understanding of the literary characteristics that the Chronicler employed has found basic agreement among contemporary scholarship.[3] The use of repetition, a characteristic of Hebrew literature, appears to be one of the most common literary techniques employed by the Chronicler.[4] Repetition also plays a role in establishing the various units of the narrative as a term may be employed to function as an *inclusio*.[5] Allen notes that the Chronicler may use a term in an almost technical sense in order to develop a theological point through anaphora. Furthermore, it is clear that the Chronicler uses keywords to draw attention to specific points. Thus the Chronicler has developed a theological commentary on the sources that he is interpreting.[6]

The Chronicler used some basic compositional techniques that need to be noted. For example, Dillard and others have seen a connection between the deliberate juxtaposition of two narrative units by the Chronicler. Dillard's specific example involving Asa and Jehoshaphat in 2 Chr 14–20 addresses these two narratives as parallel structures.[7] Thus, based on the observations of Allen and Dillard, it is clear that the Chronicler is at times using broad literary devices to structure his work.[8] The way one interprets the literary characteristics of the Chronicler also aids in determining the way the Chronicler integrates his own unique material into the narratives taken from Samuel–Kings.[9]

Preface: 1 Chronicles 15:1-24

Translation

(1) And he (David) built houses for himself in the City of David; and he prepared a place for the ark of God, and pitched a tent for it.[10] (2) Then David said, "No one is to carry the ark of God but the Levites, because Yahweh has chosen them to carry the ark of Yahweh and to minister before him forever."

(3) And David gathered all Israel together at Jerusalem, to bring up the ark of Yahweh to its place, which he had prepared for it. (4) Then David assembled the sons of Aaron and[11] the Levites:

(5) The sons of Kohath, Uriel the chief, and one hundred and twenty[12] of his brothers. (6) The sons of Merari, Asaiah the chief, and two hundred and twenty[13] of his brothers. (7) The sons of Gershon, Joel the chief, and one hundred[14] and thirty[15] of his brothers. (8) The sons of Elizaphan, Shemaiah the chief, and two hundred[16] of his brothers. (9) The sons of Hebron, Eliel the chief, and eighty of his brothers. (10) The sons of Uzziel, Amminadab the chief, and one hundred and twelve of his brothers.

(11) And David called for Zadok and Abiathar the priests, and for the Levites: for Uriel, Asaiah, Joel, Shemaiah, Eliel, and Amminadab. (12) He said to them, "You are the leaders of the Levites; sanctify yourselves, you and your brothers, that you may bring up the ark of Yahweh, the God of Israel to (the place)[17] I have prepared for it. (13) Because you did not do it[18] the first time, Yahweh our God broke out against us, because we did not seek it according to the ordinance."

(14) So the priests and the Levites sanctified themselves to bring up the ark of Yahweh, the God of Israel. (15) And the Levites carried the ark of God, as Moses had commanded according to the word of Yahweh, on their shoulders with poles.

(16) Then David told the leaders of the Levites to appoint their brothers to be the singers accompanied by instruments of music, stringed instruments, harps, and cymbals, to raise the voice with resounding joy.

(17) So the Levites appointed: Heman the son of Joel; and of his brothers, Asaph the son of Berechiah; and of their brothers, the sons of Merari, Ethan the son of Kushaiah. (18) And with them their brothers of the second rank: Zechariah,[19] Aziel,[20] Shemiramoth, Jehiel, Unni, Eliab, Benaiah, Maaseiah, Mattithiah, Elipheleh, Mikneiah, Obed-Edom, Jeiel, Azaziah[21] the gatekeepers. (19) The singers, Heman, Asaph, and Ethan, were to sound the cymbals of bronze. (20) Zechariah, Aziel, Shemiramoth, Jehiel, Unni, Eliab, Maaseiah, and Benaiah, with strings according to the voice of young women.[22] (21) Mattithiah, Elipheleh, Mikneiah, Obed-Edom, Jeiel, and Azaziah, to direct with harps

according to the bass voices.[23] (22) Chenaniah,[24] leader of the Levites,[25] was instructor in charge of carrying,[26] because he was skillful. (23) Berechiah and Elkanah were doorkeepers for the ark. (24) Shebaniah, Joshaphat, Nethanel, Amasai, Zechariah, Benaiah, and Eliezer, the priests, were to blow the trumpets before the ark of God; and Obed-Edom and Jehiah, doorkeepers for the ark.

Background

Chapter 15 opens with a note that David had built palaces for himself and had therefore established Jerusalem as his capital city. David then begins the task of preparing for the transfer of the ark a second time. Although this material is unique to the Chronicler, it seems that one could make a good case for its actually taking place within the historical time period. Several of the elements in the preparations seem to be alluded to by the Samuel narrative.[27] Indeed, when analyzing the Samuel narrative (2 Sam 6:12–20), several elements imply that David made preparations for the movement of the ark to Jerusalem that are not specifically mentioned in that narrative. Japhet has rightly identified these elements found in the Samuel passage.

> (a) David had prepared a tent as a place to receive the ark (II Sam. 6.17—note the past perfect of the verb נטה). (b) The people were assembled for the occasion (II Sam. 6.15, 18-19). (c) A different system of transporting the ark had been introduced: there is no mention of a cart, and II Sam. 6.13 speaks of 'those who bore the ark.' (d) Sacrificial animals had been provided, and the necessary personnel for their sacrifice were prepared (II Sam. 6.13). (e) Musicians for sounding the horn had also been put in readiness (II Sam. 6.15).[28]

These implications suggest that the author of the Samuel narrative understands that the preparations for the transfer of the ark, which the Chronicler here details, took place historically.

The differences between these two works suggest that they have two separate purposes and interests regarding this narrative.[29] For the author of Samuel, the importance of the narrative is to describe the transfer of the ark to Jerusalem; but for the Chronicler the intermediate preparations between the original failure to bring the ark to Jerusalem and the actual movement of it is of the utmost importance.[30]

The overall form of the ark narrative (13–16) has been identified as "an account."[31] These briefer reports support the overall theme of the installation of the ark in Jerusalem. De Vries indicates that the main genre of this section (vv. 1–24) is that of report.[32] Several other genres are also present within this section of material. These will be noted below in the specific sections regarding literary-critical issues.

Critical Issues

This large section of material has been broken down in various ways. Some sections are assigned to the Chronicler, whereas others are assigned to later pro-Priestly/pro-levitical editors.[33] The extent of these additions differs among scholars. Noth indicated that in this particular section of material there are two later additions (vv. 4–10 and 16–24).[34] This view has been followed closely by Rudolph and most significantly with regard to the cult singers in 15:16–24 by Gese.[35] This last issue will be addressed first because it is this section of material that sets up the pericope as a unified work. Both of these sections are of the genre type called "roster."[36] It seems significant that it is within these lists of names that most scholars find the majority of the redactional layers. The usual test for this type of material is whether the names appear intrusive or if they have some relationship with the narrative.

Part of the problem in this section is the fact that the singers appointed by David are Asaph, Heman, and Ethan (15:17), but elsewhere they are referred to as Asaph, Heman, and Jeduthun. Scholars have posited that there was a historical progression in the categorization of these singers in Chronicles and Ezra–Nehemiah.[37] Gese's work remains the most influential. He develops the various orders of cultic singers by building on von Rad's previous work and being highly influenced by the redaction criticism of Rothstein and Hänel.[38] He argues that there were three main stages within the development of this religious class with the third stage being subdivided into two separate groups.[39]

Gese's development is not without problems, some of which Gese himself tentatively admitted.[40] His theory is based largely on the assumption that the works of Ezra—Nehemiah and Chronicles together form a work that shows a continual progression within the postexilic period that suggests greater freedom in identifying the groups of Levitical singers. However, Levine offered the opposite opinion: the lists found actually come before the writings of any of the postexilic works.[41] There are other issues that raise questions of methodology. First, he does not address the LXX material. In fact, the textual evidence from LXX Nehemiah causes this writer to reach the opposite conclusion of Gese.[42] Further, Gese does not interact with the Qumran material either. This is forgiven, as that material was so difficult to obtain during the time of his writing, but this material should be correlated with his work. Secondly, his division of Stage 3 is questionable, especially with regard to the ark narrative. Knoppers notes that it is odd that an editor would replace Jeduthun with Ethan for genealogies during the reigns of David and Solomon but never after that. This would suggest that Jeduthun was the one who replaced Ethan in the lists.[43] Thus, it appears that Gese's theory needs to be rejected and other options need to be analyzed.

Williamson's view of the Chronicler's writing at Stage 3b argues for the Chronicler as the author of this material, but Williamson fails to address the various problems within Gese's development noted above. It appears that he believes that by moving the Chronicler's own writing to 3b that those issues are alleviated.[44] Steins argues that the positions of Rothstein and Hänel, Welch, Williamson, and Braun are untenable in light of 2 Chr 29.[45] He argues for four major layers within chapters 15–16. Steins rejects Gese's analysis of the cultic musicians as well.[46] Furthermore, he acknowledges that the role of the priesthood must have to some degree been present in the foundation layer.[47] Steins argues for these redactional layers based on the parallel texts found in the genealogies (1 Chr 5:27–6:66), where he sees two clear layers of material.[48] This, however, may be better explained by the different types of genealogies themselves rather than by different layers being present within them.[49]

Therefore, it seems better to look elsewhere for the internal literary structure of the Chronicler. On the surface there does appear to be an intrusion in the narrative at this point because the narrative indicates that the procession has already started according to v. 15.[50] However, a closer look at the narrative reveals that vv. 16–24 are an integral part of the narrative that is required in order to balance the structure. The chapter breaks the transportation of the ark into three separate units of material. These include: (1) the six families of the Levites (vv. 4–10), (2) David's commands to the Levites to carry properly the ark (vv. 11–13), and (3) the Levites' carrying out that command immediately in the Chronicler's narrative (vv. 14–15).[51] These three units then find a parallel in the musical organization of the cult, which is broken down into three subunits as well. These include (1) David commanding the heads of the Levites to appoint musicians and singers (v. 16), (2) the list of those appointed to service and their various responsibilities (vv. 17–21), and (3) the list of those that were involved in the proper procedure and safety of the ark during its transportation (vv. 22–24).[52] This suggests that v. 16 is not out of order because the parallel panels indicate that the Chronicler was not addressing the organization in chronological order; rather, the Chronicler was emphasizing the preparations for the transportation of the ark, followed by the musical organization for it.

Returning to the other disputed section of material within this literary unit (vv. 4–10), one finds in Rudolph's work a major objection to unity. Yet, there may be some methodological problems here as well. The basic issue that Rudolph identified was the fact that vv. 4–10 are juxtaposed to v. 11 and are viewed as an expansion on that verse.[53] Braun was so convinced that vv. 4–10 were an expansion that he dismissed other arguments in favor of unity without comment.[54] However, Benzinger noticed that the list found in these verses must reflect a time period older than the time of the Chronicler. He argues that the six divisions point to a time when the numbers of the Levites would have been much smaller than they were in the postexilic period.[55] Further, Welten has shown that it was common for an author or editor to repeat previous material when he moved from one of his sources back to his narrative.[56] This does not, however, necessitate this material as being original to the narrative, as a later editor could well have used this same technique. Many scholars think that this material is intrusive within the narrative and shows signs of being the work of a later pro-Priestly redactor.[57] This is because the priests are supposedly out of place in a narrative that is so focused on the Levites. Further, it does seem odd that this material (vv. 4–10) includes the same six heads of the Levitical family as these in v. 11, but with additional genealogical material for each family. Thus, if this material were original, v. 11 would be redundant. De Vries furthers this line of argumentation by stating,

> In v. 4 the 'sons of Aaron' are mentioned before the Levites, but the roster that follows is purely that of the Levites (cf. 6:16–30). In v. 11 David summons 'the Priests Zadok and Abiathar,' along with six Levites, but in addressing them he says, 'You are the heads of the fathers' houses of the Levites', which might conceivably include the priests as descendants of Levi through Aaron; but carrying the ark is exclusively the duty of the Levites according to Numbers 4, hence we are surprised to read that the priests as well as the Levites sanctify themselves for bringing up the ark (v. 14), yet immediately read that it is solely the Levites who did the carrying (v. 15), plainly marking the references to priests in v. 11, 14 as glosses.[58]

De Vries' comment makes it appear logical that a later gloss is the best way of handling the discrepancies within the passage.

It may be possible to view De Vries' argument against unity in another way that may in fact support it. While De Vries is correct in stating that the priests were descendants of Levi, there are other issues that need to be considered. The priests are the ones who are responsible for carrying out sacrificial offerings to Yahweh, as mentioned in v. 26 and 16:1. They would have gone through ritual purification before performing any cultic activity. This purification was undoubtedly practiced during David's time as well as during the time of the Chronicler; and there are places in Leviticus that would suggest this as well (e.g., Lev 8:11, 12, 33; 11:44; and 21:8). The Mishnah also includes such purification rites.[59] This fact seems to alleviate De Vries' issues and adequately reflects the context of the larger pericope, namely, proper care in cultic activities (15:1–24).[60] In addition, it also seems likely that the mention of the priests (vv. 4, 11, and 14) are necessary because the priests are appointed to blow the trumpets in v. 24.

Japhet also questions Rudolph's evaluation. She poses this question: "Is this a result of his implicit wish to bring Chronicles closer to the Deuteronomistic historiography, making it more attractive to the modern reader?"[61] She argues that the non-parallel sections are made up of narrative sections and lists of names. She then states, "However, no explanation is given why a certain literary structure, i.e. 'instruction a+b—execution a+b is authentic and admissible, while a different literary structure, namely 'instruction a—execution a; instruction b— execution b', is not."[62] While her point is well taken, it would be better received if she made a case for this list as complementing the storyline.

The list itself should not be interpreted as intrusive because it supports the story line. David is beginning to organize the cult and make preparations for worship in Jerusalem by moving the ark to his capital city. It also provides a background for these cultic orders that will be developed further in this narrative and again in 1 Chr 23–27.[63] Hence, it may be possible to see the lists of names as being used in a preliminary way to set the stage for the fuller development of the various cultic orders. The lack of order in the earlier attempt to move the ark (1 Chr 13) resulted in failure. This ordering of the various guilds serves as a means to prevent this failure from happening a second time.[64] This indicates that one of the main interests of the Chronicler was to show that David was the one who planned for national worship and Solomon his son faithfully carried out that plan in building the temple.[65] Thus, these lists in this chapter fit the Chronicler's purpose, because the transfer of the ark is the best place to introduce the Levites' various worship activities. Therefore, the lists are not intrusive but original and a major emphasis in the Chronicler's presentation of proper worship.

Finally, in this section of material Dörrfuß has noted that vv. 11–15 show some evidence of a redaction that supports Moses, rather than David. He argues that these verses are critical of David and place the blame of Uzzah's death on him.[66] He goes on to argue that vv. 11–15a are based on the earlier failed attempt to move the ark to Jerusalem (e.g., 15:2).[67] Dörrfuß argues that an important ground for the assigning the priests in this section to a later development is that David turns to the heads of the families of the Levites (v. 12). The title "heads of the fathers" is most frequently found in postexilic writing.[68] The attempt failed because the Levites were not involved. However, v. 15b comes from a different source because the ark was to be moved by poles. He sees this as a direct criticism of the first attempt of moving the ark on a new cart (1 Chr 13:7). He argues that this is an insertion that supports Moses as the cult founder.[69] Further Dörrfuß notes that the term "consecrate" was used originally for the Levites but the priests are also often present in the context as well. Thus, this term has become a technical term of the Chronicler's for both the Levites and the priests in preparing for cultic ritual.[70] After a moderate interaction with some of the specific vocabulary, he concludes that vv. 11–15a are from the original work of the Chronicler, but that v.15b represents a later development.[71] The statement about Moses places David and Moses in contradiction with one another. Moses is attributed his proper place as cult founder because it was his law that was followed that resulted in a successful transfer of the ark.

While there is certainly something to be said about the role that Moses plays in the book of Chronicles, it is incompatible with the Chronicler's purpose to see Moses and David opposing each other. True, the earlier attempt failed because the ark was not handled properly, but the narrative portrays David more as a king who was able to search out the reason for the failed attempt. He addresses the clergy in order to fix the problem so that the ark could be brought to Jerusalem. During the period between the Mosaic era and that of David, the movement of the ark is documented only a few times, and one can presume that this movement was overseen by the leading cultic officials at the time. (For example, 1 Sam 4:3 suggests that Samuel placed his sons in charge of the ark and that they accompanied the ark into battle [4:11].) Therefore, David had few examples of the proper movement of the ark. Nevertheless, after the failed attempt, David was the one who understood the problem and took steps to rectify it. David is not being contrasted with Moses; instead, he is being depicted as a truly committed reader of the Torah (Deut 17:14-20) and an accurate interpreter of the Law in his present situation.[72] The phrase in v. 2 suggests that David has searched the book of Deuteronomy. This becomes clear because the first part of the verse "No one is to carry the ark of God but the Levites," comes from Deut 10:8 and the second part of the verse "because Yahweh has chosen them to carry the ark of Yahweh and to minister before him forever" must be based on Num 4:15. This combination of these two texts suggest that David is following the Pentateuch in his statement to the Levites. Thus, it becomes clear that David has devoted himself to the study of Torah in order to discover the reason for Uzzah's death.

The Movement of the Ark: 1 Chronicles 15:25–16:3

Translation

(25) So David, the elders of Israel, and the captains over the thousands went to bring up the ark of the covenant of Yahweh[73] from the house of Obed-Edom[74] with joy.[75] (26) And when God helped the Levites[76] who bore the ark of the covenant of Yahweh, they offered up seven bulls and seven rams.[77] (27) David was clothed with a robe of fine linen, as were all the Levites who bore the ark, the singers, and Chenaniah the officer in charge of carrying, the singers. David also wore a linen ephod. (28) Thus all Israel brought up the ark of the covenant of Yahweh with shouting and with the sound of the horn, with trumpets and with cymbals, making music with harps and lyres.[78]

(29) And when the ark of the covenant of Yahweh came to[79] the City of David, Michal, Saul's daughter, looked through a window and saw King David dancing and playing music;[80] and she despised him in her heart.[81]

(16:1) So they brought the ark of God and set it in the midst of the tent that David had erected for it. Then they brought near[82] whole burnt offerings and peace offerings before God. (2) And when David had finished sacrificing the burnt offerings and the peace offerings, he blessed the people in the name of Yahweh. (3) Then he distributed to all Israelites, both man and woman, to every person a loaf of bread, a raisin roll,[83] and a cake of raisins.

Background

The source for this pericope is clearly 2 Sam 6:12-19. Nevertheless, scholars still debate about whether the Chronicler followed his text or made changes to his *Vorlage* to fit his purposes. The pericope fits the form of a report of ritual. De Vries defines a *report of ritual* as "A brief description of procedures followed in the performance of public worship, all of which has been regulated by ritual."[84]

Three major differences between the text of 2 Samuel and 1 Chronicles are very apparent.[85] These differences include: (1) David does not act alone as in Samuel; he, the elders of Israel, and the commanders of the thousands went to bring the ark to Jerusalem (1 Chr 15:25 and 2 Sam 6:12b); (2) the sacrificial offering is different. In 2 Samuel it is an ox and a fatling (2 Sam 6:13), but in Chronicles it is seven bulls and seven rams (1 Chr 15:26); (3) the singing and playing of instruments by the Levites is lacking in 2 Samuel. The Chronicler further identifies the instruments that are different from the "sounding of the horn" (found in both passages) as being the trumpets, cymbals, harps and lyres, which are the same ones mentioned in the preceding passage (vv. 19–24).

The lack of scholarly consensus causes one to remain cautious about the historical value of these changes in the text. However, the overall perspective between the text of Chronicles and Samuel along with the fact that a case can be made for this organization occurring during the time of David, at least implicitly by the text of Samuel, suggests that this organization and festival took place at the time that David brought the ark to Jerusalem.

Critical Issues

The Chronicler is clearly following his source at this point; therefore, the critical issues primarily surface around the differences between the texts of 1 Chronicles and 2 Samuel. These issues were broadly addressed in the preceding section. Because these issues do not normally raise questions of literary unity or disunity, the specific details will be reserved for further comment in the exegetical portion of this work below. There is, however, one point that does need to be addressed. Kleinig has indicated that there is an *inclusio* with the term שׂמחה in vv. 16 and 25. On this basis he argues that v. 25 belongs with the first twenty-four verses of this chapter.[86] Based on this interpretation of the data he argues that the section must be from the hand of the Chronicler.[87]

It seems difficult to arrive at this conclusion. He argues that Williamson has made a similar argument in his commentary.[88] However, Williamson does not call it an *inclusio*. He merely states that "v. 25 is not a direct continuation of v. 15.… However, v. 25 marks the start of the Chronicler's use of 1 Sam. 6."[89] If this writer is interpreting Kleinig correctly, it appears that he has confused Williamson's comment on vv. 4–10 with the present section of material.[90] In light of this, it appears that a better option may be that this is simply a repetition of the noun and nothing more. The use of repetition is common throughout the Chronicler's work and may suggest a return to his main source of Samuel at this point.[91] Such a repetition seems quite natural considering the Chronicler's emphasis on worship. The fact that in v. 16 the music and singing was to be joyful and the fact that v. 25 states that it was joyful seems too natural to be considered an intentional literary convention of the author.

Furthermore, when looking at the passage as a whole, v. 16 introduces the list of the names of the Levites, but v. 25 marks a return to a narrative sequence (note the standard narrative marker ויהי at the opening of v. 25). While Williamson's note that this verse does not explicitly resume the narrative is correct, it appears that with the sudden change of genre from that of roster back to a narrative report, the Chronicler is making a transition back to his source in 2 Samuel.[92] This becomes evident as he picks up his source at the end of v. 25 and continues with it through this section. The fact that 2 Sam 6:12 and v. 25 end with the same noun that v. 16 opens with seems arbitrary. Therefore, it should not be regarded as a valid argument for an *inclusio* in this passage.

The Cultic Appointments in Jerusalem: 1 Chronicles 16:4–6

Translation

(4) And he appointed some of the Levites to minister before the ark of Yahweh, to commemorate,[93] to thank, and to praise Yahweh the God of Israel. (5) Asaph the chief, and next to him Zechariah, then Jeiel, Shemiramoth, Jehiel, Mattithiah, Eliab, Benaiah, and Obed-Edom: Jeiel with instruments of harps and lyres, and Asaph sounding cymbals. (6) Benaiah and Jahaziel the priests regularly blew the trumpets before the ark of the covenant of God.

Background

Because this material is unique to the Chronicler, few scholars are willing to state clearly that this material has any historical value for the preexlic period, although several are willing to say that it does reflect the Chronicler's own time period and that the material should not be regarded as a later addition. Yet, one should note that the Samuel narrative does seem to leave a gap at this point. Obviously, every author makes choices as to what he wants to include or exclude from his work. The Samuel narrative is less interested in the development of the cult than that of the Chronicler's work. Thus, it would be natural for the author to leave this material out of the narrative.[94]

Since the Samuel narrative leaves a narrative gap in its text and the Chronicler's narrative as filling this gap, why must it reflect a later time period? If these lists reflect an earlier time period than that of the Chronicler himself, then it seems reasonable to think that there is at least some historical basis to the list.[95]

Critical Issues

Since 1 Chr 16:4–6 is unique to the Chronicler, many scholars have argued that it is a later addition. In fact, Willi sees nearly all of chapter 16 as a later editorial addition (the exceptions being vv. 1–3, 39, 43).[96] Willi's position is very close to that of Noth's, except Noth takes v. 4 as original.[97] Galling also sees several later additions but he sees fewer additions than Noth and Willi (he excludes vv. 5–6, 37-38, 41–42).[98] De Vries sees the names in v. 5 as being later glosses, with the exception of Asaph and Zechariah.[99] However, Curtis and Madsen view this material as being original to Chronicles.[100] The list of names is taken from 15:17–24. These officials are set aside for the purpose of transporting the ark to Jerusalem. Here, however, there is only one chief singer with seven of his brothers and two priests.

While there is little discussion of these verses being intrusive in the text, there is discussion of priestly editing and the difficulty of placing these lists in the development of cultic officials.[101] The development of these officials is difficult to know precisely. Nevertheless, the hypothesis that a priestly reviser added the material in 1 Chr 16:4–6 is difficult to sustain. First, there are only two priests mentioned. An editor that favored the priesthood would have surely included a larger number of priests to support the ark in Jerusalem, especially in light of the larger number of priests at Gibeon. Second, rather than being out of context the priests' blowing the trumpets before the ark plays an integral part of the liturgy that surrounds the ark.[102] The priests are the ones who are to sound the trumpets (Num 10:8).[103] It also appears that the trumpets were to be used for holy days and sacrifices (Num 10:10). Thus, the ark, while not being designated by the Chronicler here to be included in ritual sacrifices, required two priests to blow the trumpet before it, most likely at the time that the sacrifices took place in Gibeon.[104]

One other issue needs to be addressed. The final priest in v. 6 (Jahaziel) does not appear in 1 Chr 15:24. Japhet suggests that the only way to resolve this problem is to take Jahaziel as a corruption in one list or the other.[105] However, it could also indicate that there is a development in the cultic appointments. Yet, it is clear that the lists are not considered comprehensive in nature and it may suggest that the perceived cultic development is not as clear as some have thought. This is especially true in this instance because the name does appear elsewhere (1 Chr 12:5; 23:19; and Ezra 8:5). It also shows that Japhet's conclusion is not necessary. The Chronicler followed a source at this point because the name does differ from the list in the previous chapter. This suggests that for some reason David appointed specific individuals for the movement of the ark. Then he appointed them and at least Jahaziel to the two cultic sites. Although the addition of Jahaziel seems unexpected, it argues strongly for the fact that Num 10:1 states that two priests are to blow the trumpets. The other priests mentioned in 1 Chr 15:24 are also mentioned as taking part in the activities at Gibeon, where daily sacrifice was to take place. Therefore, the group at Gibeon required a larger number of priests than did the group at Jerusalem. They took precedence over the Jerusalem site and Jahaziel was added to meet the required number of priests there.

The Psalm of Praise: 1 Chronicles 16:7–36

Translation

(7) On that day David first appointed, for the purpose of giving thanks to Yahweh, Asaph and his brothers.

(8) Oh, give thanks to Yahweh;
Call upon his name;
Make known his deeds among the peoples.

(9) Sing to him, sing psalms to him;
Talk of all his wondrous works.

(10) Glory in his holy name;
Let the heart of those rejoice who seek Yahweh.

(11) Seek Yahweh and his strength;
Seek his face evermore.

(12) Remember his marvelous works which he has done;
His wonders, and the judgments of his mouth.

(13) O seed of Israel, his servant,
You children of Jacob, his chosen ones.

(14) He is Yahweh our God;
    His judgments are in all the earth.
(15) Remember his covenant forever;
    The word which he commanded for a thousand generations.
(16) The covenant which he made with Abraham,
    And his oath to Isaac.
(17) And he confirmed it to Jacob as a statute,
    To Israel for an everlasting covenant.
(18) Saying, "To you I will give the land of Canaan,
    As the allotment of your inheritance."
(19) When you were few in number,
    Indeed very few, and strangers in it.
(20) When they went from one nation to another,
    And from one kingdom to another people.
(21) He permitted no man to do them wrong;
    Yes, he rebuked kings for their sakes.
(22) Saying, "Do not touch my anointed ones,
    And do my prophets no harm."
(23) Sing to Yahweh, all the earth;
    Proclaim the good news of his salvation from day to day.
(24) Declare his glory among the nations,
    His wonders among all peoples.[106]
(25) For Yahweh is great and greatly to be praised;
    He is also to be feared above all gods.
(26) For all the gods of the peoples are idols,
    But Yahweh made the heavens.
(27) Honor and majesty are before him;
    Strength and gladness[107] are in his place.
(28) Give to Yahweh, O families of the peoples,
    Give to Yahweh glory and strength.
(29) Give to Yahweh the glory due his;[108]
    Bring an offering, and come before him.[109]
    Oh, worship Yahweh in (his) majestic holiness.[110]
(30) Tremble before him, all the earth.
    The world also is firmly established, it will not be moved.
(31) Let the heavens rejoice, and let the earth be glad;
    And let them say among the nations, Yahweh reigns.
(32) Let the sea roar, and all its fullness;
    Let the field rejoice, and all that is in it.
(33) Then the trees of the woods will rejoice before Yahweh,
    For he is coming to judge the earth.

(34) Oh, give thanks to Yahweh, for he is good.
    For his mercy endures forever.
(35) And say, Save us, O God of our salvation;
    Gather us together, and deliver us from the Gentiles,
    To give thanks to your holy name,
    To triumph in your praise.
(36) Praise Yahweh the God of Israel
    From everlasting to everlasting.
    And all the people said, Amen! and praised Yahweh.

Background

There is little doubt that the Chronicler relied upon the book of Psalms for his song of thanksgiving. Almost all scholars today agree that the Psalms used were already written prior to the time of the Chronicler's composition.[111] Keil argues that David is the actual composer of this psalm and that it was written specifically for the occasion of the ark being brought into the city of Jerusalem for the purpose of public worship.[112] While this may be possible, and many translations clearly adopt this position, it is necessary to note that v. 7 does not actually say that David gave this psalm to Asaph, only that he appointed Asaph and his brothers to give thanks to Yahweh.[113] Myers has a more modest view that has some following. He states, "The Chronicler here illustrates what he believed was the origin and practice in the time of David, by a concrete example from his own time and in so doing gives us an insight into certain liturgical usages in post-exilic times."[114] Most scholars, however, follow Butler and more recently the work of Hausman who argue that the psalm explains the reason for the institution of the Levitical singers in Jerusalem.[115]

The majority of scholars agree that the psalm was composed of three earlier psalms. Yet, at the same time the material the Chronicler chose clearly reflects his own interests and concerns for his own time period.[116] This of course leads to literary and other critical issues. Before addressing these issues, it is important to note that the Chronicler makes no major change in the text of the three Psalms.

Critical Issues

One of the obvious issues is whether the psalm is a later addition to the work of the Chronicler or original to the Chronicler's hand.[117] The reasons for viewing this psalm as being added by a later editor are the same as the reasons for the previous sections. The psalm interrupts the narrative flow of the text and consequently cannot be the work of the Chronicler. Here the mention of Obed-Edom in vv. 5 and 38 is taken to show that these verses are a later pro-Priestly redaction.[118] However, the mention of the priests throughout this narrative does not necessarily mean that a pro-Priestly redactor has been at work. The other sections above have shown that there are other possibilities that need consideration.[119] Kleinig and others have made a strong case for the names of the priests to be connected directly to the narrative and not as an insertion.[120]

One of the most significant works on the redaction of this Psalm is by Gosse.[121] He does not identify the editors and the time period during which they wrote, and does not comment as to whether the psalm itself went through several redactions. It appears, however, that he understands the psalm to be the product of an editor, not of the Chronicler himself. He notes four points that he sees within the Psalm, all of which are related to the covenant with Yahweh. First, he notes that the first place that the ark is mentioned is in 1 Chr 6, in the Levitical genealogy. He indicates that in this passage the Chronicler is preparing for the installation of the ark in the temple and the editors of Chronicles wanted to connect this directly with their community.[122]

Gosse also argues for continuity with the past as a theme because the Levites are connected with the Patriarchs in v. 22. The Levites are charged with making known this unique covenant with Yahweh.[123] His second point is that the people have an eternal covenant with Yahweh (vv. 8–22). He argues that there are two points that cause the reader to identify with the preexilic history. The first is the cult as it is bound to the arrival of the ark in Jerusalem. The second is the covenant and its promise of the land of Canaan forever.[124] His third point is that Yahweh's glory is found in his constant interventions in Israel's history, which is seen in the use of the second Psalm (vv. 23–33). His final point is found in the theme of חסד. He then concludes by arguing that the editor chose these Psalms to show continuity with the past. While his points are well taken, it is difficult to see why this would necessitate a later editor's inserting the psalm. His arguments, though, seem to be quite in line with the themes the Chronicler developed throughout his work.

Kleinig, on the other hand, gives reasons that support the inclusion of the Psalm as being from the Chronicler himself. The most significant of these is that the Levites are appointed to praise Yahweh. The specific terms that v. 4 lists as their function appear within the psalm itself.[125] It is more probable that the Chronicler would have chosen to insert this material into his narrative than would a later editor. This is largely because the Chronicler can use this material in two ways. First, he would have incorporated it to show the significance of song in the worship service of both the preexilic and the postexilic Jewish community. By doing this the Chronicler makes a tie that unifies both time periods, which seems to play into part of the overall purpose of his work. Second, this psalm allows him to weave into it specifics that contribute to his purpose. Thus, the function of the psalm in the text becomes extremely important. The changes he makes to his material discloses what he believes about the importance of singing in the worship of the Jewish people during the Second Temple period.

The structure of the material now needs to be addressed. This issue is debated largely because the psalm is a composition of three other psalms (Pss 105; 96; and 106). This composite composition has led some scholars to argue that it has no unity at all or that part of the psalm was original to David and that the other two sections were later added by the Chronicler.[126] This has resulted in many commentators defaulting the exegesis of the Psalm to commentaries on the Psalms.[127] Yet there is enough unity among these three Psalms for De Vries to classify this unit as a "hymn of praise."[128] Several other scholars have argued for an inner unity for this psalm.[129]

The Chronicler used several literary devices to make the psalm a unified whole.[130] These devices are evident in the major sections of the psalm itself. First, there is an *inclusio* with the phrase הדו ליהוה at the beginning of v. 8 and its second occurrence is at the beginning of v. 34.[131] The *inclusio* acts as a major stanza divider by separating the introduction and conclusion of the psalm from the main body of the psalm itself. It is also significant that it marks off the major section of the psalm as a psalm of praise.

Within this major section there is a clear *inclusio* with the phrase כל־הארץ in vv. 23 and 30. This *inclusio* separates and divides the main part of the praise psalm into three stanzas. The content of the psalm itself agrees with this evaluation. The first main stanza reflects Israel's praise (vv. 9–22); v. 8 serves as an introduction to the psalm itself; the second then reflects the praise of all nations (vv. 23–30); and the final major section is the praise of God over all creation (vv. 31–33).[132] Verse 34 then serves as a conclusion to the main section of the psalm. Further, in v. 35 the phrase "and say" breaks from the psalm citation. This was a priestly call to the people to respond.[133]

The internal composition of this psalm should not be forced into a chiastic structure as some have attempted to do.[134] A chiasmus has been seen by noting the legitimate *inclusio* in vv. 8 and 34 and the repeated imperative שירו in vv. 9 and 23; however, it seems strained to think of these repeated terms forming a chiasm when they are quotations from the Chronicler's source.[135] They are used to introduce parallel units within the poem itself, which is a common function within Hebrew poetry.[136] There are, however, several repeated terms that also seem to support this type of parallel structure within the psalm itself. A quick perusal of the text shows that six terms are repeated three times or more within this brief psalm. They are: (1) הודו (vv. 8, 34, and 35); (2) שם (vv. 8, 10, 29, and 35); (3) עם (vv. 8, 20, 24, 26, and 28); (4) הלל (vv. 10, 25, and 35); (5) קדש (vv. 10, 29, and 35); and (6) גוי (vv. 20, 24, 31, and 35).[137] It would seem that these terms' frequency in this poetic section indicates that the Chronicler purposely chose them to show that worship involved giving praise to Yahweh because of who he is and because of how he will work among the nations to bring praise and honor to himself and his people.[138] This suggests that the psalm itself has been composed with a single unified thought from these three psalms that reflects praise to God. Furthermore, it fits within the narrative context of the larger literary structure and should be considered as coming from the hand of the Chronicler. Nielsen views this psalm as illustrating the care of the Levites in carrying out their duties that David had given them.[139]

This function of the psalm suggests that the reason for the Chronicler to incorporate this material within his work is because it serves as a model for worship which he wants to see similarly expressed in the Second Temple.[140] However, the purpose does not stop there as the psalm connects other narratives around this section to itself.[141] Thus, from a literary perspective, the psalm foreshadows David's military victories that will come in the following chapters (18–20) and are here shown as being the result of Yahweh's intervention on the part of his people (v. 35).

David's Final Ordering of the Levites: 1 Chronicles 16: 37–42

Translation

(37) So he left Asaph and his brothers there before the ark of the covenant of Yahweh to minister before the ark regularly, as every day's work required. (38) And Obed-Edom with his sixty-eight brothers,[142] including Obed-Edom the son of Jeduthun,[143] and Hosah, to be gatekeepers.

(39) And Zadok the priest and his brothers the priests, before the tabernacle of Yahweh at the high place that was at Gibeon. (40) In order to offer burnt offerings to Yahweh on the altar of burnt offering regularly morning and evening, and to do according to all that is written in the Law of Yahweh which he commanded Israel. (41) And with them Heman and Jeduthun and the rest who were chosen, who were designated[144] by name, to give thanks to Yahweh, because his mercy endures forever. (42) And with them Heman and Jeduthun, to sound aloud with trumpets and cymbals and the musical instruments of God. Now the sons of Jeduthun were gatekeepers.

Background

This section of material returns to the narrative developing the cultic divisions for the two sites at Jerusalem and Gibeon. Those scholars who argue for the authenticity of the preceding narrative (vv. 4–6) also understand that these verses are original to the Chronicler.[145] In fact, the task given to Asaph is that of ministering before the ark. This task was explained in v. 4, where David states that they should commemorate, give thanks, and praise Yahweh. This is then illustrated through the psalm which shows that this duty is fulfilled through the use of psalms of praise that are found in the book of Psalms. Furthermore, the Chronicler has included within this section of material the descendants of Merari (v. 38). Jeduthun and Hosah are both Merarites.[146] This is significant as the Chronicler noted that it was the Merarites who were charged with the care of the tabernacle (Num 4:29–33). They were to perform the same duties for the tent where the ark was placed that they carried out in the tabernacle. This restatement of duties shows historical consistency and also reveals the Chronicler's purpose of showing that the ideal unity of a single temple was temporarily delayed.

The form of this pericope seems to be a type of modified roster. It clearly lists the names and duties of individuals but it also lists specific numbers of some of the families. De Vries does not comment on the genre of this unit; however, he does note that v. 40 is an authorization formula.[147]

Critical Issues

There are two major issues regarding the unity of this section. The first is the fact that the Chronicler mentions Obed-Edom, followed by the phrase "sixty-eight of his brothers," (v. 38). The problem comes in 1 Chr 26:8 which states that Obed-Edom had "sixty-two" in his family. This issue is difficult to resolve unless one chooses to resort to seeing a scribal error as there are some similarities of orthography between the two numbers.[148] However, with no manuscript evidence, it is difficult to reach such a conclusion and as a result it seems that this issue is irresolvable at this time.[149]

The second issue is that the Chronicler mentions that the tabernacle was at Gibeon. This reference to Gibeon in the Chronicler's narratives occurs only here and in 1 Chr 21:29 and 2 Chr 1:3–6. As a result some scholars view these references as secondary additions from a later hand.[150] Others think that this section is nothing more than a folktale that the Chronicler fabricated to explain why Solomon went to Gibeon in 1 Kgs 3:4; and for the authorization and authentication of Zadok as high priest because he was not known prior to this time.[151] However, it is more likely that this section of material came from the Chronicler himself. Some scholars argue that he made use of an ancient source that was historically accurate.[152] Others, while not quite as willing to see a completely historically accurate source, have argued that the Chronicler had access to a historical source and that this reflects his own variation of that source.[153] It seems that there is a good case to be made for the historical accuracy of these verses. Williamson, for example, sees 2 Sam 7:6 as implying "respect for the tent sanctuary."[154] However, the work of Görg and Hertzberg is the most consistent argument for the Chronicler's use of an earlier, historically reliable source. They base their argument on the close geographical locations of Nob and Gibeon, noting that the tabernacle was most likely moved from Nob after Saul killed the priests there because they gave David the show bread. They further argue that the tent that David had constructed for the ark could not have been the tabernacle.[155] This suggests that there must have been some source that the Chronicler was following at this point.[156] This specific passage is significant of understanding the work of the Chronicler, especially since this chapter appears to be devoted to the division of the Levites between the sanctuaries at Gibeon and Jerusalem. Historically speaking, valid reasons exist for this duality in the cult during the united monarchy. This narrative in Chronicles helps explain how the divisions of the priests and Levites were developed for the temple cultus in 1 Chr 23–27. Thus, this section of material should be viewed as being central to the work of the Chronicler.

Conclusion: 1 Chronicles 16:43

Translation

(43) Then all the people departed, every man to his house, and David returned to bless his house.

Background

This verse marks the Chronicler's return to his source in 2 Samuel. It is a quotation of 2 Sam 6:19–20. As has been noted above, virtually all scholars take this verse to be original with the Chronicler. Therefore, there are no literary-critical issues that need to be addressed here. It is significant that Knoppers notes that this verse forms an *inclusio* with 15:3.[157] Thus, the entire section of the second part of the ark narrative forms a single unit. Furthermore, Johnstone notes that the term "house," which ends this chapter connects this narrative to the following narrative in 1 Chr 17.[158] The final verse does link this chapter with what comes before and what comes after it. While it may be possible for an editor to connect the passages as a larger unit, it is more likely, because most scholars see this verse as original with the Chronicler, that the Chronicler himself has deliberately linked the passages. This linking argues for a complete unity of the work with what precedes and with what follows.

Features and Functions as a Whole

The critical analysis above has looked at specific sections of material within the second part of the ark narrative. It is now necessary to show how this narrative connects on a comprehensive scale with the narrative units around it. First, while most scholars acknowledge that this narrative properly begins in chapter 13, there are larger literary connections.[159] Mosis actually marks the beginning of the narrative unit at chapter 11 because he equates the anointing of David, the subsequent conquering of Jerusalem, and David's making Jerusalem his capital as being essential conditions for the ark narrative. The topics of anointing and conquering Jerusalem are treated only superficially and serve as an introduction to the ark narrative.[160] Eskenazi argues that the narrative unit is directly related to the Saul narrative.[161] Therefore, she argues that the beginning point of the larger narrative should be chapter 10.[162] While it is clear that the ark narrative proper begins in chapter 13, Eskenazi's view of the story of the ark as being directly related to the larger narrative including Saul's narrative stands on solid literary grounds.[163] Thus, while the ark narrative proper clearly starts in chapter 13, it is clear that the Chronicler chose his material within the second major section of his work (1 Chr 10–2 Chr 9) by introducing the need for the care of the ark and the consequences for those who did not give it proper care.[164] This suggests that the entire narrative that opens the Chronicler's second section is designed to show his concentration on the priority of proper worship.

While the ark narrative proper unquestionably ends with chapter 16, the story itself continues beyond this chapter. Braun and Japhet actually include chapter 17 in this narrative unit.[165] While this viewpoint is not without merit, Mosis and others have suggested that chapter 17 is the start of a new unit of material that is closely related to the ark narrative.[166] In fact, Eskenazi states, "I suggest that 17:1–22:19 is another ark narrative that replays, on a larger scale, some of the thematic developments of chaps. 13–16, likewise beginning and ending with the ark (17:1; 22:19)."[167] She bases this understanding not only on the *inclusio* that is noted here but also on a significant literary device that the Chronicler uses, namely, repetition of themes and similar actions. For example, the Chronicler includes within both of these episodes an opening desire to care for the ark which is then followed by two military victories. These victories are then the reason for the cultic consecration that follows and concludes the units. These two parallel units that are at work need to be viewed as closely associated with each other.[168] This association results in the ark narrative itself coming to the fore of the Chronicler's purpose.

Wright, on the other hand, argues that there is no ark narrative in Chronicles.[169] His statement is not without merit because 1 Chr 14 breaks the ark narrative into two segments. The ark narrative is not a single continuous narrative as it appears in 2 Samuel. However, 1 Chr 14 was moved between the two attempts at transferring the ark to Jerusalem precisely to show that David was being blessed by Yahweh. This blessing fits the Chronicler's purpose of Yahweh blessing those who care for the cult. Thus, chapter 14 actually lays the groundwork for chapters 15–16 because it clearly indicates that David had been blessed. David realizes that Yahweh has not judged him for moving the ark but for not moving it properly. He then takes measures to ensure proper care for the ark during its transport.[170]

Although the ark narrative itself has been defined as chapters 13–16, it has close literary connections to what comes before it and what follows.[171] However, it seems that the story of the ark does not end in chapter 22 either. The next section of material within the book (1 Chr 23–29) sets up Solomon's enthronement by showing David's motivation for arranging the cult into its final organization and his command to Solomon to build the temple so that the ark might have rest (1 Chr 28:2). Eskenazi states, "Indeed, one can label 1 Chronicles 10 to 2 Chronicles 10 as stations on the ark's way until it finally finds its rest in David's and Solomon's temple...."[172]

The literary analysis suggests that the ark narrative itself plays an important role within the Davidic and the Solomonic narratives as it pertains to the development of the cult.[173] It also appears that it is the foundational narrative that structures the book as a whole.[174] This being the case, it causes the reader to think about the implications of David's first establishing the political capital and then establishing and organizing the cult within that capital.

Summary

The broader literary context shows that the Chronicler is focused on the ark, the temple, and the city of Jerusalem. The narrower unit of the ark narrative (1 Chr 13–16) links all of these themes. Furthermore, the second part of the ark narrative (1 Chr 15–16) should be viewed as coming from the hand of a single author. The sections on the background of each of the literary units at least allow for the historicity of the material. The critical issues were able to be resolved to one degree or another and indicate that it is possible for a single author to have written the material found in 1 Chr 15–16. While it may be impossible to prove some of the arguments that support unity, it seems more probable because of the mounting evidence that this narrative, as well as those around it, are all from the same hand.

The individual units combine to emphasize the significance, aesthetics, and joyfulness of the ark's procession into Jerusalem. The Chronicler focused his attention on cultic matters and because this narrative seems to serve as the foundation of the Chronicler's work as a whole, it drives worship to the forefront of the Chronicler's concern.

Notes

1. Leslie C. Allen, "Kerygmatic Units in 1 and 2 Chronicles," *JSOT* 41 (1988): 23.
2. The reason for not treating chap. 16 seems to be based on the fact that the keyword (פרץ) found in 13–15 is not present in that chapter (ibid., 27–28). There are other literary connections that need to be addressed, however.
3. There are several recent studies that have looked at the various structural devices on a section by section basis. Kalimi makes specific points about topics like additions, omission, chiasmus, parallel panels, parallel texts, etc., but he does not comment on specific issues within specific pericopes (see Issac Kalimi, *The Reshaping of Ancient Israelite History in Chronicles* [Winona Lake, Ind.: Eisenbrauns, 2005]). Further, Strübind has done a detailed work on 2 Chr 17:1–21:1 (Kim Strübind, *Tradition als Interpretation in der Chronik: König Josaphat als Paradigma chronistischer Hermeneutik und Theologie*, BZAW 201 [Berlin: de Gruyter, 1991]).
4. H. G. M. Williamson, *1 and 2 Chronicles*, NCBC (Grand Rapids: Eerdmans, 1982), 121–22. Welten has also noted a similar literary device in Ezra–Nehemiah (Peter Welten, *Geschichte und Geschichtsdarstellung in den Chronikbüchern*, WMANT 42 [Neukirchen-Vluyn: Neukirchener, 1973], 190–92). The very fact that Ezra–Nehemiah has similar literary devices seems to support the theory that these devices were in vogue within this time period. However, these various literary conventions do not necessarily reflect common authorship. They do, however, support the idea that these devices were seen and understood by the original readers as standard literary conventions used by a postexilic author.
5. Allen, "Kerygmatic Units," 26–33.
6. Ingeborg Gabriel, *Friede über Israel: Eine Untersuchung zur Friedenstheologie in Chronik 1 10–2 36*, ÖBS 10 (Klosterneuburg: Österreichisches Katholisches Bibelwerk, 1990), 168–72; 179–80.
7. Raymond B. Dillard, *2 Chronicles*, WBC 15 (Waco, Tex.: Word Books, 1987), 129–30; and John W. Kleinig, *The LORD's Song: The Basis, Function and Significance of Choral Music in Chronicles*, JSOTSup 156 (Sheffield: JSOT Press, 1993), 172–73.
8. As the extrabiblical evidence seems to suggest, the Chronicler has deliberately developed the ark narrative in a way that reflects David's care for the ark and the city. This in turn allows God to pour out blessings on David and the nation. Therefore, it follows that the various kings and their regard for God and his ark is directly correlated to their success or failure. See Gary N. Knoppers, *1 Chronicles, 10–29: A New Translation with Introduction and Commentary*, AB 12A (New York: Doubleday, 2004), 632. Walters emphasizes the fact that a king's offences against God result in tragedy for the nation (Stanley D. Walters, "Saul of Gibeon," *JSOT* 52 [1991]: 61–76).
9. Scholars who have sought to discover how the Chronicler incorporates his material include Sara Japhet, *1 and 2 Chronicles: A Commentary*, OTL (London: SCM, 1993); and Kleining, *The LORD's Song*, 141–44.
10. In addition to the textual remarks below, one should also consult Leslie C. Allen, *The Greek Chronicles: The Relation of the Septuagint of 1 and 2 Chronicles to the Massoretic Text*, vol. 2, *Textual Criticism*, VTSup 27 (Leiden: Brill, 1974); Knoppers, *1 Chronicles 10–29*; Jared Judd Jackson, "The Ark Narratives: An Historical, Textual, and Form-Critical Study of 1 Samuel 4–6 and 2 Samuel 6" (Th.D. diss., Union Theological Seminary, N.Y., 1962); Werner E. Lemke, "Syn-

optic Studies in the Chronicler's History" (Ph.D. diss., Harvard University, 1963), microfilm; and Sebastian P. Brock, *The Recensions of the Septuagint Version of 1 Samuel*, Quaderni di Henoch 9 (Torino: Zamorani, 1996).

11. The LXX omits the *waw*, which would change the meaning of the text to "the sons of Aaron the Levites." This could be taken as excluding the priests. However, in light of no other textual evidence, and the fact that v. 11 specifies that the priests were also called, the evidence seems to favor the inclusion of the *waw* here.

12. The codices Vaticanus and Sinaiticus read "ten" instead of MT's "twenty." While the weight of these two codices is significant, the reading is difficult to follow because of the absence of other external witness to the variant. It appears that the scribe most likely dropped the plural ending thus reading "ten."

13. The LXX reads "fifty" for the MT's "twenty." It is difficult to understand how a scribe could mistake the Hebrew terms for "fifty" and "twenty." One possibility is that the variant arose as a result of an inner Greek corruption caused by the use of letters for numerals.

14. A few medieval Hebrew manuscripts read "two hundred" for the MT's "one hundred." However, the versions support the MT. Thus the textual evidence seems to favor the MT.

15. The LXX reads "150"for MT's "130." Again, the lack of other witnesses for the variant make it difficult to understand what the LXX translators were really seeing in their text. This has led some to suggestion that the original had numerals instead of the usual spelled out numbers (see Knoppers, *1 Chronicles 10–29*, 606). The suggestion is intriguing as there are several inscriptions that support this theory. However, no medieval Hebrew manuscript consulted has numerals, which suggests that the error occurred very early in the transmission of the text.

16. One medieval Hebrew manuscript reads "80" for the MT's "200." It seems that this is the result of homoeoteleuton, as "80" is in the following line.

17. The MT lacks "the place." The Syriac, Targums, Vulgate, and the Arabic versions and a few medieval Hebrew manuscripts all read "the place which." Although the MT seems broken at this point, Joüon notes that in Chronicles the article could be used as a relative and so the MT could be correct (Joüon, §158d). The versions are most likely smoothing out the Hebrew text that they are reading. The *BHS* editors also suggest that one insert the phrase "the tent which." There is no textual evidence for this insertion and it should be rejected.

18. The MT is very difficult at this point; the literal translation would be "not you." The *BHS* editors suggest inserting "with us," making the reading "you were not with us." But 1 Chr 13:2 indicates that the Levites were with the first procession. It seems that the verb was lost as a result of haplography because the ending of the verb would be similar to the pronoun.

19. "Son" is lacking in a few medieval Hebrew manuscripts and the LXX. The editors of *BHS* have suggested deleting it. It seems that here the shorter reading is to be preferred.

20. The MT reads "Jaaziel." However, the LXX reads Oziel. The MT may be the result of dittography. In this case the first /y/ was written due to waw/yod confusion as a result of the preceding conjunction. The *BHS* editors also prefer the LXX here based on the textual evidence of v. 20.

21. The LXX reading adds Ozcias, the *BHS* editors suggest Azaziah; in light of the parallel in v. 21. Allen's comments are helpful here and following his suggestion the name is included (Allen, *The Greek Chronicles*, 137-38).

22. The translation here is based on BDB, 761.

23. *HALOT*, 1562 suggests that the term may be used as a contrast to "the voice of the women" in v. 20, and that this term is used for a bass instrument.

24. There are a few medieval Hebrew manuscripts that read "Benaniah." This can be explained by the similarity between /k/ and /b/ and should be regarded as orthographic confusion.

25. The MT has "in bearing" but this seems to be the result of dittography as the same term appears later in the verse. The translation reflects the LXX reading, which omits this term.

26. The LXX renders the term as "of the odes," and the Vulgate "to chant the melody." The broader context in chapter 15 indicates that carrying sacred vessels (i.e., the ark) was part of the the Levitical duties.

27. Japhet, *1 and 2 Chronicles*, 292.

28. Ibid.

29. The ark narratives of 2 Samuel and 1 Chronicles have several differences. In Chronicles, the ark narrative follows David's enthronement in 1 Chr 12. The Chronicler moves from chapter 12 to 13 in such a way that suggests that the movement of the ark occurred immediately following the events of chapter 12. Also, 1 Chr 13:6–14 closely parallels 2 Sam 6:2–11 (vv. 1–5 are unique to the Chronicler). However, the Chronicler has transposed 2 Sam 5:11–25, which historically must have occurred before the first attempt at transferring the ark. The Chronicler has broken his source in 2 Sam 5 into two parts. The first (vv. 1–9) is found in 1 Chr 11. The remainder is placed in chapter 14. This change in the chronological development fits the Chronicler's theological purposes. By placing all aspects of Jerusalem and David's desire to care for the things of Yahweh early in David's reign makes clear that David is successful because of his faithfulness to Yahweh. The failure of the initial movement of the ark is a crushing blow to David's early success. He states that "Yahweh broke out against us," (15:13) which makes clear that David understands the death of Uzzah was not merely Yahweh's judgment against Uzzah but on the entire procession. The Chronicler moves 2 Sam 5:11–25 here in order to show that while Yahweh judged David and the procession, David was still favored by Yahweh. This shows that there is a clear since of purpose on the part of the Chronicler in changing the chronological order of his story.

30. It is clear that the movement of the ark is important. When one looks at the narratives from a chronological standpoint the issue becomes clearer still. Merrill notes that Hiram's building of David's palace (2 Sam 5:11) could have only occurred late in David's reign. The ark was clearly moved after the completion of his palace and therefore, late in David's reign. Thus, neither ark narrative is set in its chronological background. (Eugene H. Merrill, "The 'Accession Year' and Davidic Chronology," *JANES* 19 [1989]: 104).

31. Simon J. De Vries, *1 and 2 Chronicles*, FOTL 11 (Grand Rapids: William B. Eerdmans, 1989), 426–27.

32. Ibid., 143.

33. See Paul D. Hanson, "1 Chronicles 15–16 and the Chronicler's Views of the Levites," in *'Sha'arei Talmon:' Studies in the Bible, Qumran, and the Ancient Near East Presented to Shemaryahu Talmon*, ed. Michael Fishbane and Emanuel Tov (Winona Lake, Ind.: Eisenbrauns, 1992), 69–77.

34. Martin Noth, *The Chronicler's History*, trans. H.G. M. Williamson, JSOTSup 50 (Sheffield: JSOT Press, 1987), 35.

35. Wilhelm Rudolph, *Chronikbücher*, HAT 21 (Tübingen: Mohr–Siebeck, 1955), 115–25; and also Piet Dirksen, "The Development of the Text of 1 Chronicles, 15:1-24," *Hen* 17 (1995): 268–72.Hartmut Gese, "Zur Geschichte der Kultsänger am zweiten Tempel," in *Abraham unser Vater: Juden und Christen in Gespräch über die Bibel. Festschrift für Otto Michel Zum 60. Geburtstag*, ed. Otto Betz, Martin Hengel, and Peter Schmidt (Leiden: Brill, 1963), 222–34.

36. De Vries, *1 and 2 Chronicles*, 435.

37. Risto Nurmela, *The Levites: Their Emergence as a Second-Class Priesthood,* University of Southern Florida Studies in the History of Judaism 193 (Atlanta: Scholars Press, 1998), 171–73; Antonius H. J. Gunneweg, *Leviten und Priester: Hauptlinien der Tradionsbildung und Geschichte des israelisch-jüdischen Kultpersonals,* FRLANT 89 (Göttingen: Vandenhoeck & Ruprecht, 1965), 211–12; and Kurt Galling, *Die Bücher der Chronik, Esra, Nehemia,* ATD 12 (Berlin: Evangelische, 1958), 11, 49, 51.

38. Johann Wilhelm Rothstein and Johannes Hänel, *Kommentar zum ersten Buch der Chronik,* KAT 18/2 (Leipzig: Deichertsche, 1927), 304–12.

39. Gese's development is as follows: Stage 1 probably started shortly after the return from the exile and most certainly by the time that the Temple was completed. At this time the singers were called the 'sons of Asaph,' and according to Gese they were not considered to be Levites in this initial phase. He lists Ez 2:41 and Neh 7:44 as examples of this phase. Stage 2 would be around 450 B.C.E. during the time of Nehemiah. Gese believed that because of the dual groups listed in Neh 11:13–19 there were only those two groups in operation during that time period. These two groups were both identified as Levites and noted as being the sons of Asaph and Jeduthun. Stage 3 was divided into two distinct time periods. Stage 3a is the time period that Gese has associated with the time of the Chronicler (around 350–300 B.C.E.). At this time the Levitical singers form a trio. They are identified with three sons of Levi: namely, Asaph, Heman, and Jeduthun. This list is found in 1 Chr 16:4–6, 37–42. At this period the most prominent group is the sons of Asaph. Stage 3b results in some changes to the list of singers and is considered to be later than the time of the Chronicler's writing. This time period is reflected in 1 Chr 15:16–24. This is because the name Ethan has replaced Jeduthun, and Gese supposes that due to the placement of the names that Heman has become more prominent than Asaph.

40. Gese states only that Neh 12:8, 24 and Ezra 3:10–12 complicate his reconstruction as they may in fact be from a stage later than that of the Chronicler's work.

41. Baruch A. Levine, Numbers 1–20: A New Translation with Introduction and Commentary, AB 4A (New York: Doubleday, 1993), 176–77.

42. Knoppers states, "That he [Gese] fails to deal with the LXX evidence is most unfortunate, because the LXX evidence from Nehemiah undermines one of the stages in his reconstruction...." (Gary N. Knoppers, *1 Chronicles 10–29,* 657–58). Knoppers also argues for this view elsewhere (see Gary N. Knoppers, "Sources, Revisions, and Editions: The Lists of Jerusalem's Residents in MT and LXX Nehemiah 11 and 1 Chronicles 9," *Text* 20 [2000]: 141–68; and also see William H. Barnes, "Jeduthun," in *ABD,* ed. David Noel Freedman, vol. 3 [New York: Doubleday, 1992], 655–56).

43. Knoppers, *1 Chronicles 10–29,* 658.

44. Williamson, *1 and 2 Chronicles,* 121.

45. Georg Steins, *Die Chronik als kanonisches Abschlussphänomen: Studien zur Entstehung und Theologie von 1/2 Chronik,* BBB 93 (Weinheim: Athenäum, 1995), 254.

46. Ibid., 275.

47. Ibid., 254–55.

48. Ibid., 267.

49. This issue will be discussed in detail in chapter three. One should note that Steins' argument is very complex and involves more than just the differences between the cult singers found in the genealogical material (ibid., 269–70). Yet, his lengthy analysis of it, in connection with chapters 15–16, suggests that he places a major emphasis on it (ibid., 260–69). For example, Steins argues that the expansion in 1 Chr 6 is between the first and second layers in 1 Chr 15.

Thus, the expansion layer found in 1 Chr 15 can be classified by the editing process. His examination of 1 Chr 15–16, based on this concept of this second expansion, presupposes the expansion in 1 Chr 6 and then yet another redaction in which all three lead musicians are present in the text (ibid., 269).

50. See Roddy L. Braun, *1 Chronicles*, WBC 14 (Waco, Tex.: Word Books, 1986), 187–88.

51. Dirksen argues that this should be interpreted as the way the ark was about to be moved (Dirksen, "The Development of the Text of I Chronicles 15," 272). In either case the parallel panels appear to be valid.

52. While this breakdown is the author's own, one should note that Kleinig's analysis of this material is similar. However, he argues that v. 25 closes this unit in an *inclusio* with v. 16. This will be addressed in the section analyzing 15:25–16:3. His division as a result is somewhat different from that above. He sees the material in vv. 17–24 as falling under number 2. Thus v. 25 becomes number 3 and indicates the actual movement for the ark. While his analysis has much to commend it, he ignores the change of emphasis in v. 22 and the fact that most scholars rightly see a return to the Chronicler's *Vorlage* at v. 25. See Williamson, *1 and 2 Chronicles*, 126; Knoppers, *1 Chronicles 10–29*, 624; and De Vries, *1 and 2 Chronicles*, 145–46.

53. Rudolph, *Chronikbücher*, 115–22.

54. Braun, *1 Chronicles*, 188.

55. Immanuel Benzinger, *Die Bücher der Chronik* (Tübingen: Mohr, 1901), microfiche, 51.

56. Peter Welten, *Geschichte und Geschichtsdarstellung in den Chronikbüchern*, WMANT 42 (Neukirchen-Vluyn: Neukirchener, 1973), 190–91.

57. Rothstein and Hänel, *Chronik*, 274–76; and Rudolph, *Chronikbücher*, 115–122.

58. De Vries, *1 and 2 Chronicles*, 142. Williamson also argues that the reference to the priests in vv. 4, 11, and 14 is the result of a pro-Priestly editor (Williamson, *1 and 2 Chronicles*, 122).

59. For example, *m. Tamid* 1.2, which indicates that the priests had to immerse themselves before undertaking duties in the temple.

60. One wonders if this does not apply to 1 Chr 16:2, where the text states that David offered burnt sacrifice. However, 16:1 states that they (i.e., the priests) offered sacrifice. They were the ones who had sanctified themselves for the purpose of sacrificing. Therefore, David as king is the one who is credited with the sacrifices because he is the one who has authorized the priests to carry out the ritual. It was not uncommon for ancient Near Eastern scribes to attribute an act to the king that others have carried out because he authorized the action. This view of David authorizing but not sacrificing should not be viewed as an attempt to take David's priestly actions away from him. The Chronicler does in fact portray him as functioning as a priest (e.g., he blesses the people immediately following the sacrifices which is a distinct priestly act [1 Chr 16:2]).

61. Japhet, 1 and 2 Chronicles, 294.

62. Ibid., 300.

63. Knoppers draws attention to several places in 1 Chr 23–27 where the lists in 1 Chr 15–16 are referenced (see Knoppers, *1 Chronicles 10–29*, 807, 810, 847, 849, 856, 867, 869, 870, 872, 897, 910, and 912). Based on the fact that David has utilized the Levites' own division, it is logical that he continues to develop the various courses and guilds based upon the information he has from these two cultic sites.

64. Williamson certainly seems to agree with this point. See Williamson, *1 and 2 Chronicles*, 120.

65. H. G. M. Williamson, "The Accession of Solomon in the Books of Chronicles," *VT* 23 (1976): 376–79.

66. Ernst Michael Dörrfuß, *Mose in den Chronikbüchern: Garant theokratischer Zukunftser-wartung*, BZAW 219 (Berlin: de Gruyter, 1994), 133.
67. Ibid., 135.
68. Ibid.
69. Ibid., 135–36. Weinberg has written the standard work on this issue (see Joel Weinberg, *The Citizen-Temple Community*, trans. Daniel L. Smith-Christopher, JSOTSup 151 [Sheffield: JSOT Press, 1992], 48–61).
70. Ibid., 136.
71. Ibid., 137–38.
72. This also appears to be Japhet's view as well. See Sara Japhet, *The Ideology of the Book of Chronicles and Its Place in Biblical Thought*, trans. Anna Barber, 2d ed., BEATAJ 9 (Frankfurt am Main: Lang, 1997), 238.
73. Second Samuel 6:12 has "ark of God." The Chronicler's change from his source should not be seen as a variant source as they are interchanged throughout.
74. Second Samuel 6:12 adds the phrase, "to the City of David."
75. Because the Chronicler has returned to his Samuel source, there will be a few places throughout this translation where some significant differences between these two texts will be noted.
76. The Chronicler is interpreting the events of his source material here. Second Samuel 6:13 has the expected "when they moved forward." Here the Chronicler wishes to emphasize that Yahweh was with the procession and helping to move the ark.
77. Second Samuel 6:13 notes that they offered sacrifices after six steps (or every six steps). Here there is no mention of sacrifice after six steps (although there are several ANE parallels to it). Further, the animals are different. In Samuel it was one ox and one fatted sheep; here it is seven bulls and seven rams. Although significant differences are apparent, the Chronicler may have followed his source as both the LXX and 4QSam^a read "seven bulls and seven rams." The LXX of 2 Sam 6:13 shows that there was some textual confusion at this point. It reads "And there were with him bearing the ark seven bands, and for a sacrifice a calf and a lamb."
78. Second Samuel 6:15 lacks the specific instruments of the trumpets, cymbals, harps, and lyres.
79. Although several Hebrew manuscripts are lacking the preposition עד, as is 2 Sam 6:16, it would seem that this is a result of haplography because the following root is עיר.
80. Second Samuel differs here again. It has "skipping and whirling" before Yahweh instead of "dancing and playing." The context of 2 Samuel, however, may be the reason for the specific choice of words there as they develop from common ANE cosmological terms for nature's movement away from Yahweh. Seow argues that such dances represented animals and other natural elements fleeing from before Yahweh. For a brief discussion on the dance in this procession corresponding to these cosmological terms see C. L. Seow, *Myth, Drama, and the Politics of David's Dance*, HSM 44 (Atlanta: Scholars Press, 1989), 104–18.
81. The verbal altercation between David and Michal has been left out by the Chronicler. It seems that the narrative in 2 Samuel uses it to show the final end of any possible Saulide rule. The Chronicler had other intentions (i.e., the organization and incorporation of Levitical worship duties) and had no need to develop this issue in detail.
82. The text here is different from 2 Samuel, as the 3mp "they brought near" indicates that all the people were participants in the sacrifices that took places following the procession. Second Samuel 6:17 indicates that it was David who offered up the sacrifices.

83. It is difficult to determine precisely what this term means. *HALOT* suggests that it was a roll containing raisins (*HALOT*, 95; BDB, 84).

84. De Vries, *1 and 2 Chronicles*, 434.

85. There are various opinions about the number of differences found between these two texts. These differences seem to be of lesser importance for the point that the Chronicler is trying to make. For more complete lists on these differences see Japhet, *1 and 2 Chronicles*, 293–94; and Williamson, *1 and 2 Chronicles*, 119–20; 126–27.

86. Kleinig, *The LORD's Song*, 44-49.

87. Ibid., 45.

88. Ibid., 44–45.

89. Williamson, *1 and 2 Chronicles*, 122.

90. This becomes apparent as he indicates that Williamson's discussion starts on page 121; however, Williamson's discussion of vv. 4–10 continues through this page and on to the following one as well. Also see Kleining, *The LORD's Song*, 44.

91. For specific examples see Isaac Kalimi, *The Reshaping of Ancient Israelite History in Chronicles* (Winona Lake, Ind.: Eisenbrauns, 2005), 275–94. One should also note that Kalimi does not list v. 25 in his chapter devoted to *inclusio* (ibid., 295–324).

92. This specific genre form is taken from De Vries. See De Vries, *1 and 2 Chronicles*, 143.

93. The *waw* here, and those following in this verse are functioning as explanatory *waw*'s. See GKC §154a, n. 1b.

94. Japhet, *1 and 2 Chronicles*, 314.

95. One can assume that the Israelites, like the Egyptians, placed a high value on documenting the priests and Levites because improper handling of the sacred objects resulted in death (e.g., 1 Chr 13:10; Num 4:15). Thus, this list could reflect the actual individuals chosen by David.

96. Thomas Willi, *Die Chronik als Auslegung: Untersuchungen zur literarischen Gestaltung der historischen Überlieferung Israels*, FRLANT 106 (Göttingen: Vandenhoeck & Ruprecht, 1972), 196.

97. Noth, *The Chronicler's History*, 35, 57.

98. Galling, *Die Bücher der Chronik*, 51.

99. De Vries, *1 and 2 Chronicles*, 149.

100. Edward Lewis Curtis and Albert Alonzo Madsen, *A Critical and Exegetical Commentary on the Books of Chronicles*, ICC (Edinburgh: T. & T. Clark, 1910), 219. While they understand these verses as being original, they do see the names Obed-Edom and Jeiel, and Asaph in v. 5 as being glosses.

101. Williamson, *1 and 2 Chronicles*, 127–28.

102. Ibid.

103. This particular reference does not address the ark, but it does state that only the priests are to blow the trumpets.

104. Curtis and Madsen, *Chronicles*, 220–21.

105. Japhet, *1 and 2 Chronicles*, 315.

106. Although the LXX omits the entire verse, all other versions have included it. It would appear that the verse was lost due to haplography. In this case the haplography is due to homoeoteleuton due to the similar endings of the final terms of vv. 23 and 24.

107. The term חדוה is rare in the Hebrew Bible and occurs only three other places (Neh 8:10, Eccl 8:1; and Ezra 6:16). Interestingly, Rudolph notes that this word also occurs in four Hebrew manuscripts of Ps 96:6 (Rudolph, *Chronikbücher*, 122). The rarity of the word suggests its originality in this text.

108. This line is lacking in the LXX. It would seem that the similarities between the previous verse and the second line of this verse may be the cause of the error. Both v. 28 and 29 open with the same term הבו. Further complicating the issue for the scribe is that the term ending this line is also similar to the term beginning the second line שמו and שאו.

109. The Chronicler has substituted the phrase in Psalm 96:8 "to his courts" with "before him." This may be because in the Chronicler's narrative the temple has not been built at this point. This psalm was not the psalm that David had the Levites sing on the occasion of the ark's entrance into Jerusalem. The change must have been on the part of the Chronicler to reflect the narrative and his purpose.

110. The translation "in his majestic holiness" closely follows Knoppers' discussion of the translation of this phrase. See Knoppers, *1 Chronicles 10–29*, 639.

111. The exception is Ackroyd, who has argued that the Psalmist was indebted to the Chronicler. This position has not found wide acceptance (Ackroyd, *1 and 2 Chronicles*, 64–65).

112. Keil, *Chronicles*, 209–10; 218. See Goettsberger who sees only vv. 8–22 as being original to David. See Johann Goettsberger, *Die Bücher der Chronik oder Paralipomenon*, HSAT 4 (Bonn: Peter Hanstein, 1939), 128, 131. No other commentator consulted holds this position.

113. Among the more prominent translations are KJV, NKJV, NLT, NIV, and NET. However, see the translation of this passage above.

114. Jacob Martin Myers, *1 Chronicles*, 2d ed. AB 12 (Garden City, N.Y.: Doubleday, 1965), 121. Williamson also considers this psalm as being an illustration of the type of worship that was common during David's time, following the institution of the Levitical singers (Williamson, *1 and 2 Chronicles*, 128). See also Kleinig, *The LORD's Song*, 134.

115. Trent C. Butler, "A Forgotten Passage from a Forgotten Era (1 Chr. 16:8-36)," *VT* 28 (1978): 142–50; and Jutta Hausmann, *Israels Rest: Studien zum Selbstverständnis der nachexilischen*, BWANT 124 (Stuttgart: Kohlhammer, 1987), 228–29.

116. Williamson, *1 and 2 Chronicles*, 128.

117. Representative of later additions include Rothstein and Hänel, *Buch der Chronik*, 297, 312–18; Galling, *Bücher der Chronik*, 51; and Rudolph, *Chronikbücher*, 115, 127. Kittel, however, supports the view that the Psalm was original to the Chronicler. See Rudolf Kittel, *Die Bücher der Chronik* (Göttingen: Vandenhoeck & Ruprecht, 1902), microfiche, 70. It seems that for Kittel, the narrative disruption is a result of the compositional activity of the Chronicler, because the narrative itself sets up the framework for the psalm in which he has introduced the Levitical singers.

118. So Rothstein and Hänel, *Buch der Chronik*, 297; and Rudolph, *Chronikbücher*, 115.

119. It seems natural for the Chronicler to spend more time with the Levites than the priests, as the Levites are his major concern throughout his work. However, the priests are mentioned throughout this narrative in places because of their involvement in the procession.

120. Kleinig argues that the disruption of the narrative is the work of the Chronicler and not a latter addition (Kleinig, *The LORD's Song*, 135). One should note, however, that his statement regarding Williamson needs to be qualified (ibid.) as Williamson states that the mention of the priests in vv. 4, 11, and 14 is secondary (see Williamson, *1 and 2 Chronicles*, 123).

121. Bernard Gosse, "Les citations de Psaumes en 1 Ch 16:8–36 et la conception des relations entre Yahvé et son peuple dans la rédaction des livres des Chroniques," *ÉgT* 27 (1996): 313–33. This position is also argued by Loader as well. See J. A. Loader, "Redaction and Function of the Chronistic 'Psalm of David,'" in *Studies in the Chronicler*, ed. W. C. van Wyk, OTWSAOTE 19 (Johannesburg: Weeshuispers, 1976), 69–75.

122. Ibid., 314.

123. Ibid., 316.
124. Ibid., 323.
125. Kleinig, *The LORD's Song*, 135–36; Andrew E. Hill, "Patchwork Poetry or Reasoned Verse? Connective Structure in 1 Chron 16," *VT* 33 (1983): 99.
126. Gunkel sees the psalm as nothing more than a haphazard arrangement of various psalms. See Hermann Gunkel, *Die Psalmen*, 4th ed., Göttinger HKAT 2 (Göttingen: Vandenhoeck & Ruprecht, 1926), 422. Goettsberger, however, sees some unity but poor editing results in disruption of the text. See Goettsberger, *Die Bücher der Chronik*, 131.
127. For example, see Myers, *1 Chronicles*, 121.
128. De Vries, 1 and 2 Chronicles, 150.
129. Keil argued for the unity of the Psalm (Keil, *Chronicles*, 218). Scholarship today has found unity through literary analysis. Loader sees a thematic unity that supports the consistency of the narrative that surrounds the psalm (Loader, "Redaction and Function," 69–75). Butler shows that the content of the psalm is consistent with the intention of the entire work (Butler, "A Forgotten Passage," 149). Hill has also shown that the psalm reflects classical Hebrew style and poetic devices (Hill, "Patchwork Poetry," 99–100).
130. John W. Watts, *Psalm and Story: Inset Hymns in Hebrew Narrative*, JSOTSup 139 (Sheffield: JSOT Press, 1992), 155–64. Watts concludes that the best explanation of this composition is that it is from the hand of the Chronicler.
131. Pratt rightly notes that v. 34 is the first verse of Psalm 106. The Chronicler only quoted vv. 1, 47–48 of this psalm because the middle portion of it expresses mourning over sins. Thus, one wonders why v. 1 would be included within the quotation. This certainly appears consistent with an *inclusio*. See Richard L. Pratt, *1 and 2 Chronicles* (Fearn: Mentor, 1998), 144.
132. This breakdown is somewhat different from that of the majority of commentators, who see the section as being vv. 23–33 (e.g., Knoppers, *1 Chronicles 10–29*, 647). However, this breakdown fails to adequately take into consideration the fact that in vv. 23–30 the people of the earth are the ones praising Yahweh, but in vv. 31–33 it is nature that is praising Yahweh. The change of referent seems significant. The breakdown above has attempted to note such distinctions. This is also seen by others. See Kleinig, *The LORD's Song*, 143; Joachim Becker, *1 Chronik*, NEchtBAT (Würzburg: Echter, 1986), 72–74.
133. Williamson, *1 and 2 Chronicles*, 130. Japhet argues that v. 35 starts "a direct address to the people, 'Say', to which the doxology is attached" (Japhet, *1 and 2 Chronicles*, 319).
134. So Hill, "Patchwork Poetry," 99–100.
135. One could also include the imperative זכרו here that is repeated in vv. 12 and 15. However, one should avoid seeing a chaism. Kleinig rightly notes this as well (Kleinig, *The LORD's Song*, 142, n. 2). However, Kleinig's statement needs to tempered because he ignores the fact that vv. 8–18 do in fact form three clear chiasms, something which scholars who have done work in the psalms are quick to point out. See Ceresco (A. R. Ceresco, "The Chiastic Word Pattern in Hebrew," *CBQ* 38 [1976]: 305); and A. R. Ceresco, "The Function of Chiasmus in Hebrew Poetry," *CBQ* 40 [1978]: 1–3).
136. Watson notes that a repeated term often serves as a keyword that is used to express the primary point of the Psalm (see Wilfred G. E. Watson, *Classical Hebrew Poetry: A Guide to Its Techniques*, JSOTSup 26 [Sheffield: JSOT Press, 1984], 287–88).
137. One should note that this writer is listing the root term. The specific form of the root may vary from verse to verse but the term is the same. Furthermore, in v. 35, the form is a noun, but it but the same root.
138. Loader, "Redaction and Function," 70–74; and Kleinig, *The LORD's Song*, 143.

139. Kristen Nielsen, "Whose Song of Praise? Reflections on the Purpose of the Psalm in 1 Chronicles 16," in *The Chronicler as Author: Studies in Text and Texture*, ed. M. Patrick Graham and Steven L. McKenzie, JSOTSup 263 (Sheffield: Sheffield Academic Press, 1999), 332; and also Watts, *Psalm and Story*, 158. This is also noted by Kleinig, *The LORD's Song*, 135–36; and Hill, "Patchwork Poetry," 99.

140. Watts, *Psalm and Story*, 161.

141. On this see below on the section "features and functions as a whole."

142. The MT and the LXX read "their brothers." However, the Syriac, Vulgate, and Arabic versions all read with the singular "his brothers." Others explain the issue based on haplography as the lists elsewhere may support the loss of "Jehiel" (e.g., 15:24). However, this requires the term ויחי which is not present in this text. The preferred reading here seems better as the loss of a name or the transposition of it would have had to have taken place very early on in the transmission of the text for all the versions to have lost the name as well.

143. The second mention of Obed-Edom here has troubled many scholars. It seems most likely that the Chronicler has mentioned that Obed-Edom was the son of Jeduthun to distinguish him from the Obed-Edom previously mentioned. This can be maintained despite Japhet's objections (Japhet, *1 and 2 Chronicles*, 320). Her objection still does not negate the possibility that the second Obed-Edom was less well known. Therefore, the Chronicler mentions his father in order not to add confusion to the text.

144. The phrase "who were designated" is lacking in the LXX.

145. Many scholars on both sides of this issue see "Obed-Edom" as a gloss. See Curtis and Madsen, *Chronicles*, 225; Rudolph, *Chronikbücher*, 126; P. B. Dirksen, "1 Chronicles 16:38: Its Background and Growth," *JNSL* 22 (1996): 88–90.

146. Jeduthun is identified as such in the genealogical material (1 Chr 6:29–32). Williamson notes that the genealogical material here does not correspond perfectly to that in 1 Chr 6:19–30. See Williamson, *1 and 2 Chronicles*, 74. These genealogical lists may in fact go well beyond the time of the Chronicler and date back into the preexilic period. Hosah is also identified as a Merarite in 1 Chr 26:10–19.

147. De Vries, *1 and 2 Chronicles*, 437.

148. The Hebrew text has שִׁשִּׁים וּשְׁמוֹנָה in 1 Chr 16:38 and שִׁשִּׁים וּשְׁנָיִם in 1 Chr 26:8. There are enough differences to suggest that it was more than merely an error of sight or hearing on the part of a scribe.

149. It might be possible to see this difference not as a scribal error but original with the Chronicler. The names of the original sixty-eight members of Obed-Edom's family could have been specifically listed in some official court record at the time when David initiated the organization of the priests and Levites in 1 Chr 16. A subsequent list of names that listed each member of Obed-Edom's family again at the time of David's preparation of the priests and Levites for temple service in 1 Chr 26 could help explain the difference in the numbers of the family. One may posit the possibility that since there has been a number of years that have passed from the time of the ark narrative until the time of the final organization of the cultus under David that six members of the clan had died.

150. This view is represented by Welch. He argues that this division is from a secondary pro-Priestly editor (Adam C. Welch, *The Work of the Chronicler, Its Purpose and Date*, The Schweich Lectures on Biblical Archaeology [London: Oxford University Press, 1939], 30–41).

151. This view is held by Wilhelm Martin de Wette, *Beiträge zur Einleitung in das Alte Testament* (Halle: Schimmelpfennig, 1807; reprint, New York: G. Olms, 1971), 108–12; Julius Wellhausen, *Prolegomena to the History of Ancient Israel*, trans. J. Sutherland Black and Allan Enzies

(Edinburgh: A & C Black, 1885; reprint, RTS, Atlanta: Scholars Press, 1994), 183; and Curtis and Madsen, *Chronicles*, 315–16. Blenkinsopp makes the point that the Chronicler is now able to justify Solomon's visit to Gibeon without making him appear to violate the Priestly law (Joseph Blenkinsopp, *Gibeon and Israel: The Role of Gibeon and the Gibeonites in the Political and Religious History of Early Israel*, SOTSMS 2 (Cambridge: Cambridge University Press, 1972), 102; and Noth, *The Chronicler's History*, 35, 150 n. 17.

152. This view has been argued by Hertzberg and others. See H. W. Hertzberg, "Mizpah," *ZAW* 47 (1929): 176–77; and Manfred Görg, *Das Zelt der Begegnung: Untersuchung zur Gestalt der sakralen Zelttraditionen Altisraels*, BBB 27 (Bonn: Hanstein, 1967), 122–23, and 133–37. Williamson is also at least open to this view (Williamson, *1 and 2 Chronicles*, 131).

153. See Jacob Milgrom, *Studies in Levitical Terminology*, vol. 1 (Berkeley: University of California Press, 1970), 67–72; and Japhet, *1 and 2 Chronicles*, 323.

154. Williamson, *1 and 2 Chronicles*, 131.

155. Görg, *Das Zelt der Begegnung*, 121–37; and Hertzberg, "Mizpah," 161–96.

156. The debate about the Chronicler's use of non-canonical sources is far from reaching a consensus. Yet this writer finds himself reasonably close to Dillard's position on the matter. He argues that "the Chronicler is a reliable and trustworthy historian; where we are able to check his record against extrabiblical data, the picture is that of a careful author" (Dillard, *2 Chronicles*, xviii). The Chronicler's use of these sources remains an important issue in light of the various views regarding redaction throughout the book. It would seem that there are places where the Chronicler's style does change. Perhaps this change is due to his source and not to a later editor.

157. Knoppers, *1 Chronicles 10–29*, 655.

158. William Johnstone, *1 and 2 Chronicles*, vol. 1, *1 Chronicles 1–2 Chronicles 9: Israel's Place among the Nations*, JSOTSup 253 (Sheffield: Sheffield Academic Press, 1997), 197.

159. So Braun, *1 Chronicles*, 172; and Williamson, *1 and 2 Chronicles*, 113.

160. Rudolf Mosis, *Untersuchungen zur Theologie des chronistischen Geschichtswerkes*, FTS 92 (Freiburg: Herder, 1973), 51–52.

161. Tamara Cohn Eskenazi, "A Literary Approach to the Chronicler's Ark Narrative in 1 Chronicles 13–16," in *Fortunate the Eyes That See: Essays in Honor of David Noel Freedman in Celebration of His Seventieth Birthday*, ed. Astrid B. Beck et al. (Grand Rapids: Eerdmans, 1995), 263.

162. She notes that there are several keywords that link the ark narrative with chapter 10. First, the term פרץ is used throughout this section and its first occurrence in 1 Chr 13:2 is unique. Braun believes that the use of this term in 13:2 is out of context and leaves it untranslated (Braun, *1 Chronicles*, 173). Japhet has a better understanding of its usage in the context of chapter 13. She ties it to the other uses of the term in chapters 13–15 (Japhet, *1 and 2 Chronicles*, 275).

163. She also bases this view on the fact that there is a contrast between David's care for the ark and Saul's neglect of it, which "all combine to express the urgency of taking care of the ark" (ibid., 265).

164. Scholars have found a fourfold division within the Book as a whole. The breakdown is (1) 1 Chr 1–9, the genealogies; (2) 1 Chr 10–2 Chr 9, the united monarchy; (3) 2 Chr 9–28, the divided monarchy; and (4) 2 Chr 29–36, Hezekiah to the exile.

165. Braun, *1 Chronicles*, 172; and Japhet, *1 and 2 Chronicles*, 272.

166. Mosis, *Untersuchungen*, 82.

167. Eskenazi, "A Leterary Approach," 263.

168. This type of parallel structure is common to the Chronicler.

169. Wright's thesis will be discussed in detail in chapter three. However, it is necessary at this point to identify his argument as it affects his analysis of 1 Chr 15–16. He argues that chapters 23–27 are in fact the center of the Davidic narrative. John W. Wright, "The Founding Father: The Structure of the Chronicler's David Narrative," *JBL* 117 (1998): 45–49.

170. Mosis suggests that this is the case. He also notes the use of the term "to break out" as a keyword used by the Chronicler throughout this section (Mosis, *Untersuchungen*, 61; Allen, "Kerygmatic Units," 27–28). Wright acknowledges this but suggests that it is a contrast between the two narrative movements because of the disparity of themes within the two accounts (Wright, "The Founding Father," 48). However, Wright does not clearly state what these great differences between the first and second movements of the ark are. Certainly it could not merely be the fact that the initial attempt failed. He does state that the summary statement (14:17) subdivides the ark narrative (Wright, "The Founding Father," 49). The summary statement is not surprising here as this concludes his source, and reinforces the point that Yahweh made David great. In the judgment of this writer, there are no great differences between the two accounts. David begins by calling "all Israel" and states his desire to move the ark. Only the breaking forth of Yahweh because of improper care for the ark prevents the ark from reaching its destination. This is in fact one of the purposes for the narrative, the Chronicler is emphasizing David's care for the symbol of Yahweh's presence is the reason for Yahweh's blessing (chp. 14) and ultimately the reason for David becoming both the founder of the dynasty and a cult founder as well.

171. Wright too acknowledges this connection; however, he interprets the evidence entirely different from the preceding scholars (Wright, "The Founding Father," 49). For Wright there is nothing in the narrative that suggests a theological emphasis on the part of the Chronicler (ibid., 52–53). Wright's point is well taken; the Chronicler is certainly doing more than just comparing David and Saul on a theological level. However, the theme of blessing is important to the Chronicler and it is necessary here to show the reader that Yahweh has not judged David and the nation as he had Saul for lack of concern for the ark only for improper procedure in its movement. This blessing is the reason why David is successful in battle, in establishing his royal city and as a result his growing political reputation. Thus, this chapter sets up the theme of David as a cult founder quite well. This interpretation places more emphasis on the theological theme behind the narrative and acknowledges that the Chronicler's purposes are more than merely political and dynastic.

172. Eskenazi's statement here should be read as 1 Chr 10:1–2 Chr 9:31. There is nothing in 2 Chr 10 that would apply to her statement. Eskenazi, "A Literary Approach," 264.

173. While spatial considerations will not allow a full treatment of every occurrence of incidents that involve the cult and its sacred objects (both positively and negatively), these issues arise throughout the work. For example, one may well include the fact that Josiah commands the Levites to place the ark in the Temple in 2 Chr 35:3, which suggests that issues involving the cultic system take central stage throughout the entire book, not just within the major units discussed above. Furthermore, it seems that although the ark itself does not play a major role within 2 Chr 11–36, there may well be implications for it that involve the reorganization of the cult by the kings because of the lack of attention it was given by their predecessors (e.g., Hezekiah). See also, Eskenazi, "A Literary Approach," 264.

174. Wright has attempted to see the center of the work as 1 Chr 23–27 (John Wesley Wright, "The Origin and Function of 1 Chronicles 23–27" [Ph.D. diss., University of Notre Dame, 1989], 158, 165–66). However, the literary analysis seems to suggest that 1 Chr 23–27 plays a

complementary role to the ark narrative and that the ark narrative proper is the core of the work. Reading the book as a whole from this perspective may give further insight, especially in light of the extra-biblical evidence discussed in chapter three.

The Place of 1 Chronicles 15–16 within the Book

Introduction

The previous chapter outlined the critical discussion of the second part of the ark narrative. The lists, the names, the directions for worship given by David, and the composite Psalm are all controversial issues within the history of scholarship in Chronicles. These issues have been addressed in the previous chapter, largely from a literary perspective in order to uncover the unity of the passage as a whole. Knoppers emphasizes the significance of this issue when he states, "In Rudolph's reconstruction, for example, fifty-one verses (15:4–10, 16–21, 22–24; 16:5b–38, 42), or 71 percent, [of] the total seventy-two verses in 1 Chr 15–16 are later additions."[1] The previous chapter has, however, shown that it is probable that the ark narrative is a unity and that it comes from the hand of a single author.

This conclusion naturally leads one to question whether these various postulated additions are additions at all. In order to develop an argument for the unity of the book, it is necessary to reevaluate the various literary hypotheses. After a brief evaluation of each, further analysis to support a single author will be addressed. Such support is found in the section on the genealogies (1 Chr 1–9); and the section dealing with David's final organization of the cult and his commands to Solomon to fulfill that organization (1 Chr 23–27). The section which is central to this work, the second part of the ark narrative (1 Chr 15–16), was addressed in chapter two and the remaining issues there need to be addressed in the exegetical portion of this work.

Literary Hypotheses Reconsidered

Various literary hypotheses have developed, largely out of Noth's hypothesis. He takes more than half of the second part of the ark narrative as a later addition. He also assigns 1 Chr 23–27 to an editor (the only exception being 23:1-2a).[2] The genealogical material is considered late as well (the exception being 1–2:17 and a few other places that can be based on Num 26 and the genealogies of David and those of the high priests).[3] However, Noth accepts all of 2 Chronicles as being original to the Chronicler (with the exception of part of seven verses: 2 Chr 5:11b, 12a, 13a; 8:14, 15; 23:18; and 35:15).[4] Rudolph, even at that early stage in the development of the hypothesis did not agree with Noth in all details of his methodology and in some ways he had already moved beyond Noth's work.[5] Nevertheless, they often arrived at similar conclusions. Therefore, it seems fitting to speak of these critical issues as the Noth-Rudolph hypothesis since Rudolph's commentaries have articulated this literary hypothesis more clearly.

Evaluations of Hypotheses

Noth and Rudolph. Noth did not use traditional literary criteria for his study.[6] Thus, for Noth the guide to the original form of Chronicles is to be found in the major themes of the work.[7] Hence, the unique materials in these chapters are later additions because they do not support the major theme of moving the ark to Jerusalem. Rather, they slow the narrative and in his view intrude upon the narrative unit. It appears that Rudolph has broadly accepted Noth's main framework of the ark narrative without major changes to it. However, the above literary analysis in chapter three arrives at the opposite conclusion. The lists do in fact support the theme both literarily and stylistically.[8] Thus, the hypothesis of those who follow Noth and Rudolph closely can no longer be sustained.[9] Further, Rudolph does not look at repetitions as a possible literary structure, an element that is a common literary motif of the Chronicler. Such literary devices complicate his point that the Chronicler is completely consistent in his work and later editors can be found as the result of inconsistencies in their style, which for him is often found in these repetitions.[10]

Williamson. Williamson's theory differs from that of many commentators because he understands the Chronicler as writing during the time that Gese calls "stage 3b," but Gese and others see the Chronicler writing in "stage 3a."[11] Williamson's view regarding a slight pro-Priestly redaction is open to criticism, both from those who see additions to the text and those who see a single author at work. Both sides of the issue could accept some of Williamson's literary remarks and still reject his pro-Priestly redaction. Those who see various redactors at work could argue against a single redaction because he has not made specific connections between the texts that he identifies as later additions. This lack of connection leaves room for more than one hand to be present within these texts as well. Those who argue for a single author contend that Williamson fails to acknowledge the possibility of two or more types of sources that have been combined in 1 Chr 23–27, where he spends much time developing his theory.

Williamson's theory, however, goes well beyond Chronicles and addresses the work of Ezra–Nehemiah. Thus, the implications for rejecting his view are far reaching. Before addressing this broader issue, one should note that Williamson's pro-Priestly redaction in 1 Chr 15–16, in particular, needs to be rejected. The analysis of the material in chapter two indicates that the mention of the priests (15:4, 11, 14) does not imply a later addition. The priests needed to be mentioned in these places because of sacrificial issues in the text (15:26; 16:1), and they are necessary because the priests alone are required to play the trumpets mentioned in 1 Chr 15:24.[12]

Williamson's theory in its entirety is difficult to sustain.[13] Several scholars have noted that the literary and theological makeup of Ezra–Nehemiah requires a single author.[14] Japhet's arguments are important, yet it is necessary to note that she does not attempt to identify the author of the work. She states only that there are historical and theological motivations that require a single author. Williamson attempts to determine who wrote Ezra 1–6. He concludes that it is a pro-Priestly writer who writes after the rest of the composition is completed.[15] Several issues which have not found complete consensus among scholars need to be resolved before Williamson's view of the authorship of Ezra–Nehemiah can be adopted. One example is the issue of priority of Ezra or Nehemiah; another is how the two works were combined. These issues make it difficult to come to exact conclusions on the question of authorship.

Williamson's theory requires one to adopt several issues that are being debated among scholars. One of the major issues is the two lists found in Ezra 2 and Neh 7. The two lists share a number of commonalities; however, several important differences need to be noted as well. Williamson argues that Neh 7 was part of the original text because the list in Ezra 2 is a summary of Neh 7.[16] After reviewing Williamson's arguments Blenkinsopp states, "Arguments from numbers can be rather slippery, due to textual variations. In any case, 61,000 gold darics is hardly a rounding out of the 41,000 in Nehemiah."[17] He further states:

> The 'treasury of the work' also continues the theme of temple endowment, especially in view of the allusion to priestly vestments. This theme remains totally unexplained in the Nehemiah context. That the list with its narrative sequel has been adapted to a new context in Nehemiah is also suggested by the syntactic awkwardness of Neh. 7: 69 [70], which begins with the heads of ancestral houses, breaks off without giving their contributions, then begins again with a listing of donors in descending order of importance. Reference to months by numbers rather than by names is also characteristic of Ezra 1–6 (see Ezra 3:1, 6, 8; 6:19), the only exception being Adar at 6:15. In the Nehemiah memoir, on the other hand, months are invariably referred to by names (Neh. 1:1; 2:1; 6:15).[18]

While one needs to temper Blenkinsopp's evaluation somewhat, his observations still weaken Williamson's argument. For example, one can agree with

Blenkinsopp that it is difficult to understand how Ezra's list summarizes Nehemiah. This is, however, complicated by the fact that Ezra's list does appear to be a summary. Nehemiah's list gives specific details, whereas Ezra's list summarizes. Thus, it is difficult to say that Ezra is only summarizing Nehemiah. Nevertheless, it appears that Ezra is rounding out his numbers and summarizing the totals rather than listing specific details found in his source.

Blenkinsopp is also correct in noting that the narrative connection following the list in Ezra 2:68–70 and Neh 7:69–72 suggests that the author of Nehemiah borrowed the material because of the connective syntax of Neh 7:69–70. The connection in Neh 7:72 as it transitions into Neh 8 also seems to support Blenkinsopp's point. Although Williamson has not directly addressed this issue in his work, he does make the point that Ezra 2:68 is a plus and should be seen as the hand of the editor, not as an omission from Nehemiah's account.[19] Williamson's argument is based on the fact that he interprets this verse as having the same characteristics and vocabulary as that of the editor. This becomes troubling on two grounds. First, he does not comment on how this pro-Priestly editor's vocabulary and outlook differ from the rest of Ezra–Nehemiah. Further, does the author(s) of the remaining part of the work show evidence of being pro-anything else, or anti-priesthood? To put it another way, could a case be made for the remainder of Ezra–Nehemiah to be considered pro-Priestly as well? Second, while Ezra 2:68 ties together the text of the preceding chapter and the following chapter, it seems unlikely that the priestly editor of Ezra 1–6 placed v. 68 there. The point of emphasis is the building of the temple and the list of the elders giving to the project; this is not surprising because the elders are highlighted in Ezra 5–6 as being responsible for the building of the temple. The fact that Ezra does not spell out the exact amount of money given in the same manner as Nehemiah does not demand that he has borrowed from Nehemiah. In fact, the syntax of the verse is normal; however, it is Nehemiah's narrative that breaks off from the list of elders and enumerates those who gave (Neh 7:69–70). This could suggest that Nehemiah may be following Ezra and adding details.

Second, Williamson argues that the author of Chronicles wrote first.[20] This too is open for debate. Steins, for example, argues that the Chronicler had the foundational layer of Ezra–Nehemiah before him.[21] While this writer cannot accept Steins' arguments, his point serves as evidence that there is still a debate about which work was written first. If the priority of Chronicles is overturned by scholarship, Williamson's theory becomes impossible to sustain.

Third, and most damaging to the view of a pro-Priestly editor is the fact that the text indicates that both the priests and the Levites sanctified themselves in Ezra 5:19. Yet, the Levites slaughtered the lambs for the people and for their brothers the priests (5:20). This is decidedly pro-Levitical in nature, and it is difficult to understand why anyone favorable to the priesthood would include this material.

Williamson argues that the fact that the priests and the Levites had both purified themselves indicates a pro-Priestly editor because the accounts in Chronicles (2 Chr 29:34; 30:3) indicate that the priests had not purified themselves in large enough numbers.[22] Williamson makes such statements because he believes that the author used the same methods and had the same outlook as that of the author of Ezra 1–2. He argues that the method is typological; therefore, the Passover must be based on the Chronicler's narratives. This Passover, however, is represented as taking place during or shortly before the author of Ezra 1–6's own time and there is no reason to see typology here. It seems to be a straightforward historical account. Other issues are also troubling in seeing such a connection with Chronicles. For example, the editor chose not to draw on parallels between the Second Temple and that of Solomon (2 Chr 5–7). This editor also chose to give Moses authority over the ordering of the priests and the Levites, yet if there were a connection based on the Chronicler's narratives, David would be better suited as the source (1 Chr 23–27).

Williamson argues against the idea of a historical account of the Passover by saying that it is better to "take more seriously the apparent links with Haggai and Zech. i–viii, particularly as regards the leadership of the community."[23] These links could possibly be better explained by understanding that these two prophets wrote their material a few decades before the author of Ezra 1–6 and that the two works were in wide circulation and familiar to the author and his audience.[24] Finally, the priests do constitute a theme elsewhere in the work but there are other broader themes, such as that of leadership which is found in these first six chapters as well. Thus, there are only two possibilities regarding Ezra 1–6. The first is that there is a second hand present that has glossed in pro-Priestly ideas but who is not responsible for the origin of these six chapters because of the broader issues that are present in both sections of Ezra. Second, the material can be interpreted as coming from the same hand as that of the author of Ezra 7–10, which also reflects these broader themes, including the theme of the priests. Either option indicates that the idea of a pro-Priestly editor who was responsible for all of Ezra 1–6 and the various additions to Chronicles seems to be possible though it may not be the most plausible option available.[25]

Dörrfuß and Steins. Dörrfuß and Steins see major redactions throughout the Chronicler. Dörrfuß argues for a late Maccabean redaction that brings Moses and his Law into a positive light in contrast to David and the temple. He sees the Sinai traditions as being the source of hope for Israel's future. He does use literary criticism in order to find these various levels of redaction throughout the book.[26] However, he places too much emphasis on Moses. He does help identify an often overlooked issue of Moses and the Mosaic covenant; however, Moses is mentioned according to him only twenty-one times. This is a small number of occurrences for a major redaction that attacks David and the temple, which is emphasized throughout the work. Further, it is difficult to detect the redactor was critical of David in these sections. As has been shown, the Moses redaction in 1 Chr 15:11–15 should be rejected because the text seems to be portraying David as the one who sought out the reason for God's anger in the Torah and then commanded that the ark be moved properly.

Steins' work, on the other hand, is a massive attempt to see major redactions that occurred over an extended period of time.[27] He argues that Chronicles was written as the final book in the canon. Chronicles rewrites the history of Israel while staying well within the influence of the Pentateuch.[28] One is struck by these two scholars' lack of form-critical analysis, especially in Steins' work. Dörrfuß's analysis of the book might be better received if he had argued for the redactional layer in light of form-critical evaluations.[29] Steins, however, would have surely found fewer redactional layers, as many of his layers are found within the same lists of names. He breaks the lists up according to the development of the singers and gatekeepers; however, it is difficult to understand why so many minor redactions, which take place at different times, would have been authorized and/or accepted by the leadership as necessary revisions to an authoritative work. Steins' other issues are the changes in the leaders of the musicians and their classification. He notes that David appointed the leaders of the Levites; then later he told the Levites to appoint themselves. These two issues play a role in the literary development for Steins. In the development of his redactional layers, he sees the foundation layer tracing the same event as that of chapter 13, the movement of the ark. The other layers are built around this layer, based on the cultic musicians. First, there is a single head; in the next layer all three heads are present; then there is a change within the order of the three. Finally, the gatekeepers are added to the material. Some of the issues he addresses could be resolved by textual criticism, which is lacking in his treatment.

Finally, it seems difficult to accept Steins' position because of the narrative itself. For example, the gatekeepers were a para-military unit that protected the ark. It is difficult to imagine the ark's moving anywhere without such a detachment for its protection. Furthermore, his identification of the genre of the work as a "conclusion to the canon" opens his view to criticism because he fails to explain why individuals or the community as a whole felt the need to add material to a conclusion.[30] Hence, his redactional levels are at odds with his interpretation of the book.

The Genealogies

In dealing with such a large section of material, spatial limitations will not allow a full treatment of all nine chapters. Indeed, many of these individual genealogies could well be a separate treatment in their own right. Since the issues in the genealogies and the lists within the ark narrative are similar, finding unity in the genealogies may help further clarify the issues involved in the ark narrative as well.[31] Therefore, this section of material deserves a few brief comments. Braun addresses the historical value of the genealogies. He states as his conclusion, "It is clear then that the introductory chapters of Chronicles *are* useful for historical reconstruction. What is not so clear, however, is *how* this material is useful to the historian (e.g., for the reconstruction of biological, political, or other sorts of relationships or for other purposes)."[32] De Vries also sees the value of the genealogies when he states, "Closely scrutinized, they show the same 'Chronicles' linguistic traits, and their striking absorption with the Levites and the house of David is shared by the entire book."[33] This does not mean for De Vries that no secondary additions or glosses are in the text, only that on the whole these first nine chapters should be attributed to the Chronicler himself.[34] Some scholars still contend that the genealogies are entirely a secondary addition, but when the genealogies are viewed as a whole most scholars seem to be able to agree that the genealogical section originated with the Chronicler.[35]

A general overview of literary characteristics and patterns within the genealogies seems to support such findings. Knoppers has painstakingly addressed the patterns that are present within this section of material.[36] He shows that the Chronicler saw patterns that were in his sources and that he elaborated them in ways that suggest a unified work. Knoppers does see various insertions within these genealogies that are the result of later editorial activity; however, he shows that the major sections and structure appears to be from the Chronicler's own hand.[37] Furthermore, there are parallels to the Chronicler's structural patterns that are also present in other ancient Near Eastern societies.[38] This seems significant as no one questions the authorship of these documents that have been discovered in the ancient Near East. Further arguments for unity can be multiplied; however, it seems that there is enough broad agreement among scholars that one can safely say that the issues driving scholars to see the majority of the genealogies coming from a later editor are successfully challenged in the genealogical section.[39]

The work as a whole can be viewed from the prospective of the Chronicler's arguing for Jerusalem and its cult being the hope for Israel's future.[40] For example, the genealogies and the narrative that takes up the remainder of the work support the same conclusion. They end with the exile (1 Chr 9:1; 2 Chr 36:17–21). The reason for the exile is directly related to the people's unfaithfulness (1 Chr 9:1; 2 Chr 36:12–16). There is concern for the people's return to the land and the city of Jerusalem (1 Chr 9:2–34; 2 Chr 36:22–33). While it may be possible to argue that a later editor inserted the genealogies and structured them to fit this pattern, it seems more likely that the major structure was developed intentionally by a single author.

David's Institution of the Cult

Possibly more important than the discussion of the genealogical material in the first section of the Chronicler's work is the section devoted to David's institution of the cult. This importance results from many literary hypotheses that find their basic argument for additions within this section of material.[41] This position was first challenged by Williamson.[42] He arrived at the conclusion that the foundational features of these chapters must have been original with the Chronicler but that a pro-Priestly editor added several units of material to this section (23:13b–14, 25–32; 25:7–31; 26:6–8, 12–18; 27).[43] Williamson's literary argument was developed further by Kleinig, who accepted Williamson's arguments but rejected a pro-Priestly editor.[44]

It was Wright, however, who developed this issue in his dissertation.[45] He later updated this work in a brief article in which he argues that there are three foundational issues that prove a single author was responsible for the entire section of material.[46] First, he shows that there is no need to consider the assembly in 1 Chr 28:1 as a repetition of 1 Chr 23.[47] Further, the assembly that takes place in 1 Chr 28:2–29:22 should not be regarded as a repetition of the assembly in 23:2–27:34; it should be understood as a second assembly.[48] Finally, he argues that the narrative itself, in 1 Chr 28:1–29:30, shows evidence of being a smooth continuation of the narrative both from 1 Chr 23:1 and from 27:34.[49] It is the link to 1 Chr 27:34 that is significant as it indicates that there is no need to see 1 Chr 28:1 as rejoining the narrative from 23:1.[50] Japhet argues in her commentary that there are reasons for seeing this material as being original to the Chronicler, both on grounds of explicit elements in the text and implicit elements that cause scholars to reject this material.[51] Her basic premise is that there is no reduplication of the material because the genre in 1 Chr 22, 28–29 is different from that of 1 Chr 23–27. Thus, the two different genres can be completely integrated into the context of the major section as a whole (1 Chr 10–2 Chr 9).

Her statements concerning the implicit grounds on which scholars reject this section are quite significant for the ark narrative as well. She states, "I have already observed that the same scholars who advocate the 'secondariness' of 23–27 would pronounce the same verdict for all or most of 1 Chron. 1–9 or certain sections of 1 Chron. 15–16 which share the same literary characteristics."[52] Having examined the arguments for these two major sections of material, this writer believes that it is probable that the majority of the material was produced by the Chronicler himself. Many scholars believe that there are places within each where a later editor has made various additions but they still believe that the unity on the whole would best be explained as coming from the hand of the Chronicler.

The significance of this argument is substantial. Since the various lists can be regarded as being incorporated by the Chronicler, the sections of material that address the priests and Levites are part of the primary argument of the Chronicler. It is widely accepted that the Chronicler's emphasis throughout his work is on the monarchy, the temple, Jerusalem, and worship. Therefore, the ark narrative is at the heart of his purpose and may be considered the theological foundation from which everything else moves in harmony.[53] If this is the case, then it must be possible to outline reasons for taking the ark narrative as the theological and thematic foundation of the book.

Arguments for the Importance of the Ark Narrative

In order to make a case for the ark narrative's being the foundational narrative that the Chronicler used to set forth his special concerns, the narrative must reflect the emphases of the Chronicler. In order to prove such a focus exists in the ark narrative, it is necessary to look at the Chronicler's purpose for writing his book. Also, it is necessary to look at the ark narrative as one that builds themes throughout the work.[54] Therefore, the themes that are present in this section of material need to be identified.[55] A final avenue of argumentation is the tracing of these themes to show how they unify the work as a whole.

The Chronicler's Overarching Purpose

Discussion among scholars who attempt to find the main purpose of Chronicles has resulted in several conclusions. For some this issue centers around the date; however, it seems best, at least for the time being until the issue of date can be further resolved, to argue as Dyck has, that the date of the Chronicler's writing does not affect the purpose of the work.[56] The main purpose of the Chronicler's writing is continuity with the past. Many scholars have consistently acknowledged these themes.[57] Dyck's helpful article also notes major themes. He argues that the reigns of David and Solomon are closely linked to building the temple and establishing of the cult.[58] Scholars generally agree on these themes; the issues of debate pertain to the implications of these themes more than anything else.[59]

Japhet has also extensively researched the purpose of the Chronicler.[60] Her conclusions are most briefly summarized in her commentary where she states, "It is doubtful, however, whether one single and unilateral purpose would account for such an enormous enterprise, with all its complexities of content and form."[61] Yet, it seems that she too would agree with the idea of continuity as being the central point because the Chronicler is bridging the gap between the past and the present for his audience.[62] Some may wish to see a multifaceted purpose within the Chronicler's work, but it is possible to see a single theme that runs throughout, namely, continuity.[63] This term, however, seems too broad. Perhaps it is possible to see continuity though a specific element that is evident throughout the book. If so, one could support both the general idea of continuity and the specific idea that reflects that theme. Perhaps the specific idea can be found in the role of David in three areas: (1) his dynasty; (2) his making Jerusalem his capital city; and (3) his instructions for the institution and organization of the cult, which ultimately lead to proper temple worship.

The Chronicler is offering David and the subsequent kings as an illustration of this continuity. This appears to be in line with the extra-biblical evidence from the ancient Near East.[64] A significant example is that of Ashurnasirpal II (884–858 B.C.E.), who, following the reconstruction of Nineveh as his capital city, builds various temples along with his palace. He establishes festivals, offers the various deities large numbers of sacrifices, and hosts a banquet for all the people.[65] These features are quite similar to the action in the ark narrative. David has just rebuilt Jerusalem, having taken it from the Jebusites. He then prepares a tent for the ark. Upon its entrance into the city, he sets up cultic officials in charge of worship and joyful song; he then authorizes sacrifices and hosts a banquet for the people.

The king was clearly expected to be both a strong political ruler and a supporter of the cult. The Chronicler has in effect set up the ark narrative and the following section that is so closely linked to it as the standard that other kings must follow. By remembering David's organization of the cult and seeking to maintain its proper relation between God and the people, the nation will prosper.[66]

The theme of David as the pattern that has been set for other kings to follow could include the concept of calling for the temple and its services to function under the authority of the Davidic dynasty.[67] The Chronicler, in picturing the cultic services in this way, calls for a return to temple worship in the postexilic period, instituted by David himself. For the Chronicler this worship maintains the proper relationship between God and man.

The following section of narrative material (1 Chr 17–29) also gives support to this theme. For example, the Davidic covenant is given in chapter 17. David then finalizes the cultic organization that he had initiated in the ark narrative and he calls upon Solomon to incorporate it by building the temple following David's death. This is then followed by the Chronicler's portraying Solomon as completely submitting to his father's wishes by carrying out his plan.

The Davidic covenant and its accompanying narrative raises a major issue of debate among scholars concerning whether messianic implications can be found in Chronicles.[68] Since the ark narrative is followed closely by the Davidic covenant there are messianic implications for the book. The Chronicler did look forward to a time when a Davidic king would be sitting on David's throne again. However, the messianic elements within the text itself may not be as clear as some have stated and caution needs to be used in attributing messianic elements to the Chronicler.[69] For example, Townsend argues that the Davidic covenant is the center of the book and that everything else flows out of that narrative (1 Chr 17).[70] Yet, this writer believes that the Mosiac covenant plays a complementary role within the work. Elements such as the proper handling of the ark, found within this covenant, cause David to take steps to insure proper worship. While Townsend's observation is important, in that the Davidic covenant plays a major role in the work, it is always held in tension with the Mosaic covenant, especially in the narratives of the kings. Therefore, neither covenant should be considered the central theme of the book.

The Ark Narrative as Foundational to Unity

Literarily speaking, the ark narrative functions in a way that ties the narrative units of the book together. It also ties the various themes together. There is one other viewpoint toward the ark narrative as it plays a foundational thematic role for the book. This thematic role is found in the examination of some passages that have similar language as that of the ark narrative. The major passages in which similar language occurs are in the genealogical material and David's final organization of the cult in 1 Chr 23–27. One can also make a case for the theme of continuity as it develops in the narratives of subsequent kings and their parallels with ancient Near Eastern royal inscriptions.

Genealogical material. First Chronicles 6:16–17 is the initial place that one finds what some have called a "Davidic assignment formula" which includes a reference to the ark. This passage states, "And these are the men whom David appointed over the music in the house of the Lord, after the ark came to rest. And they were ministering with song before the tabernacle, the tent of meeting, until Solomon had built the house of the Lord in Jerusalem, and they served in their office according to their order." These verses seem to refer to the ark narrative, because David appoints the Levites to minister before the ark and the tent in Jerusalem and Gibeon respectively.

It is necessary at this point to look at Wright's thesis, because his work is very helpful in this discussion. However, Wright argues that the references to the duties of the Levites, both preceding and following chapters 23–27, point to that section as being part of the Chronicler's primary purpose for writing this book. Finally, he compares ancient Near Eastern documents from the Persian period that also pertain to the establishment of the personnel in the temple.[71] He arrives at the conclusion that the Chronicler is following the typical style of other ancient writers in articulating the establishment of cultic personnel and David's action legitimates his reign.[72] Wright attributes this material, 1 Chr 6:16–17, to a direct reference to 1 Chr 23–27. This ignores the original historical development of the cult.[73] Braun, who did not view this statement in the genealogies as being original, is still able to state, "The Levitical musicians were appointed to their posts by David himself when the ark was brought up to Jerusalem (1 Chr 15–16)."[74]

Wright's major point is that the Davidic narrative centers on 1 Chr 23–27, not the ark narrative. He argues that 1 Chr 6:16–17 is written with 1 Chr 25 in mind. He also argues that 1 Chr 9:22 is written with 1 Chr 26 in mind. Wright's main thesis is interesting because he sees these two places in the genealogies as relating to chapters 23–27 more so than to the ark narrative itself. If a case can be made that these two passages relate to the ark narrative, and that 1 Chr 23–27 is a direct consequence of the ark narrative, then it helps to substantiate the argument that the ark narrative is foundational not only to the Davidic narrative but that everything else is connected to it thematically. It should be noted that Wright's thesis does appear to be adequate for all of the succeeding references which address the temple and its organization (for example, 2 Chr 8:14–15). This being the case, Wright has done well in arguing for the unity of these chapters, but has failed to understand the significance of the ark narrative as the link that binds the entire Davidic narrative.

Wright sets up two criteria for attributing these two sections of material to chapters 23–27: (1) he looks for the source and (2) the literary characteristics for each of the references. He is forced to state, "1 Chr 15:17 best fulfills the first condition dealing with David's appointment of Heman, Asaph, and Ethan."[75] However, he continues to argue for 1 Chr 6:16–17 being a direct reference to 1 Chr 25 because for him the second criterion is closely linked to the temple since it is mentioned within the passage itself. The term temple being used in the passage allows him to look for another place where the temple is mentioned. Thus, for Wright the Levitical positions mentioned in the ark narrative cannot be David's basis for the final organization of the cult, because the genealogical material specifically states that the Levites were to function in the temple. Therefore, Wright denies that this list could refer to David's appointment in the ark narrative.

Not only do Braun's statements about the text seem to be better suited, but Wright cannot adequately address the issue of the difference between 1 Chr 6:16–17 and 1 Chr 25:6. There the names of the Levites have been changed from Heman, Asaph, and Ethan, to Asaph, Heman, and Jeduthun. Wright is again forced to admit that this change is a serious problem. He attempts to avoid this problem by arguing that the two names refer to the same person.[76] However, this appears to undermine his point because the latter tradition would be secondary.[77] Braun shows that to arrive at such a conclusion logically, one would have to base the change in names on a "psalm tone," which suggests a later development on the name.[78] It is better to take this reference in the genealogical material as referring to the original institution of the Levitical singers in the ark narrative. Wright has to find a connection for this change of name in the ark narrative itself.[79] He bases his argument on the fact that Ethan's name is present until the ark is moved to Jerusalem, after which Jeduthun's name is found. One wonders why, if his name were changed there, the other two names were not, and why the Chronicler did not indicate the reason for such a change. The Chronicler's ideology should have prompted him to state the reason for the renaming of Ethan, especially since this renaming would lend further credence to Ethan's line as being the one who was to carry out the daily tasks at Gibeon and later in the temple.

The Chronicler is extremely concerned about the cult, and he has taken pains to develop and authenticate it wherever possible. The renaming of an individual would certainly have been a rare honor that one would expect the Chronicler to have taken time to develop.[80] It appears that it would be better to understand 1 Chr 6:16–17 as being a direct reference to 1 Chr 15–16, especially since the name Ethan is replaced by Jeduthun in that narrative. The reference to 1 Chr 25:6 cannot explain the change. Thus, 15:17 is more likely to be the source of 6:16–17, and the list in 16:38 is included in the same narrative to help explain why all following references would be to Jeduthun, not to Ethan.

Although the genealogical material has been dealt with as a whole above, this particular section of material now needs to be addressed specifically, because some have seen it as a later insertion.[81] Those scholars who see this material as being added base their understanding on two main factors. First, there is a repetition between the material found within the larger section (1 Chr 6:16–38) and the section that precedes it (1 Chr 6:1–15). Second, there are irregularities that exist between the two sections of genealogies.[82] However, Williamson sees a very tight structure within the chapter itself that suggests that it is original to the Chronicler.[83] Williamson's point is that the chapter reflects a pattern that seems to support a unity between these two genealogies.

The introduction in the second section (vv. 16–18a) is similar to that of the first part of the chapter (vv. 1–3). The introduction in vv. 1–3 listed the line of the high priests and as a result recorded only one member of each generation. The introduction to the second part of the chapter (vv. 16–18a) is concerned with the heads of all the Levitical families. This allows for the variations and the similarities that occur within each of the genealogies presented in 1 Chr 6. While a later redactor could also be responsible for this patterning, there is little evidence to suggest that a later editor has done this. The passage itself suggests a single unified work. Curtis and Madsen, although making a different point, have noted that vv. 16–18a is most likely from the hand of the Chronicler.[84]

Wright's argument again merits further consideration, although it in and of itself does not prove unity. He argues that the term "appoint" is stylistic of the Chronicler and that he employed the term throughout his work.[85] He traces the use of the term throughout the book and notes that where the term is used elsewhere there is no question that the narrative belongs to the Chronicler himself.[86] He then argues that the phrase עַל־עֲבוֹדָתָם which is also found in v. 17, also occurs two other times in the Hebrew Bible (2 Chr 8:14 and 35:15) and that both sections are usually acknowledged as belonging to the Chronicler.[87] While one must be cautious about these observations, when combined with the general literary structure of the chapter, they do seem to lend credence to the theory that this section also came from the hand of the Chronicler himself.

Rudolph, however, raises the objection that the passage in 1 Chr 6 actually contradicts the assignment of singers in 1 Chr 16:37–42. This is no small issue that can merely be overlooked. Williamson believes that the Chronicler was working with an inherited tradition.[88] Laato indicates that the reason for these genealogies being placed here in this precise way suggests that they are "the most important cultic personnel of the time of David."[89] The difference in the order of the names may reflect the order as it appeared in the Chronicler's sources. The order in 1 Chr 16:37–42 is not of necessity in order of importance. For example, Asaph is singled out to serve the ark at Jerusalem, largely because he sings the song that welcomes the ark into Jerusalem. This indicates that the assignment reflects Asaph's association with music and does not reflect either the site at Jerusalem or the one at Gibeon as being more important. Heman and Jeduthun were then selected to serve at Gibeon. While Gibeon is the place of daily sacrifice, the ark is in Jerusalem with the king. This may account for the change in the order of the names in later material as Asaph, regardless of the original reason, was essentially promoted to a place of honor near the king.

The last passage that needs to be addressed in Wright's work is 1 Chr 9:22. The verse states, "All those chosen as gatekeepers were two hundred twelve. They were recorded by their genealogy, in their villages. David and Samuel the seer had appointed them to their trusted office." Wright has assessed the context of 1 Chr 9:22 with caution. However, there is one problem with his analysis. He notes that David and Samuel do not appoint the gatekeepers in 1 Chr 26.[90] He is correct in understanding that David is clearly behind these appointments, but Samuel is not related to the appointments in 1 Chr 26 at all.

Samuel does appear in 1 Chr 26:28 and this may be the connection Wright is drawing upon.[91] Yet, Samuel's name is listed in the context of those who had previously donated materials to the national treasuries. Samuel is not the only person included in the list of donors; Saul and others are included in this list alongside the prophet. First Chronicles 26:28 has different contextual concerns and the link is not close enough to establish Samuel as one who appointed the gatekeepers. This fact allows for the possibility that the referent came from another place.[92] It appears likely that the main referent comes from 1 Chr 16:38, especially since the Chronicler refers both to the temple and to the tabernacle in 1 Chr 9:23. Curtis and Madsen say, "This statement refers to the families of gate-keepers living in Jerusalem. The two expressions, *the house of Yahweh* and *the house of the tent*, seem used to cover both the case of the Temple and the period of David before the Temple was built."[93] The Chronicler is trying to tie the gatekeepers to both the temple itself and to the earlier organization of the gatekeepers by David.[94]

The expression "the house of Yahweh" is used in reference to the tabernacle (Exod 23:19; 34:26; Josh 6:24; 1 Sam 1:7, 24; 3:15). The similar phrase "the house of my God" also refers to the tabernacle (Josh 9:23; Jdgs 18:31; 20:18, 26; 21:2). The use of "house" elsewhere also suggests that the tabernacle was referred to as a house (Deut 26:13). While the tabernacle is referred to as a "tent" (Exod 26:7, 9, 11, 12, 13, 14; 35:11; 36:14, 18, 19; 39:32, 33, 40; 40:2, 6, 19, 29; Num 3:25; 9:15; 2 Sam 7:6), it seems that within these references the tent is referred to as a specific element of the tabernacle itself. The exception is the references that specifically state "the tabernacle of the tent of meeting." The temporary place of the ark is referred to as a "tent" elsewhere as well (2 Sam 7:2).

The examination of these verses leaves open the possibility that the Chronicler is referring to the tabernacle itself or to the tent that housed the ark in Jerusalem. One might raise the objection that since both Jerusalem and the temple are focal points of the Chronicler, the temple should be assumed; however, the statement "the house of Yahweh" is anything but clear. Perhaps the Chronicler intended to be ambiguous in order to place the temple on a strong order of continuity with the past. Yet, he would still be maintaining continuity by connecting the two sanctuaries before the temple was built, which is exactly what he did in the ark narrative.

The statement "the house of Yahweh, the house of the tent" in 1 Chr 9:23 shows that the Chronicler is connecting the gatekeepers to the remote past. Braun seems open to the idea that this verse is not a reference to the temple.[95] Thus, when the Chronicler includes Samuel, he is following the standard practice of 1 Chr 9 to tie his own time period to that of David and earlier periods wherever possible.[96]

The connection with Samuel seems to be more in line with Samuel's own concern for the cult and his activities in the tabernacle when he was a young child (1 Sam 3:1–21).[97] This allows the inclusion of Samuel to lend more authority to the gatekeepers by showing that Samuel and those before David also had concern for the cult.

It is logical then that the Chronicler is thinking in terms of either a dual sanctuary or at least a continuation between the temple and the tabernacle. Wright is hard pressed to show why, if 9:22 is a reference to 26:1–19, only an implied connection exists between the two texts. He does not explain adequately why the tradition depicted in 9:22 would not have been mentioned in 26:1–19. Finally, if the Chronicler included 1 Chr 23–27 in his original work, why would he structure chapter 26 the way he did if he intended to show a link with 9:22, when he had the source for 9:19–33 at his disposal? The connection is designed to show a link to the Davidic organization that is first developed in the ark narrative. The two notations regarding the house of the Yahweh and the tent seem to suggest that the Chronicler was attempting to tie the original ordering to David and also make a link further back with Samuel.[98]

David's organization of temple personnel. The two major instances in which the genealogies have similar language to the ark narrative support the view that the Chronicler had that narrative in his mind when he composed the earlier sections of his material. It may be that the major section of organization of the temple personnel (1 Chr 23–27) is also a result of this section. 1 Chr 23–27 should not be interpreted as being implied from the ark narrative; however, it appears to be a logical outgrowth from it. In the second part of the ark narrative, David calls for the Levites and the priests Zadok and Abiathar to sanctify themselves for the retrieval of the ark (1 Chr 15:11). Then after the ark has arrived at Jerusalem he sets up the organization of the priests and Levites between the two sanctuaries at Gibeon and Jerusalem (1 Chr 16:4–6, 37–38 [at Jerusalem]; and 16:39–42 [at Gibeon]). The organization in and of itself suggests that it would be temporary, as the Deuteronomist has clearly stated that there would be a centralization of the cult at some point in Israel's history (Deut 12:5–28), after the nation has been given rest from all its enemies (Deut 12:10). Further, the discussion of the ark narrative within the larger unit of material (1 Chr 10–2 Chr 9) in chapter two of this work suggested that the Chronicler's tightly organized material in the following chapters (17–22) is a logical outgrowth from the ark narrative.

Wright, however, argues that the ark narrative "splits into two episodes concerning the ark, each a minor theme in separate movements of the Chronicler's narrative."[99] This hypothesis is difficult to sustain in light of previous scholarship which argues for the entire larger unit of material (1 Chr 10–2 Chr 9) as being tightly connected with chapters 17–22. The connection is so tight that 1 Chr 17–22 is argued by some as a second ark narrative. Wright recognizes that the Saul narrative of 1 Chr 10 is connected with the following material as well.[100] Thus, both Wright and Eskenazi see a broader connection for the Saul narrative within the work.[101] However, Wright interprets those data in a completely different way.[102] Because of his decisions on a literary level, he is able to see only that this legitimates the king as the founder of the cult and dynasty, but not as the legitimization of the cult itself.[103] Thus, for him the cultic and theological concerns are not the primary purpose of the Chronicler in this section of material. It is probable that the Chronicler is attempting to legitimate both the Davidic dynasty and the cult. De Vries, states, "For duty at the eventual Temple David organizes all the Temple personnel (1 Chr 23–26). Finally, he oversees the installation of Solomon, which is less to the throne than to the task of building the Temple (1 Chr 28:1–8; 29:1–25)."[104] Hence, succession is part of the Chronicler's purpose but not his primary function in this material.[105]

Among other things in chapters 23–27, David is finalizing the organization of the cult that was started in the ark narrative. This has become necessary because he is now looking forward to the building of the temple. The construction of the temple will end the need for the two sanctuaries and the centralized place of worship spoken of in Deuteronomy will be completed in Jerusalem. This section of material falls within what Wright and others have perhaps correctly classified as the Chronicler's "succession narrative."[106] However, those who see succession stop short of this writer's understanding because they see this narrative as being only political in nature. Thus, the preparations that David makes in this section not only serve as an element with the succession narrative of Solomon but also as the basic structure for the narrative of Solomon. The point is that one of the underlining issues within this narrative is the legitimate succession of Solomon to the throne. The main issue, however, remains the fact that David is interested in the cult and in the establishment of a permanent house for Yahweh.

David's organization of the cultic and civil elements indicate that he is at least partially responsible for the building and institution of the temple and its cult. The first place that David begins this institution is when he establishes the ark in Jerusalem. When he develops a desire to make Yahweh a house instead of a tent (1 Chr 17), he is not permitted to do so. However, when he offers sacrifice at the thrashing floor of Ornan (1 Chr 21:26), he renews his desire to contribute to the building of the temple. As a result of this rekindled desire, he takes steps to prepare for the finalization of the cult.

In 1 Chr 23–27, the duties of the priests and Levites are given in detail with regard to the finalization of the temple. It goes without saying that there are elements present in these chapters that cannot be based on the ark narrative alone. However, there are elements within the organization of the priests and Levites that do presuppose the earlier organization of them in the ark narrative. Such an organization takes the ark narrative to its logical conclusion for the ark will soon have a permanent home.

David developed specific courses and guilds for the Levites and priests within these chapters. However, earlier in the ark narrative he divided the Levites for the purpose of singing, making music, taking care of the ark in Jerusalem, and keeping the gate. The same divisions are given for the sanctuary at Gibeon, except instead of the duties for the ark, the duties for the preparations of daily sacrifices are put into action. At the time of the ark narrative, these divisions are only general divisions with David granting the heads of the Levites the right to choose specific men to minster. It appears that this is all that was necessary for the two sanctuaries to function properly. However, when the temple was completed a more precise organization would be required.

Wright's specific argument that previous narratives were based on this section of material seems to be once again strained. He argues that this section is the focal point based on the term אסף (1 Chr 23:2) which has a parallel use in 1 Chr 15:4 and 2 Chr 29:4. One may accept Wright's analysis of the term without arriving at his conclusion. He argues that this term is used in these cases to refer to a "royal initiative to activate cultic reform...."[107] For Wright, these two narratives (1 Chr 15:4; 2 Chr 29:4) give the best explanation for the background of this term in 1 Chr 23:2. He also rightly notes that the term אסף is different from that suggested by the term קהל.[108] He argues that the former term is used by the Chronicler for the monarch's appointments and commands to the clergy. The latter term is used in reference to a cultic and civil gathering called for by the monarch.[109]

Wright's acknowledgment once again to the second part of the ark narrative finds significance for the thesis of this work. He has consistently and honestly had to address issues that have subverted his own thesis by acknowledging that the answers could easily be found in the ark narrative. Thus, while his thesis can be maintained with respect to the material that follows chapters 23–27, it suggests that the material that precedes it and the material present within it comes from the initial organization of the ark narrative.

This writer is in agreement with Wright in seeing the tight connections between chapters 23–27 and the remainder of the book. However, the preference is to regard the earlier material and that in 1 Chr 23–27 as being written with the ark narrative in mind. Perhaps it is better to think along the lines of a revision of his thesis. Rather than viewing the above passages in the genealogies as arguing for the originality of the succession narrative, one could see them as having been written because the narrator had intended to write the ark narrative. This would mean that the succession narrative was also written in direct connection with the ark narrative, which the similar terms discussed above seem to indicate. The remainder of the passages that Wright addresses seem to support quite adequately his thesis; thus, the thesis remains valid with regard to chapters 23–27 being original to the Chronicler.[110]

The Ark Narrative in Theme Building

The Chronicler was a capable writer who was able to orchestrate large parallels between his narratives. The best example of this capability may be seen in Dillard's work on the account of King Asa.[111] Taking Dillard's work as a starting point, it is possible to trace the implications of the ark narrative throughout the book. This begins in the section in which David finalizes the cultic institutions and charges Solomon to carry out those institutions. Solomon is then portrayed as faithfully carrying out those commands.[112] It seems significant that Riley notes, "The normative status of the figure of David was already present in the Deuteronomistic History, as is evidenced by its use of David as the canon by which other kings are evaluated."[113] In looking at the kings in the Chronicler's narratives, one can affirm that this type of patterning is correct. Yet, this is not the only way kings are held accountable to David's standard. Many of the royal reforms indicate that the king is also operating in light of the Davidic standard.[114]

This brief summary of the views of various scholars shows that there are many who see a developing theme that is used like a model in which the Chronicler has shaped his account of the various kings. Typological models are common in Chronicles; for example, Williamson has noted the pattern of the succession of Solomon to be based on the pattern of Joshua's succession to Moses. Further, Solomon like his father had a deep concern for the cult, the temple, and its officials.[115] The various themes in the ark narrative can be viewed from a perspective of introducing themes upon which these later narratives build. Many of these themes are well known (for example, seeking Yahweh). Therefore, there is no need to trace them throughout the work. However, in tracing the reigns of the various kings, it is important to outline the reign of Saul, especially because of the differences that the Chronicler emphasizes between him and David. The Saul narrative of 1 Chr 10 has been carefully analyzed by Riley.[116] He shows that the Chronicler has made comparisons and contrasts between Saul as a non-cultic king and David as caring for the cult from the beginning of the ark narrative. Saul is referred to negatively in the ark narrative because his daughter disapproves of David's cultic dance (1 Chr 15:29).[117] David is being portrayed as the opposite of Saul; he is indeed the king who is concerned with the cult. Thus, this theme of concern for the cult should be found throughout the Chronicler's work.

Israel's prosperity and David's dynasty should also flow within the general pattern of ancient Near Eastern royal ideology. Such royal ideology is prevalent from the start of the ark narrative (1 Chr 13) where David shows his concern for the ark and is then granted victories over the enemies who had previously defeated the nation and taken the ark from Israel. This royal ideology is heightened by the fact that following the completion of the transfer of the ark, God grants David an everlasting dynasty through the Davidic covenant (1 Chr 17). It is this royal covenant that is closely linked to common ancient Near Eastern temple theology, where the king is responsible for the temple.

It seems significant that while David himself does not build the temple, the Chronicler acknowledges David's responsibility for the temple. Kapelrud, among others, has researched temple building in the ancient Near East.[118] When one compares the Chronicler's statements about David's organization and preparations for building the temple with the general features of Kapelrud's work, there are striking similarities. It is David who sees the need for the temple. It is David who receives the plan for the temple by God. It is David who proclaims his desire to build the temple. It is David who provides the material, most notably the cedar from Lebanon, for the construction. David himself establishes the temple personnel. Finally, it is David who is granted the promise of an everlasting dynasty.[119] This dynastic link is so prevalent that it has caused some to see David as a cult founder. While David is careful to follow the Law of Moses, he is also the one who receives divine revelation. This revelation allows him to introduce new elements within the cult.[120] Welten notes that the way that the Chronicler has developed the entire David narrative, especially 1 Chr 11–16, ties the anointing of David with the ark narrative and gives the narrative a fluid flow.[121] This highlights the dynasty (as it is tied to David's anointing) and cultic development (which is evident in the organization of the priests and Levites to the two official cultic sites) of the narrative, which are in turn developed throughout the remainder of the book.

The kings that the Chronicler includes in his narrative establish a solid link between their reigns and that of David's and his institution of the cult.[122] The political and other reforms are rarely addressed in the book of Kings, and when addressed they are addressed in passing. The Chronicler on the other hand shows a broader interest in the way that the kings of Judah reformed their kingdom.[123]

Connections within the Davidic–Solomonic Narrative

The Chronicler has carefully connected the Davidic narrative with the Solomonic narrative. The same thematic elements make up both narratives: an example is the bringing of the ark into the temple (2 Chr 5:1–13). One is struck by the close parallel between 1 Chr 15 and 2 Chr 5: there, both kings called for the leaders and all people to join them (1 Chr 15:25, 28; 2 Chr 5:2, 6); both kings authorized sacrifices (1 Chr 15:26; 2 Chr 5:6); both narratives include music and song accompanying the movement of the ark (1 Chr 15:28, 16:7–36; 2 Chr 5:12–13); both narratives indicate that the priests and Levites sanctified themselves (1 Chr 15:12). In 1 Chr 15:12 the priests are not specifically listed, but they are certainly implied in light of the narrative context. In 2 Chr 5:11 the priests are mentioned as having sanctified themselves, but the Levites are clearly implied as they too would have sanctified themselves before bearing the ark in v. 4. Further, Braun notes that the Chronicler deliberately changes the building account of the temple (2 Chr 8:12–16). The Chronicler changes the account in order to summarize the major features of worship in the temple. Hence, the author gives David and Solomon the authority to order the performance of the priests and Levites at the temple.[124]

The parallels between these two accounts are significant enough to be able to say that the Chronicler was not merely interested in David as a royal political figure, but also as a king who was concerned for the cult.[125] Such parallels show that the two passages draw upon the same elements, which ultimately reveal that the proper function of the cult is the primary concern of the Chronicler.[126]

David is the litmus test for all other national polity and for true worship. The concern for cultic personnel is required because they are held under the authority of the Davidic king. Thus, the functions of the cultic personnel are given legitimacy by the king. In every place in Chronicles where there is development or change made within the cult, the king is the one who authorized the movement.[127] This is also consistent in light of the ancient Near Eastern understanding of the king and temple building. Thus, the historical and political achievements of all the kings of Judah take second place to the cultic actions that they have done.[128] Yet, one must also keep in mind that the Chronicler indicates that the kingdom and its kingship belong to Yahweh, a fact that seems to become quite clear within the ark narrative.[129]

Reforms of the Kings in Their Ancient Near Eastern Context

In addressing the specific kings, Ben Zvi's caution with regard to the building texts has merit for the material as a whole. He states, "A final note: any proposal claiming that Chr sent a single message to the audience in a particular account or set of accounts is inherently weak."[130] While this section is devoted to how the kings are tied thematically to the ark narrative, one should not think that all the various sub-motifs are being neglected. They too can be indirectly tied to the themes mentioned here.[131]

The Chronicler evidently had much knowledge of ancient Near Eastern inscriptions. McCarter has done considerable research with regard to the Assyrian inscriptions in relation to the ark narrative of Samuel.[132] The parallels between the ancient Near Eastern literature and the narrative of 2 Sam 6 cause him to state that the narrative serves as an introduction of Yahweh to Jerusalem. However, McCarter's arguments need some modification when they are applied to Chronicles.[133] Therefore, an examination of the relevant literature should help illuminate what was taking place in the ancient Near East. The parallels will then be applied to the ark narrative in Chronicles to discover the implications for reading the text. The Chronicler is showing his readers that the priests and the Levites are not completely autonomous, but they function within the national institution of Judah, originally under David and now as permitted by Persia.[134] The fact that the clergy is not completely autonomous may play an important role as Judah is not autonomous but subject to Persian authority. The Chronicler may be linking his own time to that of David's in order to show that although the Persian crown holds authority, the worship system was set up by and maintained by David and his successors. Thus, he desires for his readers to understand that the Second Temple and its cult ultimately belong to the Davidic legacy.

Inscriptions regarding city building and cult founding. A number of Assyrian inscriptions help illuminate the context of the king's building a city and also founding the cult of that city. While the original builder and cult founder's inscriptions may be of interest, it seems more significant to note the various successors' attention to the city and cult in light of the previous ruler's desire to have the city maintained. A significant number of such texts exist; however, a few examples will serve to make the point. The earliest clear reference to the building of cities and founding of the cult in the Neo-Assyrian Empire comes from Assurnasirpal II. While the festivities that accompanied his building projects and the movement of gods into his royal city also have significance for the ark narrative, as they are quite similar, it is the concluding inscription that seems to be the most significant.[135] The inscription states,

> When the temple of Ishtar, the queen of Kidmuri, which had existed in former days under the kings, my fathers, had been destroyed…I built that temple of Kidmuri anew for her. …
>
> O thou future prince among the kings, my sons, whom Assur shall call by name, (when) thou shalt behold (this) vision, restore the imperfections thereof, into a place (unsheltered from) the sun thou shalt not cause her to enter. Thou shalt not blot out my name which is inscribed (hereon) but thou shalt inscribe thy own name by the side of my name, and shalt restore it unto its place and thou shalt repair the ruins of this temple. (Then) Assur, the great lord, Shamash, judge of heaven and earth, and Ishtar, queen of Kidmuri, will hear his prayers and will surely lengthen his days! In the war of kings, upon the field of battle, may they cause him to attain to the desire of (lit., all that is in) his heart! Whosoever blots out my name (and) inscription, and writes his own name (in its place), or carries off this immemorial stele…may Assur, the great lord, and Adad, ruler of heaven and earth, and Irra (Girra), the lord of storm and destruction, overthrow his kingdom.…[136]

Although the ending of the inscription is lengthy, it serves to establish the point of the ancient Near Eastern kings and their feelings regarding the cult that was reestablished in their royal city. The restoration of royal cities and cults can be illustrated throughout the Neo-Assyrian kings.[137] However, it is interesting that the blessing on the future king is tied to their respect and restoration of the city and the temple cult, not to the king per se. Such blessing becomes clear in several inscriptions that address a king's memorial inscription.[138] It is interesting that there is no blessing of the gods for subsequent kings maintaining other king's memorials, only a curse.

It seems that the promised blessing of the gods' hearing and granting the subsequent kings every wish is conducive to his restoration of the capital city and/or the cult of that city. While further illustrations could be cited regarding the kings in building various cities, either their own capital, or rebuilding a city that was a previous king's royal city, these illustrations serve as ample evidence with regard to the Assyrian kings. The same can be said of the restoring of temples, or the building of new temples for the gods. The implications from the Assyrian royal inscriptions seem to be that it is the one who restores the capital, in whole or in part and/or the cultic temples of the city, who will be blessed by the gods. This means that if the Chronicler is developing his work in light of ancient Near Eastern royal inscriptions, then the building texts that are present in the Chronicler's account may have some significance beyond mere archaeological interest.[139]

The Chronicler's idea of reform is much broader than that of the Deuteronomist. These reforms indicate rebuilding the city wall and reorganization of the temple cult. In fact, one wonders if the places where the Chronicler notes the building of various cities to fortify the land and the capital could also be viewed in similar terms, especially so in light of the Canaanite and Aramaic building inscriptions. For example, Yehimilk of Byblos built a house, possibly a temple, and rebuilt other houses. He hoped that as a result of this building that the gods of Byblos would grant him long life.[140] The same connections with regard to a long life for the king who maintained the land in general are made in the Azitawadda inscription. There, Azitawadda claimed to have restored the Danunites and expanded their territory, resulting in blessing and well being for his people. He also established the cult and an order of priests within it. This accomplishment is followed by the king's hope of a long life, superiority over other kings, and material blessings.[141]

This inscription has certainly broadened the building texts to include, "strongholds in all the outposts at the borders…"[142] within this stated desire for blessing. Thus, when the Chronicler speaks of various building texts outside of the city of Jerusalem, he may well have had this idea of blessing in mind.[143] A similar idea is found in a text from Eshmunᶜazar of Sidon. The inscription on his sarcophagus notes that he has built temples for the gods of Sidon and Sidon by the Sea. As a result, the Lord of Kings gave him Dor and Joppa because of his deeds.[144] The same type of hope can be found in the various cultic inscriptions in this area as well.[145] This hope may mark a slight difference between the Assyrian inscriptions which focus on the future ruler and the blessing he will find for restoring the cities and cults of the land and the Canaanite and Aramaic inscriptions that focus the hope of blessing on the present king.

Implications applied to the narrative. Although the Chronicler does not give a clear statement of David's desire for Yahweh to grant him or his successors favor, the way the cultic texts noted above have such similar activities within them leaves open the possibility that the Chronicler does intend for his work to be looked at in a similar way. David's actions on behalf of Yahweh in the second half of the ark narrative certainly suggest that David has authority over both the cultic affairs and the royal affairs of the nation. Thus, like the Assyrian royal inscriptions, the Chronicler's references to the various building projects may be linking the building or reorganization of the cult (e.g., 2 Chr 26:9; 27:3; 32:5; 33:14, 16) by those kings as indicating that Yahweh heard their prayers and that they found favor in his sight.

A significant example is Manasseh. Before his exile he did not regard the temple, or David as the cultic founder of it; instead he set up altars to other gods within the temple (2 Chr 33:4–5). Therefore, the logical conclusion for the

Chronicler is that his disregard for the cult and its official founder resulted in his exile. Second Kings 21:1–19 is silent on the matter of Manasseh's exile and restoration, as well as his attention to the cult following his restoration. The writer of the account in Kings looks at Manasseh as a major contributing factor to the devastation that Assyria lays upon Judah, and the subsequent Babylonian exile; he is judged solely on the basis of the Mosiac covenant. The Chronicler, on the other hand, notes that during his exile he turned to God and God heard him and returned him to Judah (2 Chr 33:12–13). There he did give attention to the cult and the city and as a result had a long and prosperous reign.

While the Assyrian royal inscriptions also note other kings giving attention to the city of previous kings, there are no parallels with Judah, because Jerusalem was the only capital. Another case that may have similar implications, although not linked to building the capital or reorganizing the cult in explicate terms, is the Chronicler's account of Abijah's reign. Again, this is another account not included in 1 Kings. The Chronicler clearly notes that Israel should not fight against the kingdom of Yahweh which is under the Davidic king because Judah has not forsaken Yahweh. The priests and the Levites still continue to do their daily duties (2 Chr 13:8–10). The result is that God fights for Judah and allows them to prevail, despite being out numbered and ambushed.

The Canaanite and Aramaic inscriptions, however, are more pointed regarding the building of cities and temples. They focus on the blessing that the present king hopes to gain as a result of his benevolence to the people and to his god.[146] When these texts are compared with Chronicles many close connections become immediately apparent. For example, the building of cities to protect the nation and the capital result in the king's being blessed (2 Chr 11:5–12; 14:6–11; 17:12, 19; 26:6–15; 27:3–4; 32:5, 27–30; 33:14); a similar case can be made for the rebuilding or restoration of the cult as well (2 Chr 15:8; 17:8; 19:4–11; 20:5; 24:4–14; 27:3; 29:3–30:27; 31:11–21; 33:16; 34:8–21; 35:1–19).[147]

The above evidence shows that while the Chronicler is certainly doing more than just merely writing the royal annals for the Davidic line, he also takes into account royal inscriptions in his work. He has done far more in this area than his counterpart in Kings. The Chronicler sets up his account of the royal reforms in light of similar ancient Near Eastern texts. Prosperity seems to be directly linked to how these kings cared for the city of David, whether through directly rebuilding some portion of it, fortifying the country as a whole, or in the repairing or reorganization of the cult in Jerusalem. Other implications are involved within this framework as well. For example, Welten noticed that the Chronicler separates Jerusalem from all other cities in Judah with regard to building and organization of national polity.[148] The Chronicler attributes these building texts to the actual activities of these kings.[149] The reason the Chronicler allows only some kings, and not others, to build is not easily resolved.[150] However, it seems that all those kings who cared for the cult and for the God of their father David experienced similar blessings as those of the ancient Near Eastern texts discussed above. Not every king in these inscriptions is credited for building in both the capital and other cities (few at all in the same inscription); hence the Chronicler may have been selective in what he chose, but the point remains the same. Divine blessing is granted to those who care for Yahweh and his people in a similar way as did the founder of the dynasty and organizer of the cult.

Restoration of a cult in Egypt. A number of Egyptian inscriptions that date to the Persian period deal with a high-ranking Egyptian official's appointing temple workers. Although the temple is yet to be built in the ark narrative, the appointing of cultic personnel in that narrative may well have some parallels to this material. Several scholars have addressed this material but no one at present has addressed it in light of the ark narrative.[151] Wright has briefly addressed this material in light of David's final organization of the cult in 1 Chr 23–27.[152] One of the reasons it may not have been developed within the ark narrative is that the extra biblical material pertains to a temple, which is not present here. One wonders, however, if the temple was merely the only institution available and that the parallel should be noted here first because David did organize cultic officials and it was an official national organization of the cult. Wright argues that this type of information is given at the end of a king or high official's life; however, the same type of material is also found in Neh 13:14. Nehemiah, however, still seems to be a Persian official and while aged may still have functioned in that capacity for some time after the completion of the events found in the work bearing his name. Furthermore, it seems clear that the movement of the ark to Jerusalem is not in chronological order. Such a move would require time for David to build his own houses and then establish a place for the ark. This could be done only after the borders of Israel were under control and the Philistine menace was suppressed. This necessitates a date around 977 B.C.E. which would be within six years of David's death. Thus, the events of the ark narrative would have occurred at the end of David's reign and fit this broad description of such material coming at the end of the king's life.

Upon examining the Egyptian materials dating to around the first Persian domination, or the Twenty-Seventh dynasty in Egypt (525–404), it appears that the evidence has been over drawn by Blenkinsopp. Wright does appreciate the significance of the ideological background in these texts and notes that they were written to support the Persian king more than to praise the Egyptian official. The major texts coming from Egypt that deal with the restoration of a cult are the *Udjahorresnet* inscription and the *Petosiris* inscription.[153] Although Blenkinsopp's and Wright's observations are valid, it seems that this ideology is at the forefront of the biographical inscriptions found during this time period. Thus, it seems better to look at the larger picture that these texts provide; namely, that they are polemics for Persian authority in Egypt. If there is a parallel to be found in the ark narrative, it would be a polemic for David as a cult founder who was granted a dynasty by Yahweh. Yahweh is the great king, just as the Persian king is in the postexilic period, and the Chronicler is portraying David as his appointed official. Thus, the parallel asserts that the ultimate sovereign is Yahweh, whose permission to accomplish anything must be sought in order to achieve one's desired goal. While one needs to keep this type of parallel tempered with caution, it is precisely this connection that explains the link between the Saul and David narratives. Saul did not seek the great king and, therefore, was removed from office and his dynasty was never established. David sought Yahweh's approval and willingly submitted to his authority, which resulted in his being given a dynasty.[154]

Implications applied to the narrative. The implications here are significant because the inscriptions do not merely legitimate David as a royal official.[155] These inscriptions are used by the Chronicler to show that the cult was legitimated by David and ultimately Yahweh. This fits the context of the ark narrative better than the context of David's final organization of the cult. In the ark narrative proper (13–16), David insists on caring for the ark of Yahweh. Although commendable and certainly within Yahweh's own desire, he is not permitted just to move the ark under his own authority. Proper cultic procedure had to be observed. This clearly shows that while David desires to unite both the capital and the cult, Yahweh allows the unification but only when proper reverence is given to his presence.

The final ordering of the cult also acknowledges God, it does so according to standard cultic practice; an example is the use of casting lots (1 Chr 24:5). David's movement of the ark seems to provide a clearer picture of Yahweh as the true king of the nation. This may help to explain why Michal despised David. He was not trying to function as her father had, but in submission to Yahweh. Therefore, the Chronicler's narrative encourages the people to follow the leaders of that cult because in doing so they are following the great king, over whom even the Persian authorities have no power.[156] This may alleviate the long troubling issue of why the Chronicler did not put any emphasis on Zerubbabel as being in the Davidic line. He is not making a defiant stand against Persia, merely arguing that the one institution that they have allowed to function should be viewed as the people's authority and should be followed closely. It is through this pure worship that Israel will be able to maintain covenant relations with Yahweh. As a result, Yahweh will once again be able to intervene on behalf of his people. Whenever this intervention occurs, the Chronicler believes that the Davidic line would once again retake the throne and return autonomy to the nation.[157]

The Chronicler is not merely arguing for formal adherence to the cult on the part of the monarch, and by implication the nation, but he is arguing for complete devotion to Yahweh.[158] While only a few kings are noted for their maintenance of the cult, there are other kings that do not specifically reform the cult but still fit this pattern.[159] However, the key development seems to be in the reorganization of the cult. Kings such as Hezekiah and Josiah play an important role in this regard.

Hezekiah clearly reorganized the cult in 2 Chr 29–32. The Chronicler's reworking of the narrative in 2 Kgs 18–20 is not surprising. Lowery states, "For the Chronicler, Hezekiah is David and Solomon rolled into one."[160] Hezekiah consecrated and rededicated the temple after it had fallen into disuse (2 Chr 29). In a very real sense he reunited the two kingdoms after the Assyrians had taken the northern tribes into captivity and encouraged both nations to participate in the cultic festival (2 Chr 30). Then he took steps to maintain proper worship in the temple (2 Chr 31). He accomplished this by reorganizing the priests and Levites in the same way that David had commanded. The Chronicler portrays Hezekiah as a king that brought the glorious days of David and Solomon back to the nation (2 Chr 30:26). This is given support by Hezekiah's desire to maintain proper worship which is evident in his specific commands regarding the musical instruments, the offerings, his prayer, and the great rejoicing that went on during the worship service.

Josiah serves as a final major example of cultic reorganization. In many ways Josiah's reformation was developed along similar lines as Hezekiah's: the removal of high places (2 Chr 34:3–7) and his command to the Levites to reorganize themselves (2 Chr 35:4) were according to the Mosaic and Davidic standards for the cult. However, Josiah's reorganization of the cult may also have specific interest for the Chronicler, because Assyrian rule in the West was over, and Josiah is the first king of Judah to have political freedom from a foreign power. Thus, this new freedom called for clear political and cultic direction. By reorganizing the cult and reaffirming the covenant with the people, Josiah was taking the proper steps to maintain proper worship and cultic purity. Therefore, the Chronicler may be illustrating his point that since the temple has been rebuilt and the people of Yehud have the ability to worship Yahweh once again like their fathers, they should do so properly so that they can maintain proper covenant relations with Yahweh and not be driven from the land. This cultic reform serves as the last cultic act of any king. The following kings then serve as a clear illustration that an improper attitude toward Yahweh would result in exile. This is precisely the reason for the Chronicler's including the Passover account, which emphasizes the nation's freedom from slavery. Hence, Josiah's reform was a clear attempt on the part of the king to reform the cult and through it change the national culture to one that served Yahweh alone.

There are other kings who reorganized the temple cult. They too do so with the authority of their Davidic heritage.[161] Thus, the Chronicler is showing his readers that no matter how badly the cult was ignored by some of Israel's kings, the cultic activities were reorganized later by a Davidide who had the authority to do so. Therefore, the elements present in the postexilic period are assured the same legitimacy because the cult is functioning under the same guidelines as the preexilic temple was. As a result it too functions under the authority of the Davidic dynasty, despite the fact that there is no Davidic ruler present.

Summary

This chapter serves two functions. First, it pulls together the major literary hypotheses and demonstrates that there were methodological problems within each one based on the literary analysis of the preceding chapter. Further evidence was given from the genealogies and David's final organization of the cult to demonstrate that both of those major sections should be considered original to the Chronicler as well. Thus, all places where major objections to the possibility of single authorship are debated were addressed. On the whole these sections support single authorship. It is at least plausible that the various places where the priests and the Levites are found in the text stem from the hand of the Chronicler alone.

The second function of this chapter is to begin to show the way the ark narrative functions thematically throughout the book. The purpose of the Chronicler's work is discussed and the findings there supported the general idea of continuity. Yet that theme is far too broad; therefore, it became necessary to see more specific emphases that carry that theme through. It seems that the role of David is being consistently emphasized in three areas: (1) his dynasty, (2) his making Jerusalem his capital city, and (3) his instructions for the institution and organization of the cult.

Following the examination of the Chronicler's purpose, arguments for the ark narrative's being the thematic center of the work were examined. This was accomplished first by looking at similar language in the genealogies and in examining David's final ordering of the cult. Second, in addressing the narratives of the kings. The implications for the ark narrative clearly show that the Chronicler was arguing for David as a cult founder who had charged those to come after him to care for the cult.

Notes

1. Gary N. Knoppers, *1 Chronicles, 10–29: A New Translation with Introduction and Commentary*, AB 12A (New York: Doubleday, 2004), 655.
2. Martin Noth, *The Chronicler's History*, trans. H. G. M. Williamson, JSOTSup 50 (Sheffield: JSOT Press, 1987), 31–35.
3. Ibid., 36–42.
4. Ibid., 35–36.
5. For example, Rudolph would see more literary connections than Noth. He states, "His [the Chronicler's] ability to create larger units, I would rate higher than does Noth; he shows it as much in his presentation of the post-exilic period as in his construction of the David narrative; and in his descriptions of the reigns of individual kings (for example, Ahaz or Hezekiah), produces a more unified picture than that in his canonical original" (Wilhelm Rudolph, "Problems of the Books of Chronicles," *VT* 4 [1954]: 403–4).
6. Noth, *Chronicler's History*, 30.
7. Ibid., 31.
8. Although Noth's literary analysis addresses the Chronicler's work as a whole, it is not possible to address it fully here due to spatial considerations. One should see Wright's helpful critique of Noth's analysis of 1 Chon 23–27 (John Wesley Wright, "The Origin and Function of 1 Chronicles 23–27," [Ph.D. diss., University of Notre Dame, 1989], 148–57). One should note that he does not address Rudolph in his critique.
9. Two major scholars in this field attempted to refine Rudolph's basic analysis of the Chronicler. The first was Willi, who went beyond those before him by arguing that 1 Chr 23:25–32 and 2 Chr 35:3–4 were based on the editor's reading of 1 Chr 15:2. See Thomas Willi, *Die Chronik als Auslegung: Untersuchungen zur literarischen Gestaltung der historischen Überlieferung Israels*, FRLANT 106 (Göttingen: Vandenhoeck & Ruprecht, 1972), 196–97, 203. While Willi does move the hypothesis beyond that of Rudolph, the same criticism applies to his analysis. Hence, although Wright does not address Willi's position directly, his statements on 1 Chr 23:25–31 apply to Willi as well (Wright, "The Origin and Function," 103–5). The second attempt is by Braun, who has followed Rudolph but harmonized the hypothesis with that of Freedman and Cross. Braun leaves the issue a bit unclear as he does not develop the point in his commentary on a consistent basis (See Roddy Braun, *1 Chronicles*, WBC 14 [Waco, Tex.: Word Books, 1986], xix–xxi; xxvi–xxix).
10. Rudolph, "Problems of the Books of Chronicles," 401–9.
11. Williamson, *1 and 2 Chronicles*, 14–15.
12. Dirksen has noted also that the priests play an important role in this chapter and should not be considered secondary (Piet Dirksen, "The Development of the Text of 1 Chronicles, 15:1–24," *Hen* 17 [1995]: 273).
13. One should note that by rejecting Williamson's pro-Priestly redaction one does not, and should not, reject his view of separate authorship of Ezra–Nehemiah and Chronicles.
14. Sara Japhet, "Composition and Chronology in the Book of Ezra–Nehemiah," in *Second Temple Studies, vol. 2, Temple Community in the Persian Period*, ed. Tamara C. Eskenazi and Kent H. Richards, JSOTSup 175 (Sheffield: JSOT Press, 1994), 214.
15. H. G. M. Williamson, "The Composition of Ezra 1–6," *JTS* 34 (1983): 29–30.
16. This fundamental issue was challenged by Blenkinsopp and continues to be debated in scholarship (see Joseph Blenkinsopp, *Ezra–Nehemiah: A Commentary*, OTL [Philadelphia: Westminster, 1988], 43–44).

17. Ibid., 43.
18. Ibid., 43–44.
19. Williamson, "Composition," 3.
20. It should be noted that Williamson argues that the material original to the Chronicler was written first. The pro-Priestly redaction was written a generation later than the original work.
21. Georg Steins, *Die Chronik als kanonisches Abschlussphänomen: Studien zur Entstehung und Theologie von 1/2 Chronik*, BBB 93 (Weinheim: Athenäum, 1995), 210–11. For his complete discussion regarding the foundational layer that was at the disposal of the Chronicler, see ibid., 175–211.
22. Williamson, "Composition," 29.
23. Ibid., 23.
24. It appears that the priests had the responsibility of teaching the people (Lev 10:8; 2 Kgs 17:27; 2 Chr 15:3, 17:7; and Ezek 44:23). This would likely include the reading of authoritative texts before the people (see Ezra 3: 2-4, Dan 9:1-2; Ezek 4:24–5:2).
25. It seems that the best explanation at this time is that the author of Ezra 1–6 also wrote 7–10. However, there are a number of issues regarding authorship of Ezra that are distinct enough from Chronicles that one must admit that such a conclusion is tentative at best.
26. Ernst Michael Dörrfuß, *Mose in den Chronikbüchern: Garant theokratischer Zukunftserwartung*, BZAW 219 (Berlin: de Gruyter, 1994), 277.
27. Steins, *Die Chronik als kanonisches Abschlussphänomen*. Steins has limited his work to 1 Chr 11–29; and 2 Chr 1–9; 29–32; and 34–35. He also attempts to justify his work in these sections of material as being representative of the final form of the work.
28. For example, see ibid., 254–55.
29. McKenzie indicates that Dörrfuß's lack of form criticism allows him to employ "hypercritical" literary divisions throughout his work (Steven L. McKenzie, "The Chronicler as Redactor," in *The Chronicler as Author: Studies in Text and Texture*, ed. M. Patrick Graham and Steven L. McKenzie, JSOTSup 263 [Sheffield: Sheffield Academic Press, 1999], 80). For additional criticisms of Dörrfuß's work, see Gary N. Knoppers, "Review of Ernst Michael Dörrfuss, *Moses in den Chronikbüchern*," *CBQ* 58 (1996): 705–7.
30. McKenzie also raises this objection against Stein's argument ("The Chronicler as Redactor," 80).
31. For a good overview of genealogical material see Robert R. Wilson, "The Old Testament Genealogies in Recent Research," *JBL* 94 (1975): 169–89; and Robert R. Wilson, *Genealogy and History in the Biblical World*, YNER 7 (New Haven, Conn.: Yale University Press, 1977).
32. Roddy Braun, "1 Chronicles 1–9 and the Reconstruction of the History of Israel," in *The Chronicler as Historian*, ed. M. Patrick Graham, Kenneth G. Hoglund, and Steven L. McKenzie, JSOTSup 238 (Sheffield: Sheffield Academic Press, 1997), 105. Although Braun's primary issue is the historical value of the genealogies, yet his argument supports unity as well. On the historical reliability of the genealogies see Gary A. Rendsburg, "The Internal Consistency and Historical Reliability of the Biblical Genealogies," *VT* 40 (1990): 185–206; and John W. Kleinig, "Recent Research in Chronicles," *CRBS* 2 (1994): 45.
33. Simon J. De Vries, *1 and 2 Chronicles*, FOTL 11 (Grand Rapids: William B. Eerdmans, 1989), 13.
34. For De Vries list of glosses and secondary assertions, see ibid., 13–14.
35. For example see Ran Zadok, "On the Reliability of the Genealogical and Prosopographical Lists of the Israelites in the Old Testament," *TA* 25 (1998): 228–54.

36. Gary N. Knoppers, *1 Chronicles, 1–9: A New Translation with Introduction and Commentary*, AB 12 (New York: Doubleday, 2003), 245–65; also see Gary N. Knoppers, "Classical Historiography and the Chronicler's History: A Reexamination of an Alleged Nonrelationship," *JBL* 122 (2003): 627–50.

37. Ibid., 254, note 8.

38. Avraham Malamat, "King Lists of the Old Babylonian Period and Biblical Genealogies," *JAOS* 88 (1968): 168–73; Marshall D. Johnson, *The Purpose of the Biblical Genealogies: With Special Reference to the Setting of the Genealogies of Jesus*, 2d ed., SNTSMS 8 (Cambridge: Cambridge University Press, 1988).

39. In general Kartveit's discussion is quite illuminating. Magnar Kartveit, *Motive und Schichten der Landtheologie in 1 Chronik 1–9*, ConBOT 28 (Stockholm, Sweden: Almqvist & Wiksell, 1989), especially 19–23; Manfred Oeming, *Das wahre Israel: Die "genealogische Vorhalle" 1 Chronik 1–9*, BWA(N)T 128 (Stuttgart: Kohlhammer, 1990); Thomas Willi, *Chronik*, BKAT 24 (Neukirchen-Vluyn: Neukirchener, 1991); and Sara Japhet, *1 and 2 Chronicles: A Commentary*, OTL (London: SCM, 1993).

40. This does not neglect other themes found in the genealogies and the remainder of the book. For example the theme of all Israel is a major theme as well as the connection between the tribes and their respective territories. The point here is that the genealogies ultimately point toward Jerusalem and the cult.

41. For example, Wilhelm Rudolph, *Chronikbücher*, HAT 21 (Tübingen: Mohr–Siebeck, 1955), 152–85; Frank Michaeli, *Les Livres des Chroniques, d'Esdras et de Néhémie*, CAT 16 (Neuchâtel,: Delachaux & Niestlé, 1967), 118–38; Willi, *Die Chronik als Auslegung*, 194–204; Braun, *1 Chronicles*, 228–64; Dörrfuß, *Mose in den Chronikbüchern*, 158–71; and Steins, *Die Chronik als kanonisches Abschlussphänomen*, 283–335.

42. H. G. M. Williamson, "The Origins of the Twenty-Four Priestly Courses: A Study of 1 Chronicles 22–27," in *Studies in the Historical Books of the Old Testament*, ed. J. A. Emerton, VTSup 30 (Leiden: Brill, 1979), 251–68.

43. It should be noted that some scholars prior to Noth argued that the lists were inserted by the Chronicler but that he was not the author of them (i.e., they preceded his work). See Immanuel Benzinger, *Die Bücher der Chronik*, (Tübingen: Mohr, 1901), microfiche, 68–81; and Johann Goettsberger, *Die Bücher der Chronik oder Paralipomenon*, HSAT 4 (Bonn: Peter Hanstein, 1939), 165, 191.

44. John W. Kleinig, *The Lord's Song: The Basis, Function and Significance of Choral Music in Chronicles*, JSOTSup 156 (Sheffield: JSOT Press, 1993), 55.

45. Wright, "Origin and Function,"83–218.

46. John Wesley Wright, "The Legacy of David in Chronicles: The Narrative Function of 1 Chronicles 23–27," *JBL* 110 (1991): 229–42.

47. Wright, "Origin and Function," 152.

48. Ibid.

49. Ibid.

50. One caveat needs to be stated here. Many scholars who see this section as being secondary also see some of chapters 22, 28–29 as secondary. Much of this discussion is valid only if one sees chapters 22, 28–29 as original to the Chronicler. For a good overview of this position see Adam C. Welch, *The Work of the Chronicler, Its Purpose and Date*, The Schweich Lectures on Biblical Archaeology (London: Oxford University Press, 1939), 81–96.

51. Japhet, *1 and 2 Chronicles*, 406–11. See also Martin J. Selman, *1 Chronicles: An Introduction and Commentary*, TOTC 10a (Downers Grove, Ill.: Inter-Varsity Press, 1994), 218–48; Knoppers,

1 Chronicles, 10–29, 788–98; and William M. Schniedewind, *The Word of God in Transition: From Prophet to Exegete in the Second Temple Period*, JSOTSup 197 (Sheffield: Sheffield Academic Press, 1995), 165–70.

52. Japhet, 1 and 2 Chronicles, 408.

53. The position that the ark narrative is the center of the Chronicler's work is also argued by Barker. See David G. Barker, "The Theology of the Chronicler a Synoptic Investigation of 1 Chronicles 13, 15-17 and 2 Samuel 6-7" (Th.D. diss., Grace Theological Seminary, 1984), microfiche.

54. As noted in Chapter two, the Chronicler frequently uses literary devices such as similar language in other narratives to emphasize his point. In this narrative the Chronicler has set up the ark narrative in a way that it gives direction to the remainder of the work both literarily and theologically.

55. This writer wishes to distinguish here between narrative themes and theological themes. The focus here is on the narrative itself; the theological themes will be treated in chapter five.

56. The clearest examples of attempts at dating with regard to purpose come from Freedman, Cross, and Newsome. See Frank Moore Cross, "A Reconstruction of the Judean Restoration," *JBL* 94 (1975): 4–18; David Noel Freedman, "The Chronicler's Purpose," *CBQ* 23 (1961): 436–42; and James D. Newsome Jr., "Toward an Understanding of the Chronicler and His Purposes," *JBL* 94 (1975): 201–17. Dyck nevertheless, argues that date is not the central issue. Jonathan Dyck, "Dating Chronicles And the Purpose of Chronicles," *Did* 8 (1996–97): 26; and Jonathan E. Dyck, *The Theocratic Ideology of the Chronicler*, BIS 33 (Leiden, Boston: Brill, 1998).

57. See for example, Peter R. Ackroyd, *1 and 2 Chronicles, Ezra, Nehemiah: Introduction and Commentary*, TBC (London: SCM Press, 1973), 28.

58. Dyck, "Dating Chronicles," 21.

59. For example, Freedman argues that because of these themes, the setting must be the restoration under Zerubbabel and Jeshua. Thus, the purpose is the legitimacy of the Jerusalem cultic institutions by David and therefore his dynasty's authority over the temple and the cult during that time (Freedman, "Chronicler's Purpose," 439). Noth, on the other hand, sees the same themes but views them as being anti-Samaritan (Noth, *Chronicler's History*, 100). Williamson states that the temple theme is not, "a litmus test of an orthodoxy that would exclude the non-conformist but rather a focus of unity for the people of Israel as a whole" (i.e., all Israel not just Judah. See H. G. M. Williamson, "The Temple in the Books of Chronicles," in *Templum Amicitae: Essays on the Second Temple Presented to Ernst Bammel*, ed. W. Horbury, JSNTSup 48 [Sheffield: JSOT Press, 1991], 21).

60. Sara Japhet, *The Ideology of the Book of Chronicles and Its Place in Biblical Thought*, trans. Anna Barber, 2d ed., BEATAJ 9 (Frankfurt am Main: Lang, 1997).

61. Japhet, 1 and 2 Chronicles, 43–44.

62. Ibid., 49; and Sara Japhet, "Exile and Restoration in the Book of Chronicles," in *The Crisis of Israelite Religion: Transformation of Religious Tradition in Exilic and Post-Exilic Times*, ed. Bob Becking and Marjo C. A. Korpel. OTS 42 (Leiden: Brill, 1999), 33–44.

63. While the discussion addresses the main reason for the Chronicler to write, it should be noted that other major themes do function with the idea of continuity. For example, the theme of seeking Yahweh could be viewed as the same way that the nation would be blessed in both the preexilic and the postexilic periods (On seeking see Christopher T. Begg, "'Seeking Yahweh' and the Purpose of Chronicles," *LS* 9 [1982–83]: 128–41.)

64. A full discussion of this material will be offered below. However, for the sake of clarity one brief example is given here.

65. See *ARI* II §§ 679–82.

66. Abadie has some helpful insights on David and his function in Chronicles. See Philippe Abadie, "La figure de David dans le livre des Chroniques," in *Figures de David à travers la Bible: XVIIe Congrès de l'ACFEB* 177 (Paris: Cerf, 1999), 157–86; and Philippe Abadie, "Le fonctionnement symbolique de la figure de David dans l'oeuvre du Chronist." *Transeu* 7 (1994): 143–51.

67. William Riley, *King and Cultus in Chronicles: Worship and the Reinterpretation of History*, JSOTSup 160 (Sheffield: JSOT Press, 1993),166–68.

68. The view that there are no messianic elements in the book is represented recently by Kenneth E. Pomykala, *The Davidic Dynasty Tradition in Early Judaism*, SBLEJL 7 (Atlanta: Scholars Press, 1995), 77–111.

69. Several scholars believe that the Davidic throne once again occupied by a Davidic king. Magne Saebø, "Messianism in Chronicles? Some Remarks to the Old Testament Background of the New Testament Christology," *HBT* 2 (1980): 90. Saebø's article is quite helpful here as he lists and treats numerous scholarly views.

70. Jeffery L. Townsend, "The Purpose of 1 and 2 Chronicles," *BSac* 144 (1987): 287.

71. Ibid., 240–46.

72. Ibid., 247.

73. Wright argues that this passage is one of the seven passages in Chronicles that are direct references to 1 Chr 23–27. He bases this on what he calls "Davidic assignment formulae," which are used to legitimate the assignment of the priests and Levites. He attempts to argue for the originality of 1 Chr 23–27 based on this formula. He argues that the formula in 1 Chr 6 is used as an expansion in order to clarify the clerical assignments for the temple, which did not yet exist. Therefore, it must refer to 1 Chr 25, because it too deals with these assignments. It seems better to this writer to understand 1 Chr 6 as referring to 1 Chr 15, where the original assignments for the clergy are stated. The names appear in the same order and it seems logical that David by dividing the clergy between two cultic centers intends to eventually join them as one. The genealogical section refers to that time as it has clearly come and gone; however, the ark narrative is presented as if in real time. The Chronicler is writing as if the events have just occurred and shows how the cultic organization develops according to his understanding of those past events.

74. Braun, *1 Chronicles*, 94. See also Japhet, *1 and 2 Chronicles*, 156. Knoppers makes a clear statement regarding this phrase, "'House of Yhwh.' Either the tent shrine David established for the Ark in Jerusalem (1 Chr 15:1–16:1; cf. 2 Sam 6:1-17) or the Tabernacle (1 Chr 6:17)" (Knoppers, *1 Chronicles 1–9*, 422).

75. Wright, "Origin and Function," 163.

76. Ibid., 164.

77. Braun, *1 Chronicles*, 193.

78. Ibid.

79. Ibid., 164–65.

80. Few individuals in the HB have had their names changed. Those who do are all bestowed some type of honor. For example, Abram's name was changed to represent the fact that he would be the father of many nations (Gen 17:5). Jacob's name was changed to Israel which was followed by a blessing from God (Gen 32:28–29). There is honor in being given a new

name and one would suspect that the Chronicler would have used such an event to argue further for the authority of the cult musicians in his own day.

81. Rudolph, *Chronikbücher*, 58. Both Noth and Rudolph argue that 1 Chr 6 represents the final form of a long editorial process, which was added to the original much smaller core (Noth, *Chronicler's History*, 39–40; Rudolph, *Chronikbücher*, 51–64).

82. For a good overview of this issue see Braun's commentary which charts the differences between these two sections (Braun, *1 Chronicles*, 91–93). Braun concludes that the genealogies of Kohath are the closest of all the genealogies in this passage.

83. Williamson argues that the differences between the two passages are due to two different types of genealogies: the first is vertical, the second is horizontal. These different types of genealogies serve different interests; therefore, there is no reason to see both stemming from the hand of two different editors. The supposed repetition is not a repetition in the sense of added material but reflects a change in the genealogy and the intention of the Chronicler (Williamson, *1 and 2 Chronicles*, 68–69). For a more detailed discussion regarding these different types of genealogies see Knoppers, *1 Chronicles 1–9*, 246–50. One should also note, however, that Knoppers does see this chapter as being one of "composite authorship" (ibid., 428).

84. Edward Lewis Curtis and Albert Alonzo Madsen, *A Critical and Exegetical Commentary on the Books of Chronicles*, ICC (Edinburgh: T. & T. Clark, 1910), 135.

85. Wright, "Origin and Function," 168–70.

86. Ibid., 169. Wright's other term that he uses to tie this passage to the Chronicler himself must be rejected. He attributes the specific form of the term מכתפם with the 3mp suffix to a unique use by the Chronicler. However, this specific form occurs only nine times in the MT (Num 29:6, 33; 1 Kgs 18:28; 2 Kgs 17:34, 40; 1 Chr 6:17; 24:19; 2 Chr 4:7; 30:16). The infrequent number of times that it occurs and the fact that when the term itself is used elsewhere in the book, further hinders a technical use for the literary purposes. Finally, his argument about the ark "resting" and attributing it to Solomon, although plausible, seems a little strained. The term "rest" is not present in this passage. However, Josiah says that the ark will "no longer be a burden on your shoulders" (2 Chr 35:3). It is at this point in the Chronicler's narrative that "rest" for the ark finally occurs.

87. Ibid.

88. Williamson, *1 and 2 Chronicles*, 131. In this section of material the MT's versification is different from that of English translations. Williamson's reference to v. 31 is to the English which corresponds to the MT's v. 16.

89. Antti Laato, "The Levitical Genealogies in 1 Chronicles 5–6 and the Formation of Levitical Ideology in Post-Exilic Judah," *JSOT* 62 (1994): 81. Note that while Laato does not argue for a purely historical genealogy here, he does indicate that the Chronicler had access to an earlier source and used it ideologically (ibid., 77).

90. Wright, "Origin and Function," 171–72.

91. Ibid., 172.

92. Curtis and Madsen, *Chronicles*, 176.

93. Ibid.

94. See Japhet, *1 and 2 Chronicles*, 216; and Knoppers, *1 Chronicles 1–9*, 506. The Chronicler attempts to show continuity from the oldest times of Israel's history until his own present situation. This is clear in verses like 9:18, where the Chronicler is speaking of his own time, and 9:23 which is speaking of David's time. The statements about the tabernacle may well be the writer's attempt to show such continuity with the Mosaic period as well.

95. Braun, *1 Chronicles*, 141.

96. Curtis and Madsen, *Chronicles*, 176.

97. Williamson, *1 and 2 Chronicles*, 91; and Braun, *1 Chronicles*, 137.

98. While somewhat beyond the scope of this work, Wright's analysis of the use of the term באמונתם seems difficult to agree with (Wright, "Origin and Function," 173). He argues that in the other seven times that it is used in Chronicles it is used as term where the priests and the Levites receive commands from superiors. While this is true, if the Chronicler were using this term as a technical term, one would expect it to also be incorporated in other major texts in which the priests and Levites are commanded to perform various duties. Most specifically, one would expect the term to appear in the context of the Chronicler's narrative of Hezekiah's restoration of the cult.

99. John W. Wright, "The Founding Father: The Structure of the Chronicler's David Narrative," *JBL* 117 (1998): 49.

100. Wright, "The founding Father," 49–50.

101. Tamara C. Eskenazi, "A Literary Approach to the Chronicler's Ark Narrative in 1 Chronicles 13–16," in *Fortunate the Eyes That See: Essays in Honor of David Noel Freedman in Celebration of His Seventieth Birthday*, ed. Astrid B. Beck et al. (Grand Rapids: Eerdmans, 1995), 258–74.

102. Wright, "The Founding Father," 54.

103. Ibid. However, this is clearly the opposite position of this writer and others. In fact, Freedman states, "To summarize, the Chronicler establishes through his narrative of the reigns of David and Solomon the proper, legitimate pattern of institutions and their personnel for the people of God; and they are the monarchy represented by David and his house, the priesthood, by Zadok and his descendants, the city and the temple in the promised land" (David Noel Freedman, "The Chronicler's Purpose," *CBQ* 23 (1961): 437.

104. De Vries, "Moses and David," 632. De Vries' argument shows that it is David whose concern for the cult is one of the reasons for the Chronicler's idealization of him. The statement correctly assesses the content of 1 Chr 23–27. Its primary purpose is on the cult, not on Solomonic succession as Wright suggests.

105. This also finds some support in Bar's understanding of Solomon in general. He argues that Solomon is being portrayed as the legitimate king but in so doing he notes the factors that were involved in that legitimization. For example, in Solomon's public worship at Gibeon, the Chronicler's omission of the word "dream" in his narrative, and the changes in the dream motif idealize Solomon. For Bar this idealization is the point of the entire passage (see Shaul Bar, "A Better Image for Solomon," *TBT* 36 [1998]: 221–26). Yet it seems clear that Solomon finds legitimization through cultic activity in this passage, not through royal activity.

106. Wright, "Origin and Function," 222. Also see Roddy Braun, "Solomon, the Chosen Temple Builder: The Significance of 1 Chronicles 22, 28, and 29 for the Theology of Chronicles," *JBL* 95 (1976): 581–90. Norbert Lohfink, "Die deuteronomistische Darstellung des Übergangs der Führung Israels von Moses auf Josue," *Schol* 37 (1962): 32–44; Dennis J. McCarthy, "An Installation Genre?" *JBL* 90 (1971): 31–41; and H. G. M. Williamson, "The Accession of Solomon in the Books of Chronicles," *VT* 23 (1976): 375–79.

107. Wright, "Origin and Function," 155.

108. Ibid., 156.

109. Ibid.

110. This writer does wish to state that while he is in agreement with Wright that 1 Chr 23–27 is indeed original to the Chronicler, it seems that Wright would argue that all of the text of this section is original. While one should be open to this view, there are places where glosses or additions seem to be the only way to elevate tensions within the narrative itself (e.g., 27:23–24).

111. Raymond B. Dillard, "The Reign of Asa (2 Chr 14–16): An Example of the Chronicler's Theological Method," *JETS* 23 (1980): 207–18.

112. David is by far the most idealized of all the kings. Yet Solomon is also idealized to a lesser extent. See Riley, *King and Cultus in Chronicles*, 31; and Raymond B. Dillard, *2 Chronicles*, WBC 15 (Waco, Tex.: Word Books, 1987), 1–7.

113. Ibid., 31.

114. Gary N. Knoppers, "History and Historiography: The Royal Reforms," in *The Chronicler as Historian*, ed. M. Patrick Graham, Kenneth G. Hoglund, and Steven L. McKenzie, JSOTSup 238 (Sheffield: Sheffield Academic Press, 1997), 180–81.

115. H. G. M. Williamson, "The Accession of Solomon in the Books of Chronicles," *VT* 23 (1976): 375–79.

116. Riley, *King and Cultus*, 39–53; and G. Johannes Botterweck, "Zur Eigenart der chronistischen Davidgeschichte," *TQ* 136 (1956): 412.

117. Riley, *King and Cultus*, 45.

118. Arvid S. Kapelrud, "Temple Building, a Task for Gods and Kings," *Or* 32 (1963): 56–62.

119. When compared with Kapelrud's summary, these elements were all present in ancient Near Eastern temple building. He states, "In the cases where a king is the actual temple builder the following elements are most often found: 1. Some indication that a temple has to be built; 2. The king visits a temple overnight; 3. A god tells him what to do, indicates plans; 4. The king announces his intention to build a temple; 5. Master builder is engaged, cedars from Lebanon, building-stones, gold, silver, etc. procured for the task; 6. The temple is finished according to plan; 7. Offerings and dedication, fixing of norms; 8. Assembly of the people; 9. The god comes to his new house; 10. The king is blessed and promised everlasting domination" (ibid., 62). This seems to suggest that David is to be given partial credit for building the temple, although the remaining elements here suggest that the remaining credit still belongs to Solomon. This suggests that the Chronicler is, as von Rad has argued, tracing the temple building back to David (Gerhard von Rad, *Das Geschichtsbild des chronistischen Werkes*, BWA(N)T 54 [Stuttgart: Kohlhammer, 1930], 130).

120. Myers argues that this is restricted to the cult and mainly the temple itself. This suggests that the theme of David as a second Moses is tightly connected to the Davidic covenant (Myers, "The Kerygma of the Chronicler," 269). Others have also addressed this issue (e.g., De Vries, "Moses and David," 619–39; and Dörrfuss, *Mose in den Chronikbüchern*).

121. Peter Welten, "Lade-Temple-Jerusalem: Zur Theologie der Chronikbücher," in *Textgemäss: Aufätze und Beiträge zur Hermeneutik des alten Testaments: Festschrift Ernst Würthwein zum 70. Geburtstag*, ed. A. H. J. Gunneweg and Otto Kaiser (Göttingen: Vandenhoeck & Ruprecht, 1979), 172.

122. A helpful work in this area that has helped shape this writer's thinking is G. W. Ahlström, *Royal Administration and National Religion in Ancient Palestine*, SHANE 1 (Leiden: Brill, 1982).

123. See R. H. Lowery, *The Reforming Kings: Cult and Society in First Temple Judah*, JSOTSup 120 (Sheffield: JSOT Press, 1991), 37–156.

124. Roddy L. Braun, "Solomonic Apologetic in Chronicles," *JBL* 92 (1973): 510–11.

125. This of course can also be applied to Solomon. As stated earlier the Chronicler idealizes both kings. More importantly the Chronicler states that Solomon plays a significant role in developing the cult along with David (2 Chr 35:4).

126. On a related note, Cancik attempted to show the religious festivals found in the Chronicler's narratives are specific objectives that the Chronicler has included as a major motif. These festivals point exclusively to the cult and its proper function is the Chronicler's primary theme. See Hubert Cancik, "Das jüdische Fest: Ein Versuch zu Form und Religion des chronistischen Geschichtswerkes," *TQ* 150 (1970): 339.

127. Brueggemann argues that such royal authorization shows a royal prominence that establishes a legitimation for the postexilic cult by showing royal involvement at its beginning. See Walter Brueggemann, *David's Truth in Israel's Imagination and Memory* (Philadelphia: Fortress, 1985), 100, 107. See also Newsome, "Toward a New Understanding," 215.

128. Similarly, Freedman, "The Chronicler's Purpose," 437.

129. Regarding the kingdom see Michaeli, *Les Livres des Chroniques*, 32. Regarding kingship in particular see Simon J. De Vries, "The Schema of Dynastic Endangerment in Chronicles," *PEGLMBS* 7 (1987): 62–64.

130. Ben Zvi, "Building Texts," 149.

131. Some other key themes in the narratives of the kings include (1) retribution, (2) all Israel, (3) foreign alliances, (4) lack of concern for Yahweh and his prophets. These can be found within the ark narrative proper. The theme of immediate retribution can be seen in the broader elements in the ark narrative; for example, Uzzah is killed. The same can be said of the lack of concern for Yahweh in the statement that Saul did not seek the ark (13:1). The idea of total dependence upon Yahweh instead of dependence on foreign nations may be linked to chap 14.

132. P. Kyle McCarter, "The Ritual Dedication of the City of David in 2 Samuel 6," in *The Word of the Lord Shall Go Forth: Essays in Honor of David Noel Freedman in Celebration of His Sixtieth Birthday*, ed. Carol L. Meyers and M. O'Connor (Winona Lake, Ind.: Eisenbrauns, 1983), 273–77.

133. Knoppers, *1 Chronicles, 10–29*, 630.

134. Lisbeth S. Fried, *The Priest and the Great King: Temple-Palace Relations in the Persian Empire*, BJSUC, San Deigo 10 (Winona Lake, Ind.: Eisenbrauns, 2004).

135. *ARAB* II §§467–68, 511, which notes that when Assurnasirpal II built his capital at Calah, he also erected various temples. He invited the gods into their dwellings. He offered sacrifices to the gods and banqueted ten days. Sargon II; when he built Sargon City, he established offerings, appointed priests, and had musicians in attendance (*ARAB* II, §§72–74). Sennacherib also has a similar account (*ARAB* II, §§363, 399).

136. *ARAB* I, §§ 528, 529.

137. See Ibid. regarding Shalmaneser III §§ 675–77; 698–710, but note especially §704, as he hopes that Assur will hear the prayers of the one in the future who restores the ruins and returns the inscription that he has left. On Tiglath-pileser III, §§824–27. Also see *ARAB* II On Sennacherib, §§ 363–371. This description ends with the request regarding the building of the palace, and it seems that the gods had been invited into the palace in particular (§370, 403, 416). The inscriptions continue and note the rebuilding of the temple as well (§§435–42). It is interesting that the gods took up their abodes in peace (§436). Esarhaddon also has a royal inscription that touches on this issue. See *ARAB* II, §§647–59, which describes Esarhaddon's rebuilding of a temple, with a similar blessing and curse for those who restore or remove his name from the work. A similar inscription, K. 192, also shows the attention

he has given to restoring the cult, and the same formula of blessings and curses follow (§§659–59). This becomes clearer in §694, where the inscriptions tells the future king that Esarhaddon had restored the temple of Nineveh and that when it was in ruins, it and the inscriptions of both he and his father should be restored, then Assur and Ishtar will hear that kings prayers. In §§699–700, the temple is dedicated and the details that the inscription lays out is strikingly similar to the ark narrative of 1 Chr 15–16. Also §§734, 741, 751.

138. Ibid., §189, and also see 745, 872; and *ARAB* I, §737.

139. See Zvi, "Building Texts," 132–49.

140. *KAI* § 4.

141. Ibid., § 26.

142. Ibid.

143. Although Ben Zvi arrives at a similar conclusion without the aid of these texts, his conclusion is still quite in keeping with the evidence from these inscriptions listed above. See Ben Zvi, "Building Texts," 148–49.

144. *KAI* §14. The attribution of Dor and Joppa is found in lines 18–19.

145. *KAI* notes a number of these. For example, Yehawmilk of Byblos, after erecting an alter to the Lady of Byblos, states that she heard him, and he now hopes that she will grant him long life and the favor of the gods and man (*KAI* §10).

146. There has been much discussion about immediate retribution as a theme of the Chronicler; this may well support such discussions. However, the theme of immediate retribution moves outside the scope of this discussion; therefore, such points cannot be discussed here.

147. Although restoration could involve the destruction of pagan cults and shrines, in order to keep close parallels with the Canaanite and Aramaic inscriptions these texts will not be included here. However, when one looks at these texts as well the number of texts is significantly increased. Furthermore, more exact parallels to the Canaanite and Aramaic inscriptions could be made. For example the inscriptions speak of cities holding shields and spears, and the prosperity of the king and people with regard to gain and wine. The Chronicler also includes these references in various places as well (e.g., regarding shields etc.: 2 Chr 11:12; 12:9–10; 14:8; 26:14; 32:5, 27; regarding wine and grain: 2 Chr 11:11; 31:5; 32:28). The point is that the Chronicler attributes blessing in similar terms as other ANE inscriptions do.

148. Peter Welten, *Geschichte und Geschichtsdarstellung in den Chronikbücher*, WMANT 42 (Neukirchen-Vluyn: Neukirchener, 1973), 52–78.

149. The historicity of these texts cannot be discussed here. It seems unlikely that any clear and definite conclusions regarding actual kings and their respective building projects will be cleared up to the satisfaction of every scholar. The point here, however, is that the Chronicler has attributed certain building projects to specific kings in order to show how Yahweh blessed the reign of that king. Therefore, the Chronicler has represented his text as being historical in nature.

150. Ben Zvi is certainly correct when he states, "The answer cannot be the 'pious kings' build" (Ben Zvi, "Building Texts," 140, n. 14). To Ben Zvi's credit, he is dealing only with building texts outside of Jerusalem proper. The study above has noted kings that he has listed in their reforms as builders in Jerusalem, or as maintaining the cult to some degree or another. So the above analysis still seems to be quite in keeping with the various ancient Near Eastern texts.

151. Gerhard von Rad, "Die Nehemia-Denkschrift," *ZAW* 76 (1964): 176–87; Joseph Blenkinsopp, "The Mission of Udjahorresnet and Those of Ezra and Nehemiah," *JBL* 106 (1987): 409–21; Mary Francis Gyles, *Pharaonic Policies and Administration, 663 to 323 BCE*, JSSHPS 41

(Chapel Hill: University of North Carolina, 1959); Miriam Lichtheim, *Ancient Egyptian Literature: A Book of Readings,* vol. 3, *The Late Period* (Berkeley: University of California, 1980); and Alan B. Lloyd, "The Inscription of Udjahorresnet: A Collaborator's Testament," *JEA* 68 (1982): 166–80.

152. John Wesley Wright, "The Origin and Function of 1 Chronicles 23-27" (Ph.D. diss., University of Notre Dame, 1989), 241–45.

153. For translations of these inscriptions see Lichtheim, *Ancient Egyptian Literature*, 36–41; and 44–49, respectively.

154. Riley, *King and Cultus*, 67–68.

155. This is contrary to Wright's thesis. He sees this material as legitimating David as a good king and as directly connected to his political impact and little else (Wright, "Origin and Function," 246; Wright, "The Founding Father," 59; and Wright, "The Legacy of David in Chronicles," 237, 242).

156. Although no other source consulted arrived at this same conclusion, there are several scholars who appear to see similar issues in the text. See for example, Riley, *King and Cultus*, 193–94; also see Rudolph, *Chronikbücher*, xxiii.

157. Although Riley does not see any need for a future Davidic king. However, in light of the fact that the Chronicler is arguing for continuity with the past, it seems likely that he is looking for a new Davidic king to rule the nation.

158. J. N. Schumacher, "The Chronicler's Theology of History," *TT* 13 (1957): 16.

159. Regarding the cult, von Rad notes that blessing is based on the king's faithfulness to the cult because it is viewed as direct faithfulness to Yahweh. See Gerhard von Rad, *Old Testament Theology*, vol. 1, *The Theology of Israel's Historical Traditions*, trans. D. M. G. Stalker, OTL (Louisville: Westminster/Knox, 2001), 353. See also Riley, *King and Cultus*, 111–12.

160. Lowery, *The Reforming Kings*, 161.

161. Ibid., 126–27. He argues that there are kings who not only reorganize but change the cultic regulations (ibid., 132). This presses the Chronicler's point too far and should be avoided. See Williamson, *1 and 2 Chronicles*, 120–21; and Baruch Halpern, "Sacred History and Ideology: Chronicles' Thematic Structure—Indications of an Earlier Source," in *The Creation of Sacred Literature, Composition and Redaction of the Biblical Text*, ed. Richard E. Friedman, NES 22 (Berkeley: University of California Press, 1981), 46.

CHAPTER FOUR

Exegetical Analysis

Analysis of Material

Preface: 1 Chronicles 15:1–24

Chapter 15 opens with a statement about David building houses for himself and establishing a place for the ark.[1] The ark had long been associated with the tent of meeting.[2] Thus, it seems appropriate for David initially to bring the ark into his royal city and house it in a tent. This would help calm any misgivings on the part of "all Israel" because he is maintaining an important link to earlier traditions by placing the ark in a tent. This link with earlier traditions shows David's political genius as he begins to make Jerusalem both the political and religious center of the nation.[3] Further, the place that he is preparing for the ark is a holy place. The term מקום frequently carries the idea of holiness being associated with the site.[4] This site is clearly different from David's living quarters and is set aside for the ark and the cultic functions that were to take place there after the ark was placed in its tent. By bringing the ark into his royal city, David is fulfilling the expectation of ancient Near Eastern kings in supporting the cult. It is interesting that the ark is referred to throughout this narrative in various ways. Here, it is called "the ark of God." The text itself seems to suggest that one should not regard the phrases "the ark of God" and "the ark of Yahweh" as having different connotations.[5] However, Eskenazi notes that there are instances where the phrase "the ark of the covenant" is used consistently, instead of the former phrases, suggesting that there is possibly a theological reason for that particular phrase.[6] This phrase does not, however, suggest that the various names for God should be viewed as different sources which are often associated with the Pentateuch.

Verse 2 opens with the term אז. This term can be interpreted in various ways. It can be viewed as pointing to the time that the ark had spent in the house of Obed-Edom, or to a time after David had completed his building projects.[7] In light of the preceding verse, the latter is the better option. After the completion of the tent that housed the ark, David again showed interest in bringing the ark to his royal city. In order to make this venture a successful one, he needed to identify what went wrong in the first attempt. David, apparently after a three-month period (2 Sam 6:11), explained the reason for the unsuccessful attempt as the fact that the Mosaic ordinances were not properly followed.

The Chronicler has shown David as a king who is able to identify the religious problem that resulted from the initial transfer of the ark. David is able to explain the problem to his officials before he gathers all Israel to move the ark (v.3). Thus, David is portrayed as one who has authority over cultic matters.[8] In fact, he is a priest-king who has control over cultic functions: it is his acknowledgment of the improprieties of the previous procession that changes failure into success.[9] The verses that follow are the commands of David to the priests and Levites so that the ark may be brought to Jerusalem safely.

David's statement regarding the Levites is very important within the narrative framework as a whole.[10] He states that Yahweh chose the Levites to carry the ark.[11] The Levites' devotion to Yahweh stands out as the primary reason for Yahweh's choosing them.[12]

Verse 3 then indicates that after David had instructed the officials who would be involved in the processional he called all Israel to the occasion. The Chronicler is including all the people in the moving of the ark. This allows the reader to understand that the people supported David's decision to bring the ark to Jerusalem and that they participated joyfully during the occasion.

Verse 4 shows the Chronicler's concern for acknowledging the sons of Aaron along with the Levites. While the Chronicler is distinguishing between the priests and the Levites the distinction is not always this clear throughout the narrative. At times it appears that the Chronicler can combine the two types of clergy under the heading "the Levites."[13]

Verses 5–10 comprise a list of the leaders of the Levites along with the number of their families. The list does have some differences in it when compared to the genealogies and the final organization of the cult for service in the temple. Verses 5–7 open with the same three names that are found in the Levitical genealogy (5:27–41; 6:1–66). These three names are expected; however, they are in a different order from the genealogical material. First Chronicles 5:27 has the same order as that of Gen 46:11 (Gershon, Kohath, and Merari), while 1 Chr 15:5 places Gershon last (Kohath, Merari, and Gershon).

The Chronicler further adds the families of Elizaphan, Hebron, and Uzziel (vv. 8–10), representing a further division that was not previously made within the family of Kohath.[14] This division may indicate that the Chronicler's change of order in the three main Levitical families is an outgrowth of the Levitical families' own development. The family of Kohath now controls four of the six divisions within the Levitical hierarchy and are, therefore, the most prominent clan. The change in order may also suggest that the Chronicler had an older source available to him for the genealogies. Because the genealogies have the same order presented as that of the Genesis account, one would think it most probable that that list was based on birth order. This was an important issue within the social structure of the Israelites for determining property rights; thus it appears that Gershon was first born, but over the course of time the clan of Kohath stood out among the Levities with respect to their various cultic duties. Num 3:27–31 notes that it is this family that is to care for the ark, the table, the lampstand, the altars, and the sacred furnishings.[15]

Verse 6 identifies those in the family of Merari. Their duties are found in Num 4:29–33. They were to carry the items from the tabernacle. These items include the following: (1) the boards, (2) the bars, (3) the pillars, (4) the sockets, and (5) the pillars around the court with their sockets, pegs, and cords, with all their furnishings. Since they were responsible for carrying these items on ox-carts, this type of moving automatically excludes them from being able to move the ark.

Verse 7 identifies those in the family of Gershon. According to Num 4:24–28, they were to carry the curtains of the tabernacle, the covering of badger skins, the screen for the door of the tabernacle, the screen for the door of the gate of the court, the hangings of the court and the altar, their cords, and all the furnishings for their service. They too were allowed to carry these items by ox-cart. It seems intriguing that the first attempt to bring the ark to Jerusalem resulted in failure because the ark was placed on a cart. According to McCarter, neither Samuel nor Chronicles makes a connection between Uzzah and Ahio with the priests.[16] The names are common among the tribe of Benjamin (1 Chr 8). More importantly, Knoppers notes that they are also common in Levitical contexts.[17] It is difficult, if not impossible, to know whether these men should be considered part of the family of the Levites.

There are two options: either they were Levites, but not Kohathites; or they were not Levites, but because they were the ones responsible for the care of the ark while it was in their father's house, they were allowed to move it.[18] If the first option is taken, this may suggest some kind of an attempt on the part of either the family of Gershon or Merari to usurp the Kohathites' right to carry the ark. They would have certainly carried it on an oxcart because that was according to their tradition. However, during the period of pre-monarchal and monarchal Israel, there were few documented attempts on the part of priestly families to usurp one another.[19] The source clearly predates the Chronicler here; therefore, the second option seems to be the better one with the evidence currently available. The two men were closely associated with the ark and therefore they were allowed to move it. This is at least possible since David says that only the Levites may carry the ark. He does not qualify the Kohathites at that time.

Verse 11 specifies the two priests that were called by David in v. 4. Both Zadok and Abiathar are found within the Samuel narrative as well (e.g., 2 Sam 8:17; 15:29). Olyan, among others, sees them as representing separate priestly clans.[20] Zadok, according to Kings, takes control after Abiathar is removed from that office by Solomon (1 Kgs 2:27). In Chronicles, the picture is slightly different, but the ultimate result is the same: Zadok wins the priesthood, and Abiahtar and his sons disappear from the scene. The names of the Levitical officials are the same as those in vv. 5–10. The evidence presented in chapter two suggests that there is no reason to see this repetition as evidence of a later editor. The author often used repetition within his work.[21] Japhet notes that the similarity in repetition finds parallels between 1 Chr 15 and 1Chr 29 and 35. These parallels are only in Chronicles, not in Samuel–Kings. It is difficult to see how an editor could have structured all these elements in each narrative so consistently.[22] However, some clarification of Japhet's point needs to be made. While she has placed the priests in a secondary role here, this might not have been the intent of the Chronicler. Indeed, he gives less space in his work to the priesthood; however, the amount of attention to the priesthood does not necessarily imply a change of status.[23]

In v. 12, the opening phrase, "the heads of the fathers," according to Knoppers, "refers to a form of social organization that appears in the literature dealing with the Persian period: ancestral houses."[24] These heads of the clans within the tribe of Levi are told to sanctify themselves and their family members so that they may bring the ark up to Jerusalem. Williamson links this act of sanctification to Exod 19. Exodus indicates that this ritual involved the washing of clothes and abstinence from sexual relations. Also, in light of Lev 16:26 one may include the washing of the body and anointing with oil as well (Lev 8:12). Williamson links Exod 19 closely with the ark narrative particularly with the use of פרץ in 1 Chr 13:2, 11 and 14:11 and 1 Chr 15:13.[25] This sanctification involved both the priests and the Levites, which suggests, cooperation between the priests and Levites.[26]

Verse 13 indicates that David's statement that the Levites had not carried the ark the first time was the key problem in that procession. Thus, because of the lack of these cultic officials' involvement in the procession, David now establishes their roles in moving the ark. This verse explains why David is so fixated on ensuring that the proper cultic officials are present and that the proprieties are observed at all times. The previous attempt had resulted in Yahweh "breaking out" against Israel. David was afraid and wondered how he could bring the ark to Jerusalem (1 Chr 13:12). Here, David has arrived at a conclusion. It was not that his desire was wrongly founded, but it was the lack of attention to proper care and handling of the sacred object that caused the earlier failed attempt. For the Chronicler, this would have had tremendous significance because proper attention to the cult in general is the only way that the people can maintain a covenant relationship with Yahweh. The ark narrative as a whole serves as a wonderful illustration of this point.

The interest of the Chronicler in proper worship also raises another issue in this verse. The phrase "because we did not seek it," could also be translated as "because we did not seek him," making Yahweh not the ark the subject. Although there is evidence that supports both views, it is difficult to see the referent being Yahweh.[27] While the points raised regarding "seeking" as referring to Yahweh have some validity, such as Yahweh being the nearest antecedent and the verb in cultic contexts normally refers to Yahweh. However, within the ark narrative itself (1 Chr 13–16) the verb has been used to refer to the ark (13:3).

This link, from a literary standpoint, is quite difficult to get around but the very context of the passage forces the issue. This is certainly the point of the passage; however, the debate is difficult because the ark is so closely associated with the presence of God. Yet, seeking Yahweh properly is closely tied to following the proper means of doing so.[28] Therefore, it seems that proper care of the symbol of God's presence is the issue. This proper care involves moving the ark in the prescribed way. The term כמשפט is used commonly throughout the book, usually within cultic contexts.[29] This term is used by the Chronicler here to show that the earlier failure to bring the ark to Jerusalem was a direct result of the lack of attention to Mosaic legislation.

Verse 14 is literarily tied to David's statement in v. 12.[30] Thus, the Chronicler is showing that the priests and the Levites are following David's command precisely as he had delivered it to them, which portrays David as a cult founder alongside Moses.[31]

Verse 15 states that the Levites carried the ark according to Mosaic prescription. It is important to qualify the statements made regarding David as a cult founder. Moses is everywhere attested as having a foundational tie to the cult. Hence, the idea is that David is a "second Moses."[32] In this verse, the Chronicler is following Num 7:1–9. The Chronicler further states that the Levites carried the ark on their shoulders with poles (cf. Num 7:9).

Verses 16–24 show David's giving the heads of the Levitical clans authority to appoint their own families to the various duties that worship required. This is interesting because in the early list (vv. 5–10) David appointed the officers. These verses then indicate that David, after initially appointing the officers over the Levites, delegates to the officers the right to appoint their own people at their discretion. The appointment of singers is given in extensive detail. While the Pentateuch does not specifically say anything about singers and musicians, Deuteronomy does state specific provisions for the whole tribe of Levi (Deut

18:1–8); this would certainly apply to the singers and musicians as they are Levites in Chronicles.

These singers play a central role in the domestic government that David develops. In fact, 1 Chr 25:1–31, states that they are to prophesy (25:1).[33] This prophecy is to take place with musical accompaniment. Music played a role in prophecy before David's own day (1 Sam 10:5), and would not have been out of place within the prophetic functions within the cult. Singing, therefore, is more than just merely praising Yahweh, although this too is a legitimate function.

When David tells the Levites to sing before the ark in the procession, they do praise Yahweh. They also minister to the people on behalf of Yahweh.[34] Furthermore, the Levitical singers play a major role in the reigns of subsequent kings (e.g., 2 Chr 23:18; 29:28).

This emphasis on the Levitical singers naturally leads to the question of whether the Chronicler was drawing from the tradition in his own day or if he is representing worship in the preexilic period. While there is no reason to doubt that the Chronicler was drawing from the events that took place in his own day, the cultic worship system has been seen throughout ancient Near Eastern cultures.[35] Further, some of the Chronicler's sources and other biblical passages also note singers; for example, 2 Sam 6:5; 1 Kgs 10:12; Pss 68:26; 87:7; 150:4; Isa 38:20; Amos 5:23; 6:5; Hab 3:19; and Eccl 2:8.[36] Therefore, the Chronicler has not formulated the tradition of singing and music. He has a special interest in this aspect of worship which he developed in light of Pentateuchal traditions.[37] For the Chronicler, this primary role of the Levites, instituted under David's authority, requires the same central cultic function be given to the Levites in the postexilic period.

The specific mention of the musical instruments in this verse (harps, lyres, and cymbals) suggests that the Levitical clans have been grouped into musical guilds.[38] Braun describes these instruments as well. He notes that the harp is a type of lyre.[39] While it seems that the "harp" of the Hebrew Bible may be directly linked to the "lyre," there are some significant differences.[40] The "lyre" is the next named instrument.[41] The final musical instrument mentioned in this verse is the cymbal. Braun argues that cymbals "were often used together with other cultic instruments, but only in connection with cultic events such as the transfer of the ark (1 Ch. 15:28)...."[42] However, Braun suggests that the replacement of the term צלצלים in 2 Sam 6:5 with the term used in this verse is used to show the same instruments were used in the preexilic period as in the postexilic period.[43] This may not necessarily be the only option; given the frequent pagan contexts that this term is found within, the Chronicler may have opted for a clearer term that had no other connotation than pure cultic worship.

Verse 17 states that the individuals that the Levites appointed over themselves were Heman, Asaph, and Ethan. Verse 18 further describes the appointees but with the clarifying phrase "of the second rank," indicating that these officials were not considered the leaders within the Levitical clans.[44] This list of names is specified as "gatekeepers." The main function of the gatekeepers was to guard the sanctuary from ritual violation and enemy attack. Samuel must have preformed this duty while at Shiloh (1 Sam 3). It seems that there were a large number of duties that were involved for a gatekeeper. First Chronicles 9:26–32 indicates that they were in charge of the following: (1) the care of the chambers and the treasuries; (2) the opening of the doors; (3) the serving vessels and furnishings in the tent; (4) the flour, wine, oil, incense and spices; (5) the making of ointment; and (6) baking. Wright notes that a guard was given to the ark when it returned from the Philistines (1 Sam 7); therefore, part of a gatekeeper's duty was militaristic in nature.[45] This militaristic nature of the gatekeepers was, according to Wright, still in practice during the Chronicler's own day with respect to the Second Temple.[46] They protected the temple and the sacred vessels from thieves and served as a deterrent against disruptive behavior in the temple complex.

The reason for the clarification of these fourteen individuals as gatekeepers is to indicate their class. Thus, "second rank" should not be regarded as a statement of lesser value, only that they are not the heads of the clans and that they are classified as gatekeepers. In fact, Knoppers concludes that these gatekeepers must have been the choicest of men from the clans.[47]

In verses 19–21 the names of the singers are listed, and the list is identical to the previous one.[48] This list also indicates that there is a three-fold division within the ranks according to their various musical instruments.[49] These individuals are to lead the singers in praising Yahweh.[50]

Verses 22–24 give additional information about various Levitical responsibilities. These officials are different from those of the above lists. The appointments are also somewhat broader than the Davidic command for the Levites to appoint for themselves singers (v. 16). This list opens with Chenaniah, who was appointed to supervise the ark procession, and the seven priests who were to accompany the ark during the procession are also named, along with the gatekeepers who were to attend the ark.[51]

Movement of the Ark: 1 Chronicles 15:25–16:3

The Chronicler now picks up his Samuel narrative (2 Sam 6:12–15) and describes how the ark was brought to Jerusalem.[52] The account has been changed somewhat from the MT of Samuel. First of all, the Chronicler mentions the elders and commanders of the people. This indicates that the entire nation was involved in retrieving the ark. This is one of the more important differences between the two accounts. The Chronicler emphasizes the unity of the nation, not just David's faith as the account in Samuel does. Another difference that is noteworthy is that the ark is called the "ark of the covenant" (vv. 25, 26, 28, 29). One should also note that the Chronicler states that the procession went forward with joyful singing and music.

Verse 26 also has some significant differences from the Samuel narrative. First, the Chronicler notes that "God helped the Levites." Eskenazi notes that this balances the earlier account in 1 Chr 13 because the God who had hindered the advancement in the first account now helps the Levites bring the ark into Yahweh's chosen city.[53] This emphasizes for the Chronicler's readers that in order to worship Yahweh, proper procedures must be maintained at all times. Yet, ultimately it is Yahweh's own actions that are the the reason for the Levites success.[54] Also, the Chronicler has linked this narrative to what proceeds it by connecting the help that God gave the Levites here and the help he gave to David in 12:18.[55]

Second, the sacrifice is different. In the Samuel narrative it is "an ox and a fatted calf," and this sacrifice was carried out after the first six steps. Here the sacrifice is "seven bulls and seven rams," with no mention of any number of steps, which leaves the reader to see this sacrifice as a single event, not a repetitive one. These differences could be a result of the Chronicler's changing and adapting his text to fit his purposes.[56] However, Curtis and Madsen offer two possibilities regarding the differences between the two narratives. They include: (1) the two sacrifices represent two separate occasions; the Samuel narrative is the start of the procession, while the Chronicler's is the end. This is difficult to sustain because the sacrifice is portrayed at the beginning of the procession and additional sacrifices are mentioned in 1 Chr 16:1 after the ark is inside the city. (2) The small sacrifice was David's alone, but the larger was for David and the elders.[57] This too seems out of character for David to separate himself from the people in this narrative. In fact, the Chronicler's narrative takes pains to emphasize that he included "all Israel." Furthermore, it is possible to interpret the sacrifice in Samuel as being a repetitive one which took place every six steps.[58] If that were the case, the sheer number of sacrifices would make it impractical for one man to perform by himself. One can argue that the syntax of Samuel allows for a single offering after the first six steps, but the ancient Near Eastern analogy argues against this view, complicating the issue. It is interesting that the terminology of 2 Samuel is non-priestly and the sacrifice is not specific to the cult; however, the sacrifice in 1 Chronicles of a "bull and a ram" is standard cultic offerings.[59] Hence, the Chronicler may be placing an emphasis on the priestly functions of the cult over David's own right as a priest-king.

This raises several issues regarding the nature and function of sacrifice in Israelite religion.[60] It is profitable to explain some salient features that apply directly to the worship system.[61] Without doubt, sacrifice was the central cultic ritual. Although the Chronicler is looking back at a preexilic time during this narrative, it is also necessary to understand the significance of sacrifice during the postexilic period.

The clearest example of the official order of sacrifices in Chronicles is found in 2 Chr 29:20–35.[62] In fact, v. 35 indicates that this passage is a description of "the service of Yahweh's house." This description of the worship system provides the fullest example of how sacrifice and music were combined within the cult.[63] Kleinig argues that there are two separate but related stages of public sacrifice, each with its own official ritual procedure.[64] The first stage is the blood rite. Blood ritual involved the killing of the animal and the proper disposal of the blood by the priests (Lev 4:16–18). The second stage is the burnt offering, which is accompanied by cereal offerings and the libation of wine. While this ceremony is taking place, the singers and musicians are performing, and the people are bowing down in worship (2 Chr 29:27–29). In addition to this sacrifice, on this occasion, the people are offering individual sacrifices (vv. 31–35). These offerings are not completely burnt and the people are allowed to eat the meat that is leftover at a feast in the temple. Kleinig argues that the central rite was the burnt offering, and that all other festive offerings were included in that offering.[65] If this is the case, it is interesting that David has arranged the singing and the presentation of the morning and evening offerings to take place at the same time (1 Chr 16:39–41, and 23:30–31). Thus, the singing should be viewed as enhancing the ritual sacrifice.[66]

The sacrificial system, when viewed from a history of religion perspective, functioned within the common Semitic traditions.[67] This may be true when comparing actual forms and types of sacrifice in the various cults in this broad geographical setting. However, as Kraus has noted, "The great achievement of the Old Testament is the inclusion of the whole sacrificial system within the saving events and the fact of the ברית."[68] The sacrifice that took place in this verse seems to correspond with a free will offering. It would indicate the people's thankfulness to God for allowing the ark to proceed without incident. The sacrifice also acknowledges that Yahweh is in complete control and that he is allowing the symbol of this presence to be moved into the royal city.

Verse 27 indicates that David and all of the Levites are clothed with linen robes. This marks a difference between this text and that of 2 Sam 6:20, where David is wearing an ephod but here the ephod is mentioned in addition to the robe. While the mention of the ephod is without question priestly in the Chronicler's day, he is undoubtedly following his source at this point. The ephod in

Samuel's day may not have been exclusively used by priests.[69] The robe itself is not necessarily priestly, although it could be.[70] Galling may well be correct when he notes that this is probably reflecting the clothing of all cultic officials in the postexilic period.[71] Thus, it seems that David is portrayed as actively taking part in a cultic role, one that was expected of an ancient Near Eastern king.

Verse 28 indicates that there were several other instruments that were played besides the "horn" which is also mentioned in 2 Sam 6:15. This addition shows that not only the priests were playing the horn (15:24) but the Levites were also actively playing the cymbals, harps, and lyres (15:19–21). The account is intended to reflect the grandeur of this cultic high point.

Verse 29 ends the chapter with Michal's despising David because of his dancing before the ark. Curtis and Madsen see this note as being a mark of poor editing.[72] However, it would seem that the Chronicler is reinterpreting the event. Therefore, as Mosis has pointed out, the verse is representative of Saul's line despising the ark.[73] Further, this verse does not imply that there is anything wrong in David's dance. It is quite in line with the king and other cultic officials within its ancient Near Eastern context. David is performing an expected function in bringing Yahweh into his royal city.

1 Chr 16 continues with the 2 Sam narrative. Verse 1 has three issues that need to be discussed. First, one should note that there are several parallels to a tent shrine in the ancient Near East. The evidence indicates that the divine image, in this case the symbol of Yahweh's presence, was housed in a temporary structure, such as a tent. The important emphasis is that this structure was never intended to be permanent.[74] Although the ark has always been sheltered in a tent, David raises the issue of adequacy in the following chapter (1 Chr 17:1). The Chronicler does not state whether David had already planned to build a temple before this time. The text as presented by the Chronicler shows that David is consistently concerned about the sacred and that he desires to be pleasing to Yahweh. He is not content to dwell in a palace when Yahweh dwells in a tent.

Second is the significance of the ark's coming to Jerusalem which indicates Yahweh's favor on David and the nation.[75] Shiloh, the former cultic center, has been rejected by Yahweh as the place where he would cause his name to dwell. Until the temple was built, there is a tension that leaves open the possibility for multiple sanctuaries in Israel. However, the movement of the ark, the symbol of Yahweh's presence, to Jerusalem clearly foreshadows that Jerusalem will become that central sanctuary.

Third, the text indicates a plural "they," but the 2 Sam text clearly refers to David. In the judgment of this writer the Samuel narrative is emphasizing David's kingly authority; however, the Chronicler seems to be emphasizing the people. The phrase "all Israel" is the nearest plural antecedent, which suggests that the priests were to offer sacrifice on behalf of all the people, not just David. Myers argues that this verse is present because the Chronicler does not like the implication of the 2 Sam text that David offered sacrifices himself.[76] However, he does not adequately explain why v. 2 would specifically say that David had offered sacrifices. Japhet does by stating, "it seems more likely that in any case the Chronicler would interpret these statements as referring to David only as the person who authorized the offerings and on whose behalf they were offered."[77] This allows the sacrifices to be for the entire nation. Nevertheless, David is the one who blesses the people in the name of Yahweh which is a common duty for ancient Near Eastern kings.

This blessing following the burnt offerings undoubtedly reflects David's priestly function in the capacity of the ancient Near East. More importantly the author links David's act of blessing with his institution of the musical guilds, indicating that David is functioning in the capacity of a cultic authority. This becomes especially clear when the parallel between Moses and David is taken into consideration (Exod 39:42–43).[78] Knoppers notes, "The parallel between Sinai and Zion undergirds royal Davidic authority and the notion that the Ark finds its rightful place in Jerusalem."[79] Then v. 3 indicates that David distributed to the people a fairly large sum of food. This underscores the cultic activities and makes a logical transition toward the cultic appointments and the song of praise that follows.[80]

Cultic Appointments in Jerusalem: 1 Chronicles 16:4–6

This unit of material describes David's cultic appointments following the transfer of the ark to Jerusalem. In this short pericope the reference to the division is only the ordering of the cult at Jerusalem. The division in the Gibeon sanctuary will be developed following the Psalm. Williamson suggests, "Taken together with the temporary arrangements of ch. 15 for the transfer of the ark, these factors demonstrate the Chronicler's awareness that institutions did develop through history, and that it is hazardous to take any one passage in isolation as expressing his understanding on a given matter."[81] The emphasis on the Jerusalem site is important. The Levites are given their respective musical roles that are to be carried out at the tent that houses the ark. The Chronicler needs to identify these activities here because it assures the Levites a role in the temple that is both important and necessary (for example, 2 Chr 7:5–6 and 29:25–30).

The Chronicler takes care in v. 4 to note that David appointed the Levites to the position at Jerusalem to praise Yahweh, but it is interesting that he does not say that David appointed singers at the tent sanctuary. This is also different from the earlier occasion, where David allowed the Levites to appoint them-

selves (1 Chr 15:16–24). The difference reflects the fact that David alone is responsible for the cultic appointment of officials at Jerusalem. These officials are
not involved in sacrifice at the tent sanctuary in Jerusalem, but they are to sing
in order to "bring to remembrance, give thanks, and praise."[82] The term "to
bring to remembrance" could either be referring to cause the people to remember (e.g., Exod 23:13; Josh 23:7; Isa 26:13; 48:1; 62:6); or it could be referring to
cause Yahweh to remember his covenant with his people. Eising argues that by
calling on Yahweh to remember his covenant invokes his presence.[83] Either
view would be a form of worship. The first view is supported by the fact that
Yahweh is referred to by name in the Psalm that follows; therefore, the song is
not addressed to him but to the people. The point is that the song, at least in
this passage, speaks to the people and calls Yahweh's acts to their remembrance.[84] Nevertheless, as Gosse has pointed out, the song in this passage clearly reflects covenant themes that could be considered as calling upon Yahweh to
remember.[85] Thus, the Psalm may have a dual function calling both Yahweh
and the people to remembrance.

This worship is also supported with music. Asaph according to v. 5 is the
head of the cultic guild that is to function at Jerusalem. Asaph's position helps
explain why the playing of the cymbal is emphasized in this verse. Asaph was to
sound the cymbals while the ark was being transported to the Jerusalem sanctuary (1 Chr 15:19). This new appointment, however, seems to suggest more
permanent functions; hence, it shows the need for Asaph to be included in David's final ordering of the cult. The result is that this appointment places Asaph
and his clan as the leaders who offered praise to Yahweh.

The remainder of vv. 5–6 includes the names of specific members of the
family of Asaph. It should be noted that not all of the members listed in the
procession are assigned to the cultus at Jerusalem. Some are assigned to the cultus at Gibeon in this chapter (1 Chr 16:41). The larger assignment was undoubtedly a result of the fact that sacrifice was carried out there, but not at Jerusalem
until the temple was built. However, they were to "regularly" conduct musical
services at the tent sanctuary. Thus, the singing and praise to Yahweh were central parts of worship in Israel's cultic tradition and also ties this passage to the
genealogies (1 Chr 6) and the final ordering of the cult by David (1 Chr 25).[86]

Psalm of Praise: 1 Chronicles 16:7–36

There are several points of interest that this psalm brings into the discussion of
worship from an exegetical prospective. Before proceeding to the details of this
psalm in its respective sections, it is necessary to make some general observations about the text itself. Verse 7 does not actually start the quotation of the
psalm. However, it serves as a literary connection to its introduction. David

appoints Asaph to sing now that the ark has been placed in its tent. While this appointment is in keeping with the list of names that occur throughout the work, it is intriguing that David is not the one who sings the song. David is well known for his musical ability (1 Sam 16:14–23) and many of the Psalms are credited to him, yet here he is not portrayed as a singer in any sense. This may suggest that for the Chronicler, David's function as a cult founder is more important than some of his other well known qualities.[87] Historically speaking, David's delegation of the song indicates that although he was capable of functioning in a cultic capacity, he recognized the importance of the Levites and understood that it was their role, not the king's, to carry out this function.

The Psalm itself begins in v. 8. It is a skillfully connected piece of poetry that takes on a slightly different meaning than the three Psalms that were used in its compilation. Thus, those who have ignored the exegesis of this psalm have missed the Chronicler's purpose for including it here. There are five ways that this Psalm can be interpreted.[88] Watts addresses the first issue in his summary. He states, "the narrator's periodic repetition of a refrain from the psalm, and its appropriateness for postexilic worship settings all work together to make the medley a summary of the Chronicler's theology and a model for worship."[89]

The second issue is that the Chronicler has followed his psalm sources very closely. He does, however, change the final verse more noticeably than all others. This change reflects the Chronicler's own purposes and is therefore somewhat expected.[90]

The third issue indicates that by selecting certain portions of the three psalms, the Chronicler makes a new point and has a unique purpose that is not seen in the three psalms when read separately.[91] The Chronicler's selected use of these psalms results in this psalm becoming an illustration of proper worship. Watts' comments also address the fourth and fifth issues as well. The psalm is used to show the significance of the establishment of the cult. Finally, most scholars agree that the Chronicler has written this psalm to illustrate the type of worship that was proper in David's day and also in his own.[92]

The psalm has a genre that is typical of a hymn of praise.[93] Most of the discussion regarding this psalm addresses the relationship of this psalm and the three Psalms that it is taken from. Nielsen aptly concludes, "The general answer is that Chr. drops the themes that are of little interest to his contemporaries or do not serve the purposes related to the *Sitz im Leben* that he provides for the psalm in 1 Chr 16."[94] However, the way the three psalms have been placed together is a key issue that needs development. The structure of the psalm supports the Levites as the proper leaders of the worship.[95] Hence, this song is placed in the narrative to emphasize the praise that is associated with worship. Placed here it emphasizes the same terms that David has commanded the Levites to carry out in the preceding pericope; namely, to remember, to give thanks, and to praise. It truly serves as a model for worship within the postexilic cultic community. This being said, it seems prudent to look at the psalm from this prospective. However, the Psalm is more than an example of worship. It clearly shows some of his purposes for writing.[96]

The psalm opens with a call to praise (v. 8). Those singing praised Yahweh and called for the congregation to do the same. Praise was not limited just to calling on Yahweh's name; it also was done for the acts that Yahweh had done for the nation in the past (vv. 8b, 9b, 12, 14, 21, 23, 26b 31b, 33c), for his words (for example, vv. 15–19), and for other attributes (for example, vv. 25, 27, 34).[97] Thus, through praise Yahweh is represented to the people. Furthermore, as Gosse has pointed out, the opening of this psalm with the connections of the patriarchs is an important function in calling the people to remember the covenant.[98]

This first stanza (vv. 8–22) then calls the people to praise Yahweh. Nevertheless, v. 11 may well speak directly to the movement of the ark in the narrative itself. The song states that the people are to "seek Yahweh and his strength." One of the major motifs throughout the book is that of seeking Yahweh. The idea of also seeking his strength could be tied to the ark itself. The Psalms speak of Yahweh's strength being associated with the ark (for example, Pss 78:61; 132:8). Thus, the Chronicler's readers, in light of the context, would be thinking of seeking out Yahweh's presence before the ark.[99] This seems to emphasize the role that Yahweh plays in the cult. The Chronicler has also taken pains to associate the praising of Yahweh with the Abrahamic covenant (Gen 15:1–21; 17:1–27) which he has made with Israel (v. 15). The covenant remains forever because of Yahweh's faithfulness, not the people's.[100] The unconditionality of this covenant is evident in Yahweh's oath to Isaac (v. 16), and when Yahweh confirms that oath with Jacob (v. 17); but ultimately it is seen in the land of Canaan (v. 18). The theme of the land fits the Chronicler's emphasis of continuity between the past and the present.[101] The emphasis on the Abrahamic covenant is thus not unexpected; yet by breaking off the psalm at v. 15, the Chronicler omits the praise of the exodus in that psalm (vv. 16–41). This may indicate that the cultic singers were allowed some degree of creative ingenuity in developing songs for the cult. It also raises the issue as to why the Chronicler would exclude the exodus section of material here. In the original psalm the "overall theme is Yahweh's faithfulness to his eternally valid promises concerning the land."[102] Hence, the Chronicler wished to make the tie to the patriarchal age clear because it was with the patriarchs that Yahweh made his promise. The Chronicler has effectively reworked the Psalm to fit the transfer of the ark to Jerusalem.[103]

The second stanza of this psalm (vv. 23–33) is taken from Psalm 96. This psalm is quoted in its entirety. It is a psalm of praise, which speaks of the universal rule of Yahweh. This is quite in keeping with the Chronicler's purposes. It shows how Israel, the creation, and the nations are to give praise and honor to Yahweh. In the Chronicler's own time, this song seems to represent the hope that Yahweh would return to the restored Temple.[104] If the Chronicler had such a visual connection in mind, this would place Yahweh's presence in the Second Temple, where he is ruling over his people and has the ability to judge all the earth (v. 33). This, of course, would include the Persians and other nations who were suppressing Israel.

The final stanza of the Chronicler's song (vv. 34–36) is taken from Psalm 106:1, 47–48. It opens with a call to the people to give thanks to Yahweh. It seems significant that the Chronicler has chosen to include only the beginning call to praise and the ending call to confession. The psalm in its original context is an historical psalm, but that history has been omitted. Within the context of the ark narrative the omission seems strange. The Chronicler does at times reference the exodus tradition; however, in the psalm he has consistently omitted it. Yet, the exodus typology seems fitting, especially in light of the Chronicler's postexilic readers. Perhaps, the Chronicler is more interested in the elements of proper worship than in the development of his exodus typology. If so, this once again helps to affirm that the Chronicler's major purpose in writing is to show a continued line of proper worship between the preexilic and postexilic periods. Nielsen argues that the Chronicler is using Psalm 96, and one could add the end of Ps 106, because it reflects the circumstances in postexilic Israel.[105] Thus, the end of the psalm is quite fitting for the Chronicler's audience.[106] Israel is a people who have been scattered and the cry for deliverance and for gathering the nation together brings home the hope of the postexilic nation. They desire to have a place among the nations and for Yahweh to return them to their land. The concluding statement (v. 36) indicates that the people took part in the praise through the response of specific refrains that the singers led them in.[107] Thus, an important element in the Chronicler's presentation of worship is the corporal element. The congregation that gathered at this festive occasion was called upon to participate in the worship through their response in praise.

David's Final Ordering of the Levites: 1 Chronicles 16:37–42

Verses 37–38 restate the previous narrative (vv. 4–6). This repetition indicates that the Chronicler is returning to his own material once again. It is interesting that the Chronicler has added this material to his Samuel source. The mention of Obed-Edom and Obed-Edom the son of Jeduthun may be an attempt to distinguish the two individuals from one another. It is important to realize that

Obed-Edom occurs only here as the son of Jeduthun. It seems that the normal use of the name would imply Obed-Edom the Gittite (1 Chr 13:13). Scholars suggest that the Samuel narrative indicates that Obed-Edom came from Gath (2 Sam 6:10).[108] However, Obed-Edom's Levitical connections could possibly be older than the Chronicler.[109] In the judgment of this writer, however, it appears that there was more than one individual named "Obed-Edom." The text in the second part of the ark narrative (1 Chr 15–16) and (1 Chr 26:4–8) never refer to this Obed-Edom as being a Gittite. In fact, the only place that Obed-Edom is referred to as a Gittite is in 1 Chr 13:13.[110] Thus, the Chronicler and his Samuel source may well be distinguishing where Obed-Edom originated from. After this initial clarification the Chronicler merely calls him Obed-Edom. He is a Levite who is also a Gittite; that is, he is from the city of Gath Rimmon, the Levitical city of refuge in the territory of Dan.[111] In 1 Chr 26:4–8 Obed-Edom is tied to the line of Korah.[112] The "son of Jeduthun" indicates that this second Obed-Edom was the son of the singer associated with the cult at Gibeon (16:41). Thus, he is from the line of Merari. His appointment here would then need some clarification, which the Chronicler has tried to do. This seems to argue for two individuals having the same name. There is no reason to think that Obed-Edom is an uncommon name. Furthermore, the "sons of Jeduthun" also serve as gatekeepers for the tabernacle at Gibeon (16:42). Therefore, the function of the gatekeepers would be an expected function for this individual as well, despite the fact that he had been assigned to the sanctuary of the ark in Jerusalem.

The Chronicler then sets forth the assignment of priests and Levites to the tabernacle at Gibeon (vv. 39–42). Now David, with two legitimate places of worship in Israel, had to reorganize the cult in order for both sanctuaries to have proper cultic personnel.[113] There are some major differences between the two cultic sites. For example, Zadok the high priest is appointed to the Gibeon sanctuary.[114] He and the remaining priests that helped bring up the ark to Jerusalem are appointed there.[115] Such a large appointment to Gibeon suggests that it is the major cultic sanctuary at that time.[116] Yet, the emphasis that the Chronicler places on Gibeon is often "dismissed as a fabrication of the Chronicler."[117] Gibeon's inclusion in the narrative should not be interpreted as merely a fabrication by the Chronicler.[118] While it is true that Solomon's later journey to Gibeon has been sanctioned by David's organization of the cultic officials there, the main emphasis here suggests that the Chronicler is primarily interested in the fact that David appointed officials at both places. The tabernacle required that the Mosaic altar be present for the morning and evening sacrifice to be burned upon it (v. 40).[119] While Chronicles is the only document that indicates that the tabernacle was at Gibeon, Josh 9:27 indicates that an altar was present there.[120]

The Chronicler goes on to indicate that not only is a large group of priests appointed to the sanctuary, but also two groups of singers are appointed. Thus, the Gibeon sanctuary has twice as many singers as does the one in Jerusalem, because both Heman and Jeduthun were assigned there. Both sanctuaries have similar singing and musical instruments appointed to their cultic worship. Furthermore, the reference to the "sons of Jeduthun" (v. 42) serving as gatekeepers, in keeping with the above interpretation, is not a gloss. It reflects the singers' own family involvement in the safekeeping of both sanctuaries.

The separation of the cult into two official sanctuaries is significant. First, Samuel–Kings does not state that Yahweh's name dwelt at Kiriath Jearim, where the ark was placed (1 Sam 6:21–7:2), or at Nob or Gibeon, where the tabernacle was stationed (1 Sam 21; 1 Chr 16:39-40). Jeremiah 7:12–15 suggests that Shiloh was once the place where Yahweh's name dwelt. Yet, David's statement that the daily offerings were to be carried out at Gibeon according to Yahweh's law (v. 40) suggests that Gibeon was the place where Yahweh caused his name to dwell.[121]

Gibeon clearly is the place of central sacrificial worship because of the number of priests and Levites assigned to it.[122] Thus, it appears in keeping with the analysis of this work, that the Chronicler, by taking time to organize these two cultic centers, provides a background for the final organization of the cult in chapters 23–27. This is particularly interesting because for the Chronicler the unified cult is the point of his writing. The temple as the only legitimate sanctuary could be considered the climax of the story for him in many respects.

The climax of a story, however, should not be regarded as the central structural piece within a narrative but its ultimate goal. This small pericope adds to the literary conflict and genius of the work by giving tension to the storyline because it now appears that the cult has two legitimate places of worship. By having two functional cultic sites the Chronicler has done much to further his theme of continuity with the past. It creates links with the exodus tabernacle and also with the First Temple because both resided there upon its completion. Thus, for the Chronicler the Second Temple functioned in the same capacity as the first. It is the only legitimate sanctuary for carrying out sacrificial worship.[123]

The clear separation of the ark and the tent suggests that the period was a transitional one.[124] Thus, once the temple was built, it was necessary to bring both the ark and the tabernacle into it. This would in essence show that the temple had superseded both sanctuaries and has finally connected both sacred objects.[125] This transitional period necessitated two cultic centers because of the chaotic conditions during David's reign. The borders were far from controlled, and David had to suppress the Philistines as well as Saul's house (2 Sam 2–5). Thus, the conditions for building a temple were not right.

Tracing this political aspect from the early part of Samuel may be helpful at this point. There is no clear condemnation of high places in Samuel as long as the worship was reserved for Yahweh (for example, 1 Sam 7:3–4). Samuel offers sacrifices in what appears to be a high place devoted to the worship of Yahweh (1 Sam 9:11–14). It also appears that he offered sacrifice at various other local altars (1 Sam 7:17; 10:8), which indicates for the Chronicler that the legitimation of two cultic sites in Gibeon and Jerusalem has limited worship to only these two sites. Yet, only the ark is the symbol of Yahweh's dwelling place (2 Sam 7:5–7 may confirm this if only by implication).[126] The fact that there are several viable altars is clear in light of 1 Kgs 3:2 which states, "The people sacrificed at the high places, because there was no house built for the name Yahweh until those days." It should be noted that the book of Kings speaks negatively of high places only after the temple was built; for example see, 1 Kgs 15:14; 18:30; 22:44; 2 Kgs 12:3; 14:4; 15:4, 35. Thus, it appears that there is a general movement from any high place that was sanctified for Yahwistic worship during the period of judges and the early monarchy, toward centralization. This temporary duality within the cult was unavoidable because of the political situation at that time and was rectified soon after Solomon took the kingship.

Conclusion: 1 Chronicles 16:43

This verse marks a return to the Chronicler's *Vorlage*. It picks up the narrative at the exact place that his Samuel narrative ended so that he could address the cultic appointments and give an illustration of proper worship through the psalm. It should be noted that while the previous blessing by David to the people (16:2) may well be considered a priestly blessing showing David's cultic authority, this seems more likely to be a common blessing that may have been issued by anyone in a position of authority.[127]

Summary

The exegetical analysis reveals the Chronicler's purposes for this narrative. In the first pericope (15:1–24), the Chronicler portrays David as a cultic authority who is consistent with ancient Near Eastern kings. He organizes the cultic officials so that the movement of the ark will be done according to proper Mosaic procedures. The care involved in this preparation suggests that inattention in cultic matters is unacceptable. Hence, the ultimate desire of the Chronicler is for the postexilic nation to take pains to protect proper worship.

The second pericope (15:25–16:3) focuses on the actual movement of the ark into Jerusalem. This focus indicates the joy and praise that took place as the symbol of Yahweh's presence being brought to David's royal city. It also emphasizes that the Chronicler is not interested in proper procedure alone. He is also keenly aware that Yahweh's sovereign will is ultimately the reason for the Levites' success in moving the ark. Nothing that David can do is outside of Yahweh's own desire to allow his presence to dwell in Jerusalem. In this pericope David continues to function as a cultic authority by blessing the people. It seems that while the Chronicler's picture of David is certainly different from that of Samuel, the purpose for including David's office of priest-king for the Chronicler is to show David as a submissive vice-regent doing the will of Yahweh. This serves to validate that Yahweh's ark was to be brought to Jerusalem because it was the place Yahweh had chosen. Thus, it could be viewed as a subtle polemic for the postexilic nation to worship only at the temple in Jerusalem.

The cultic officials are then given their respective roles (16:4–6). The Chronicler carefully details the appointments because they are important to the purpose which becomes clear in light of the fact the he emphasizes the Jerusalem site here. The Levites are given their respective musical roles that are to be carried out at the tent that houses the ark. It would seem that the Chronicler needs to identify these activities here because it assures the Levites a role in the temple that is important and necessary. David appoints them, thus arguing for their proper legitimation. It is also important to understand that no sacrifice took place in the tent sanctuary at Jerusalem. Nevertheless, the singing of the Levites is considered proper worship regardless of the fact that there was no sacrifice.

The call to worship in this prescribed way is then reflected in the psalm that the Chronicler has created for his readers. He has written this psalm to illustrate the type of worship that was proper in both David's day and in his own, and he reflects the same terms found in David's command to Asaph to sing (16.4). David is well known for his abilities as a singer/composer, but he does not participate in the song. David's lack of participation in the song suggests that his function as a cult founder is more important for the Chronicler. It also shows that David, although capable of functioning in a cultic capacity, recognized the importance of the Levites and understood that it was their role to carry out this function, not the king's.

Following this psalm David appoints cultic officials at Gibeon (16:39–42). This small pericope adds tension to the narrative as it leaves two legitimate places of worship in Israel. This was necessary historically speaking because of the political turmoil that was going on during the period of David's reign. The inclusion of Gibeon suggests that it was the main cultic site. These appointments to two functional cultic sites heighten his theme of continuity with the past. It creates links with the ark and the tabernacle and also with the First Temple because both the ark and the tabernacle reside there upon its completion. The Second Temple is to function in the same capacity as the first. After the delegation of cultic officials by David, the Chronicler picks up his *Vorlage* exactly where he left off to take up the psalm (16:43).

Notes

1.   Please note that the translation of this material has been provided under the appropriate sections in chapter two and should be referred to there. 1 Chr 14:1 notes that Hiram has built David a house (i.e., a palace). This would be additional building on David's part which helps to establish him as king in his royal city.

2.   Exod 40:2-3, 5, 21; Lev 16:2; Num 7:89; etc.

3.   This is an important aspect in this narrative. See Gary N. Knoppers, *1 Chronicles 10–29: A New Translation with Introduction and Commentary*, AB 12A (New York: Doubleday, 2004), 612.

4.   A. Cowley, "The Meaning of *Māqōm* in Hebrew," *JTS* 17 (1916): 174–76. The term frequently refers to a sacred place throughout the Hebrew Bible (BDB lists places where the ark rests, various temples and shrines, even pagan ([BDB, 880]).

5.   Gerhard von Rad, "The Tent and the Ark," in *The Problem of the Hexateuch and Other Essays*, trans. E. W. Trueman Dicken (London: Oliver and Boyd, 1966), 115–16. Also, Wouldstra argues that one should not see a division of sources based on divine. See Marten H. Woudstra, *The Ark of the Covenant from Conquest to Kingship* (Philadelphia: Presbyterian and Reformed, 1965), 81–83.

6.   Tamara C. Eskenazi, "A Literary Approach to the Chronicler's Ark Narrative in 1 Chronicles 13–16," in *Fortunate the Eyes That See: Essays in Honor of David Noel Freedman in Celebration of His Seventieth Birthday*, ed. Astrid B. Beck et al. (Grand Rapids: Eerdmans, 1995), 270–71.

7.   Benzinger believes that it refers to the time the ark was in the house of Obed-Edom. Immanuel Benzinger, *Die Bücher der Chronik* (Tübingen: Mohr, 1901), microfiche, 52. Curtis and Madsen understand this to be a reference to David's building projects. See Edward Lewis Curtis and Albert Alonzo Madsen, *A Critical and Exegetical Commentary on the Books of Chronicles*, ICC (Edinburgh: T & T Clark, 1910), 213.

8.   The Chronicler portrays David as a king who knew the Mosaic legislation. One should note that there is no evidence that David received any direct communication from Yahweh at this time. The Chronicler does, however, indicate that David may have had some direct communication with Yahweh elsewhere (1 Chr 28:11–19).

9.   Riley notes that the king is portrayed as a priest within this narrative (William Riley, *King and Cultus in Chronicles: Worship and the Reinterpretation of History*, JSOTSup 160 [Sheffield: JSOT Press, 1993], 59).

10.   Since there is no longer any reason to argue for pro-priestly or pro-Levitical redactions in this text, it appears that Knoppers' note regarding the influence of Priestly law and Deuteronomy is a logical conclusion based on this presentation of the text here. See Gary N. Knoppers, "Hierodules, Priests, or Janitors? The Levites in Chronicles and the History of the Israelite Priesthood," *JBL* 118 (1999): 49–72.

11.   Deut 10:8–9 is a clear example of Yahweh separating out the Levites for this special service. This is a direct reference to Exod 32:26–29, where the Levites came to Moses after the Israelites sinned by making a golden calf. It is here that the Levites are first separated, appar-

ently because they were not worshiping the idol that Aaron had made. Deut 10:8–9 then points out that it was at this time that the Levites were appointed to the duties of carrying the ark.

12. Deut 10:8 notes that the Levites were to minister to Yahweh and praise him forever (see also Deut 17:12; 18:5; and Jer 33:21). Elsewhere in the Pentateuch the priests are to serve Yahweh, and the Levites are to attend the needs of the priests (e.g., Exod 28:35; Num 3:6). While there is little hope of a scholarly consensus regarding the priestly classes, it seems that the Chronicler is attempting to show that both the priests and the Levites have respective duties that they are required to perform before Yahweh.

13. Japhet states, "The term 'Levites' is used in this context in its two primary meanings, also attested elsewhere: the first use denotes those of the tribe of Levi who are not priests; this is surely meant in all cases where the priests are mentioned separately, in addition to the 'Levites' (vv. 4, 11, 14). The other reference is to all the members of the tribe of Levi including the priests, as in v. 12 (cf. v. 14). The double usage of the term causes ambiguity in some of the verses;…A more homogenous terminology may be achieved by regarding all the references to the priests as secondary (vv. 4, 11, 14…), but even then the reference to the Levites themselves would not be standardized. Moreover, the variations in the presentation of the priests—three terms of reference, all different—would suggest the hand of an author characterized by an inclination for stylistic variety, rather than stereotyped editing" (Sara Japhet, *1 and 2 Chronicles: A Commentary*, OTL (London: SCM, 1993), 300.

14. Ibid., 299.

15. Curtis and Madsen argue that this is the reason for the Kohathites to be mentioned first. They base this assumption on Numb 4:15. See Curtis and Madsen, *Chronicles*, 213. This is without doubt a major part of the clan coming to prominence. In fact, it helps support the reason for further division within the family and is a probable explanation because the Chronicler is focusing in on the movement of the ark. Furthermore, the list returns to the original order in 1 Chr 23:6.

16. P. Kyle McCarter, *2 Samuel*, AB 9 (Garden City, N.Y.: Doubleday, 1984), 168–69.

17. Knoppers, *1 Chronicles 10–29*, 587.

18. Scholars debate about whether or not Uzzah and Ahio were brothers of Eleazar, the one who was in charge of the ark during this time (see McCarter, *2 Samuel*, 169). However, 1 Sam 7:1 calls Eleazar the son of Abinadab, at whose home the ark stayed. Abinadab is also the father of Uzzah and Ahio in 2 Sam 6:3. The text is at least linking them to the same father.

19. It may be possible, for example, to view Abiathar's involvement with Adonijah as an attempt on his part to take the high priesthood from Zadok (1 Kgs 1:7-25).

20. Saul Olyan, "Zadok's Origins and the Tribal Politics of David," *JBL* 101 (1982): 177–93.

21. Japhet shows parallels regarding the king's summons and the priests and Levites here with 2 Chr 29 and 35. See Japhet, *1 and 2 Chronicles*, 299.

22. Rudolph suggests a slightly different structure in the Chronicler's presentation. He sees complete instruction followed by complete execution; however, this forces him to take v. 16 as secondary because it is out of place. See Wilhelm Rudolph, *Chronikbücher*, HAT 21 (Tübingen: Mohr–Siebeck, 1955), 115.

23. The Chronicler's primary concern is the role of the Levites; however, the priests need to be included because of their involvement. The priests activities have not changed: they are still playing the trumpets (15:24, 28), offering sacrifices (15:26), and play a key role in bringing the ark into David's tent.

24. Knoppers, *1 Chronicles 10–29*, 616.

25. Williamson, *1 and 2 Chronicles*, 124.

26. Knoppers, *1 Chronicles 10–29*, 617.

27. Begg has a good discussion regarding the term "seeking" as it is used in Chronicles. See Christopher T. Begg, "'Seeking Yahweh' and the Purpose of Chronicles," *LS* 9 (1982–83): 128–41; Knoppers also addresses the material pertinent to this issue as well (Knoppers, *1 Chronicles 10–29*, 618).

28. Ibid.

29. For example, 1 Chr 6:17; 23:31; 24:19; 2 Chr 4:7, 20; 8:14; 30:16; 35:13.

30. Japhet, *1 and 2 Chronicles*, 301.

31. Ronald E. Clements, *God and Temple* (Philadelphia: Fortress, 1965), 129; Jacob Martin Myers, "The Kerygma of the Chronicler: History and Theology in the Service of Religion," *Int* 20 (1966): 269; Gerhard von Rad, *Das Geschichtsbild des chronistischen Werkes*, BWA(N)T 54 (Stuttgart: Kohlhammer, 1930), 130-31; and Simon J. De Vries, "Moses and David as Cult Founders in Chronicles," *JBL* 107 (1988): 626–30.

32. Myers, "The Kergma of the Chronicler," 268–69. The text also makes this point in 1 Chr 15:15; 21:9; and 22:13.

33. Scholars debate about whether the sons of Asaph, Heman, and Jeduthun should be called cultic prophets. Several argue for continuity between the cultic prophecy from the preexilic to the postexilic period (von Rad, *Das geschichtsbild des chronistischen Werkes*, 113–15; Jacob Martin Myers, *1 Chronicles*, 2d ed. AB 12 [Garden City, N.Y.: Doubleday, 1965], 171–73; and Williamson, *1 and 2 Chronicles*, 166). Others note that the differences between the preexilic community and that of the postexilic returnees are dramatic and that these socio-political conditions affected the office of prophet (Rainer Albertz, *A History of Religion in the Old Testament Period*, vol. 2, *From the Exile to the Maccabees*, trans. John Bowden, OTL [Louisville, Ky.: Westminster/Knox, 1994], 443–522). De Vries also argues that there is some kind of change within the prophetic office during the postexilic period (Simon J. De Vries, *1 and 2 Chronicles*, FOTL 11 [Grand Rapids: Eerdmans, 1989], 207).

34. John W. Kleinig, *The LORD's Song: The Basis, Function and Significance of Choral Music in Chronicles*, JSOTSup 156 (Sheffield: JSOT Press, 1993), 190. See also Roddy Braun, *1 Chronicles*, WBC 14 (Waco, Tex.: Word, 1986), 245.

35. Braun notes the cultic use of music in Egypt in the 18th and 19th dynasties as well as Canaanite music during the Bronze Age. He concludes that cultic ritual in the ANE had musical traditions that began well before this and are still present today. See Joachim Braun, *Music in Ancient Israel/Palestine: Archaeological, Written, and Comparative Sources*, trans. Douglas W. Stott, The Bible in Its World (Grand Rapids: Eerdmans, 2002), 85–99.

36. To this list others could be added. For example, the various psalm titles have been excluded from consideration at this point. Furthermore, although doubtful that the Chronicler had Assyrian royal inscriptions at his disposal, Sennacherib notes that Hezekiah sent his male and female musicians as part of his tribute (see ARAB II, §240).

37. Kleinig, *The LORD's Song*, 30-39. He convincingly shows that David instituted the singers in the cult through the prophets Gad and Nathan by David. This institution was in line with the Pentateuchal traditions (ibid., 39).

38. Braun, *Music in Ancient Israel/Palestine*, 11.

39. Ibid., 22–23.

40. The Mishnah notes that there must be two "harps" for worship and no more than six at any one time (*m. 'Arak.* 2:5). Furthermore, the strings were made from a different part of sheep intestine than that of the "lyre" (*m. Qinnim* 3:6). The lbn was made from the large intestine; the "lyre," from the small intestine. This would cause the instrument to have a deeper sound

than that of the "lyre,"as the strings would be thicker coming from the large instead of the small intestine. See Braun, *Music in Ancient Israel/Palestine*, 24.

41. Ibid., 16–18.
42. Ibid., 20. Braun also argues that these cymbals should not be seen as synonymous with the cymbals in the parallel account in 2 Sam 6:5.
43. Ibid., 21.
44. This term is rare in the plural, occurring in only two other places (2 Sam 15:9 and Ezra 1:10 [both disputed]). It seems to mean second in rank. The reconstruction of the text by Curtis and Madsen is unwarranted (Curtis and Madsen, *Chronicles*, 215, 217).
45. John Wesley Wright, "Guarding the Gates: 1 Chronicles 26:1-19 and the Roles of Gatekeepers in Chronicles," *JSOT* 48 (1990): 69–81.
46. Wright argues that they were a security force inside Jerusalem. Ibid., 69. Braun arrived at the opposite conclusion, where the nomenclature of a warrior was honorific for what they once were (see Braun, *1 Chronicles*, 249).
47. Knoppers, *1 Chronicles 10–29*, 872. Williamson does not seem to see it this way as he indicates that Obed-Edom and his family were later "demoted to the rank of gatekeepers" (Williamson, *1 and 2 Chronicles*, 125).
48. It is possible grammatically to see the term "singers" as referring only to the three leaders of the three guilds. However, the context suggests that all the listed members are singers and that this is a summary heading for all the singers in vv. 19–21.
49. Williamson notes that "Alamoth" and "Sheminith," must "have most often been taken as referring to soprano and bass respectively…" (ibid.).
50. The infinitives used here and in v. 19 both refer to the main verb in v. 17. Thus, it appears that it refers only to the Levites in vv. 20–21.
51. Regarding the procession proper, the normal use of the term משא is "bearing" (BDB, 672). The LXX, however, translates this term musically. Rothstein and Hänel understand it as referring to both the carrying of the ark and to the music of the singers (Rothstein and Hänel, *Chronik*, 278–80). Myers' understanding is better. He notes that Chenaniah was in charge of the ark procession, thus making him responsible for both the physical carrying of the ark and the music accompanying it while the ark was being moved. This may also have some support in the fact that the following term יסר should be taken as an active /qātōl/ noun (GKC §84ᵃk; and Rudolph,*Chronikbücher*, 119).
52. There are several attempts to connect this transfer to an annual cultic festival that includes a liturgical procession. This is frequently linked to Psalm 132. While there are several ANE parallels with this, in the judgment of this writer, the cultic festival would be an outgrowth of this historical event and it should not be viewed as part of the cultic tradition, but rather the reason behind that tradition. Yet, it seems significant that the parallels of other ANE monarchs are so numerous and clear, but there is no extant evidence that Israel participated in such cultic festivals. This lack of evidence, although one should not completely rule out such events, demands that more caution be exercised in arguing that the narrative is based on the Psalm (see Hans-Joachim Kraus, *Psalms 60–150*, trans. Hilton C. Oswald, CC [Minneapolis: Fortress, 1993], 475–79; and C. L. Seow, *Myth, Drama, and the Politics of David's Dance*, HSM 44 [Atlanta: Scholars Press, 1989]). Thus, while there is no question that Psalm 132 is cultic in nature, drawing the parallels from ANE literature as Seow and others have done is helpful, but should not be viewed as the cause of this narrative in either Samuel of Chronicles. The issue of whether Psalm 132 had any influence on the sequence of events in Chroniclers remains difficult to know precisely. On the one hand, it is clear that the Chronicler knew the psalm and had access to Psalm 132 (2 Chr 6:41–42 follows Ps 132:8-10; and possibly 1 Chr

28:2). On the other hand, the Chronicler could have had other theological reasons for shaping the. In the judgment of this writer, the parallels between Psalm 132 and the Chronicler's ark narrative are not close enough to presume that the psalm was used in such a way. For example, the psalm states that David vowed that he would not sleep until he found a place for Yahweh (132:3–5). The Chronicler does not mention this vow, nor that David remained away from his palace during the three months that the ark was in the house of Obed-Edom. Furthermore, it may be possible to view David's building in Jerusalem and siring children there following the initial move as being the parallel with the psalm with regard to the initial movement of the ark. However, that would result in a broken vow. David does build and move into his palace and bring up offspring for himself. The Chronicler does not indicate that such a vow would no longer be in effect just because of a failed attempt. In fact, it would be logical that David would make such a vow following the first attempt (Ps 132:10), or more likely still in light in view of the phrase present in the psalm "resting place" (vv. 8, 14) that the Psalm reflects the movement of the ark into the temple, not into the tent David prepared for it. This is based on the fact that the phrases "resting place" and "footstool" in Ps 132:7 also occur in 1 Chr 28:2. Thus, it appears that the Chronicler is closely associating the movement of the ark into the temple with this psalm, especially since he quotes it there (2 Chr 6:41–42). It is this lack of connection that causes one to suspect that the Chronicler had other reasons for structuring the ark narrative. Most likely the narrative is structured as it is to show that although the first attempt failed, Yahweh was still blessing David.

53. Eskenazi, "A Literary Approach," 268.
54. Knoppers, *1 Chronicles 10–29*, 625.
55. Martin J. Selman, *1 Chronicles: An Introduction and Commentary*, TOTC 10a (Downers Grove, Ill.: Inter-Varsity, 1994), 165; Japhet, *1 and 2 Chronicles*, 305–6.
56. Japhet, *1 and 2 Chronicles*, 306.
57. Curtis and Madsen, *Chronicles*, 218.
58. Patrick D. Miller and J. J. M. Roberts, *The Hand of the Lord: A Reassessment of the "Ark Narrative" of 1 Samuel*, JHNES (Baltimore: Johns Hopkins University Press, 1977), 96 note 157.
59. Japhet, *1 and 2 Chronicles*, 306.
60. Many of the cultic events find parallels in the ANE background and are discussed in the ark narrative found in Samuel. However, in the judgment of this writer, Anderson's statement is correct, "The bringing of the ark to Jerusalem was a unique event, not part of an established Jebusite cultic ritual" (A. A. Andersen, *2 Samuel*, WBC 11 [Waco, Tex: Word, 1989], 106).
61. The arrangement of the various sacrifices has been developed by Rainey. He argues that the order for the presentation of these sacrifices in texts that discuss the procedure of sacrifice differs from the order found in texts that seem to be given in other texts. He believes that this order is "the key to understanding the religious significance of the sacrificial system" (Anson F. Rainey, "The Order of sacrifices in Old Testament Ritual Texts," *Bib* 51 [1970]: 498). In addition to this article there are numerous works on sacrifice as an act of worship. For example, David Janzen, *The Social Meanings of Sacrifice in the Hebrew Bible: A Study of Four Writings*, BZAW 344 (Berlin: de Gruyter, 2004); Mark Harold McEntire, *The Function of Sacrifice in Chronicles, Ezra, and Nehemiah* (Lewiston: Mellen, 1993); and H. H. Rowley, *Worship in Israel: Its Forms and Meaning* (Philadelphia: Fortress, 1978). Marx holds a different view from that of Rainey in this passage. He argues that the passages regarding sacrifice are not directed to the priests but to the "sons of Israel" (Alfred Mark, *Les systèmes sacrificiels de l'Ancien Testament: Formes et fonctions du culte sacrificiel à Yhwh*, VTSup 105 [Leiden: Brill, 2005], 105–6).
62. The unity of this passage is debated (e.g., von Rad sees vv. 25-30 as being added by a Levitical redactor to help solidify their status as singers. See von Rad, *Das geschichtsbild des chronistis-*

chen Werkes, 104). Welch believes that vv. 20-24 show evidence of a later pro-priestly redactor (Adam C. Welch, *The Work of the Chronicler: Its Purpose and Date*, The Schweich Lectures
on Biblical Archaeology [London: Oxford University Press, 1939], 105–6). However, Rudolph, among others, argues for a single author in this pericope. See Rudolph, *Chronikbücher*,
293.

63. Kleinig, *The LORD's Song*, 101.
64. Ibid., 102–3.
65. Ibid., 108.
66. Psalms mentions singing during sacrifice on a few occasions (e.g., 27:6; 50:14, 23; 61:8; 66:1–
15; 96:8; and 107:22). Some of the prophets also mention this practice (Isa 51:3; Jer 33:11;
and Amos 5:21–24).
67. Hans-Joachim Kraus, *Worship in Israel: A Cultic History of the Old Testament*, trans. Geoffrey
Buswell (Richmond, Va.: Knox, 1966), 122.
68. Ibid.
69. Williamson states that it was "no more than a loin cloth," (Williamson, *1 and 2 Chronicles*,
126). Also see 2 Sam 6:14, which may not be referring to any kind of priestly activity.
70. The chief priest wore a blue robe (Exod 28:31); all others wore robes of fine linen (Exod
39:27). See also Japhet, *1 and 2 Chronicles*, 307.
71. Kurt Galling, *Die Bücher der Chronik, Esra, Nehemia*, ATD 12 (Berlin: Evangelische, 1958), 49.
72. Curtis and Madsen, *1 and 2 Chronicles*, 219.
73. Rudolf Mosis, *Untersuchungen zur Theologie des chronistischen Geschichtswerkes*, FTS 92 (Freiburg:
Herder, 1973), 26; also see Japhet, *1 and 2 Chronicles*, 307–8; and Knoppers, who outlines the
context of Chronicles with regard to Saul's line. (Knoppers, *1 Chronicles 10–29*, 626).
74. Victor A. Hurowitz, "Temporary Temples," in *Kinattūtu ša dārâti: Raphael Kutscher Memorial
Volume*, ed. Anson Rainey (Tel Aviv: Institute of Archaeology, 1993), 37–50.
75. Antony F. Campbell, *The Ark Narrative (1 Sam 4–6; 2 Sam 6): A Form-Critical and Traditio-
Historical Study* (Missoula, Mont.: Scholars Press, 1975), 244.
76. Myers, *1 Chronicles*, 119.
77. Japhet, *1 and 2 Chronicles*, 314. It is often presumed that the Samuel narrative portrays David
as offering the sacrifices himself. While this is possible and well within the authority of a
priest-king, it does not necessarily have to be the case. The Chronicler is interpreting his
Vorlage in light of David's cultic authority. He seems to be inclined to see David as the one
who authorizes and sanctions the priestly sacrifices
78. Myers, "The Kerygma of the Chronicler," 259–73. Myers argues that the portrayal of David
as a new Moses is directly linked to the Davidic covenant in 1 Chr 17 (ibid., 269); and Simon
J. De Vries, "Moses and David as Cult Founders in Chronicles," 619–39. For the broader
connections with Chronicles and the exodus traditions in particular see William Johnstone,
Chronicles and Exodus: An Analogy and Its Application, JSOTSup 275 (Sheffield: Sheffield Academic, 1998).
79. Knoppers, *1 Chronicles 10–29*, 627.
80. Cakes of raisins seem to be associated with cultic activities outside of the worship of Yahweh (e.g., Hos 3:1). Although not quite as clear as the passage in Hosea, Jeremiah also mentions cakes made for the queen of heaven (Jer 7:18; and 44:19).
81. Williamson, *1 and 2 Chronicles*, 127.
82. Some have attempted to argue for specific sacrifices that correspond to these specific terms
for singing (e.g., Rothstein and Hänel see the specific sacrifice as the אזכרה in connection
with the command "to remember," Rothstein and Hänel, *Chronik*, 287).
83. Eising, "zākhar," *TDOT* 4:74.

84. Other passages in Chronicles seem to support that this is the view of the Chronicler (e.g., 2 Chr 5:13; 7:3; 20:21).
85. Bernard Gosse, "Les citations de Psaumes en 1 Ch 16:8-36 et la conception des relations entre Yahvé et son peuple dans la rédaction des livres des Chroniques," *EgT* 27 (1996): 313–33.
86. Knoppers, *1 Chronicles 10–29*, 643.
87. It seems significant that the psalms that make up the song (105; 96; and 106) do not have David (or Asaph for that matter) in there superscriptions. Perhaps the Chronicler has chosen not to include songs from Israel's major singers and composers in order to stress the fact that while the people involved are important, it is the object of the songs themselves that one needs to keep focused upon.
88. Knoppers, *1 Chronicles 10–29*, 644–45.
89. James W. Watts, *Psalm and Story: Inset Hymns in Hebrew Narrative*, JSOTSup 139 (Sheffield: JSOT Press, 1992), 161.
90. Dennerlein notes that the Chronicler's main use of the Psalms throughout his work is to place the postexilic cult in the same tradition as that of the preexilic one, thus serving as a legitimation for the cult in the Chroniclers own day (see Norbert Dennerlein, *Die Bedeutung Jerusalems in den Chronikbüchern*, BEATAJ 46 [Frankfurt am Main: Lang, 1999], 240).
91. This issue will be addressed below within the various sections of the psalm.
92. Ibid.
93. See Howard N. Wallace, "What Chronicles Has to Say About Psalms," in *The Chronicler as Author: Studies in the Text and Texture*, ed. M. Patrick Graham and Steven L. McKenzie, JSOTSup 263 (Sheffield: Sheffield Academic Press, 1999), 283. This writer prefers Craigie's argument. The classification of psalm types is essential, but the classification system needs to be more flexible (Peter C. Craigie, *Psalms 1–50*, WBC 19 [Waco, Tex.: Word, 1983], 47).
94. Kristen Nielsen, "Whose Song of Praise? Reflections on the Purpose of the Psalm in 1 Chronicles 16," in *The Chronicler as Author: Studies in Text and Texture*, ed. M. Patrick Graham and Steven L. McKenzie, JSOTSup 263 (Sheffield: Sheffield Academic Press, 1999), 328.
95. Watts, *Psalm and Story*, 161. Also see Nielsen, "Whose Song of Praise," 332; Rudolph, *Chronikbücher*, 127; and Myers, *1 Chronicles*, 121.
96. Williamson, *1 and 2 Chronicles*, 128.
97. Kleinig, *The LORD's Song*, 146.
98. B. Gosse, "L'Alliance avec Abraham et les relectures de l'histoire d'Israël en Ne 9, Pss 105–106, 135–136 et 1 Ch 16," *Transeu* 15 (1998): 123–35.
99. Knoppers, *1 Chronicles 10–29*, 646.
100. Gosse, "L'Alliance avec Abraham," 124–34.
101. See Trent C. Butler, "A Forgotten Passage from a Forgotten Era (1 Chr. 16:8-36)," *VT* 28 (1978): 144; and Braun, *1 Chronicles*, 191–92.
102. Leslie C. Allen, *Psalms 101–150*, WBC 21 (Waco, Tex.: Word, 1983), 42.
103. Japhet, *1 and 2 Chronicles*, 317.
104. A. F. Kirkpatrick, *The Book of Psalms* (Cambridge: Cambridge University Press, 1902; reprint, Grand Rapids: Baker, 1982), 577. In the judgment of this writer, Kirkpatrick's dating of this psalm is too late and should be reevaluated. Nevertheless, his comments are well suited for the Chronicler's time and reflect the Chronicler's emphasis.
105. Nielsen, "Whose Song of Praise," 335.
106. Klaus Seybold, *Studien zur Psalmenauslegung* (Stuttgart: Kohlhammer, 1998), 107.
107. Kleinig, *The LORD's Song*, 139.

108. McCarter, *2 Samuel*, 170. He bases his argument on the fact that Obed-Edom is a non-Yahwistic name. Anderson offers a possible understanding for the name when he states, "Thus, "Edom" in this context may be a divine name...rather than a reference to the *land* of Edom...(Andersen, *2 Samuel*, 105).

109. Japhet, *1 and 2 Chronicles*, 281.

110. Since the term "Gittite" is used only here in reference to Obed-Edom many scholars presume that the Obed-Edom spoken of throughout the remainder of the book is the Gittite. Most presume that this is a reference to Gath (see 1 Chr 20:5). This may not necessarily be the case. The house of Obed-Edom the Gittite is now serving as a temporary sanctuary for the ark. Hurowitz notes that even the temporary housing of sacred objects, such as the ark, function as the dwelling place of the god that was associated with that object (see Hurowitz, "Temporary Temples," 37–50). The point is that the house of the Gittite would be treated as a sanctuary, and therefore, some form of cultic assignment would have been assigned to the place as well. The text is silent on this matter and the presumption that a Philistine functioned in this capacity seems unlikely, especially since the ark is being housed there because of the tragedy of Uzzah mishandling the ark.

111. See Josh 21:24. While it is not possible to argue conclusively that the Chronicler is referring to the specific Levitical town that Obed-Edom's clan was originally associated with. It would seem out of David's character to allow a Philistine, even one on friendly terms to house such an important cultic object as the ark. Furthermore, it suggests that the Chronicler has not made up Obed-Edom's Levitical heritage, and may indicate that he is following some genealogical source at his disposal

112. Levitical city of Gath Rimmon was given to the clan of Kohath (Josh 21:20), and the Chronicler has indicated in his genealogical material that Korah is among the family of Kohath (1 Chr 6:22). This clearly argues for Obed-Edom's being in the line of Korah.

113. Dennerlein, *Die Bedeutung Jerusalems*, 64.

114. There are several helpful studies on Zadok and the priesthood, although some attempt to see Zadok's enigmatic origins as being evidence that he was a Jebusite. See Deborah W. Rooke, *Zadok's Heirs: The Role and Development of the High Priesthood in Ancient Israel*, OTM, (Oxford: Oxford University Press, 2000).

115. The only priest not appointed to the Gibeon sanctuary was Benaiah because he was already appointed to the tent that housed the ark (16:6).

116. One should note that there is no reason to see Gibeon as secondary material as Welch does (Welch, *The Work of the Chronicler*, 30–41).

117. Williamson, *1 and 2 Chronicles*, 130.

118. See Joseph Blenkinsopp, *Gibeon and Israel: The Role of Gibeon and the Gibeonites in the Political and Religious History of Early Israel*, SOTSMS 2 (Cambridge: Cambridge University Press, 1972), 102. Japhet, however, understands that the Chronicler includes Gideon for specific purposes. See Japhet, *1 and 2 Chronicles*, 323.

119. See Exod 29:38; and Num 28:3.

120. Japhet acknowledges that Josh 9:27 suggests that there was a sanctuary at Gibeon (Japhet, *1 and 2 Chronicles*, 322). It is impossible to tell if the altar at Gibeon was once used for pagan worship. Soggin at least confirms that the original statement could have been about Gibeon. J. Alberto Soggin, *Joshua: A Commentary*, trans. R. A. Wilson, OTL (Philadelphia: Westminster, 1972), 111.

121. Blenkinsopp, *Gibeon and Israel*, 69.

122. Knoppers, *1 Chronicles 10–29*, 659.

123. There are theological reasons for the Chronicler to include Gibeon as a cultic center. This will be discussed in the following chapter.
124. Terence E. Fretheim, "The Ark in Deuteronomy," *CBQ* 30 (1968): 9. This statement is also supported by Ps 78:60.
125. Ibid., and also see Hurowitz, who notes that by bringing old material into a new temple that the old sanctuary is linked to the new one. See Victor A. Hurowitz, *I Have Built You an Exalted House: Temple Building in the Bible in Light of Mesopotamian and Northwest Semitic Writings*, JSOTSup 115 (Sheffield: Sheffield Academic Press, 1992), 264–65.
126. This does not mean that the place of the ark is the only place where Yahweh's presence could be found. Exod 20:22–26 indicates that Yahweh could appear before an altar. Yet, at these sites, the presence of God was not assured. See Baruch A. Levine, *Numbers 1–20: A New Translation with Introduction and Commentary*, AB 4A (New York: Doubleday, 1993), 199.
127. Such blessings were common in Israel. In Ruth 2:4 Boaz greets his harvesters with a common greeting. The blessing is typical and comes from one in a place of authority to those below him.

CHAPTER FIVE

Theology of the Ark Narrative

The Function of the Narrative within
the Davidic Narrative as a Whole

As noted in chapter two, the ark narrative has tight literary connections that reach back to the beginning of the Chronicler's narrative and on into Solomon's narrative as well. These connections will be explored from a theological perspective in the following section.[1] In this section it seems important to address the theological function that the ark narrative plays within the larger Davidic narrative (1 Chr 11–29), of which it is a part. The way the ark narrative functions should find its major support in the Davidic narrative. The Davidic narrative falls into two sections. The first addresses the founding of the Davidic dynasty (11–22:1). The second section addresses David's final organization of the cult, instructions regarding the temple, and the organization of the government (22:2–29:30).

First Chronicles 10 has major theological significance as it is attached to David's anointing in the following chapter. It shows Yahweh's sovereignty quite clearly. Yahweh brought about Saul's death and gave the kingdom to David.[2] Chapters 11–12 are necessary in order to set the stage for the ark narrative. David is anointed king of all Israel because Yahweh had chosen him according to the word of Samuel (11:3). After being established as king, he takes Jerusalem (11:5) and makes it his capital city. The cursory treatment of such major issues as David's anointing and subsequent victory over the Jebusites indicates that the Chronicler's major emphasis is not found in this section of material. Chapters 10–12 then serve as an introduction to the story which sets David apart from his predecessor and portrays him as a strong king who has Yahweh's blessing. Chapters 11–12 further explain that David was accepted by all Israel and took his royal city; both elements point toward the importance of the ark narrative.[3] Once the ark narrative begins, the narrative then slows and care is taken in the development of the Chronicler's own special emphases that he will continue to develop throughout the book.[4]

First, the Chronicler is careful to note that David's actions are exactly the opposite of those of his predecessor, Saul (13:3). Another interesting feature of 1 Chr 13 is that it notes that Yahweh's presence is with the ark; it dwells between the cherubim where his name is proclaimed" (v. 6), which establishes the importance of the ark, because it is a symbol of his presence. The major theological issue in this chapter is the death of Uzzah. It is undoubtedly connected with the holiness of Yahweh. Yahweh is a holy God and as such neither he nor his sacred objects can even have incidental human contact without following proper cultic procedures which Yahweh himself has revealed to the nation through Moses and David. Nevertheless, proper adherence to the cult is not enough to please Yahweh. Chapter 14 clearly shows that David continues to be blessed by Yahweh with the building of his palace and with his multiple children and military victories. This indicates that Yahweh is not displeased with David's desire to bring his presence into the city of Jerusalem.

The second part of the ark narrative continues to emphasize the joy and festivities that occurred when Yahweh allowed the symbol of his presence to be brought into Jerusalem. The cult is given sanction by David, who is Yahweh's vice-regent. The initial ordering of the various cultic officials serves as a background and guides the final ordering of the cult (23–27). Hence, while the temple is of the utmost importance for the Chronicler, the ark narrative provides the cultic officials with their royal appointments to their various duties. These duties will ultimately serve as a pattern that will be used in the ordering of the temple officials. The ark narrative then functions both as a legitimation of David and the cult by Yahweh. Worship now clearly includes music and singing along with sacrifice. This suggests that proper worship comes out of joyous praise and thanksgiving to Yahweh.[5] This narrative with its emphasis on bringing to remembrance, on giving thanks, and on praising (16:4, 8–36), emphasizes that there is no compulsion by Yahweh for the nation to worship him. True worship is a result of thankfulness for what Yahweh has done and the hope that he will continue to work on the nation's behalf.[6] The narrative itself makes a major tie between the First Temple and the Sinai traditions and also links the First Temple with the Second Temple, which is now completed.[7]

The link between major traditions of Israel's past shows some of the Chronicler's theological motives. First, the Chronicler ties centralized sacrifice to Gibeon because the tabernacle and the Mosaic altar were there. Thus, the Chronicler indicates that proper sacrifice must be carried out according to Mosaic legislation. At the same time David's appointment of the priests and Levites to only Gibeon and Jerusalem limits legitimate cultic worship to these two sites. Second, although the Pentateuch indicates that music was present during worship (Num 10:10), the ark narrative emphasizes worship in Jerusalem and Gibeon with music and song (16:4–38). Once the temple is built, this musical tradition will remain but it will be reorganized for temple worship. The regulations that David institutes in 1 Chr 23–27 serve as the guideline for his own day, for that of the monarchy, and for the Chronicler's time as well.

Chapter 17 begins a new unit of material that is closely associated with the ark. The main topic is the Davidic covenant: it is Yahweh's making of the covenant that is the point of the passage. David's desire to build a temple for Yahweh is not Yahweh's desire. However, David's concern results in Yahweh acting on his behalf.[8] David's response to Yahweh sets the standard for the nation and also bridges the past with the present.[9] Chapters 18–20 depict David's military success and indicate that David is following divine guidance in his various conquests. These successes suggest that there is blessing in following the commands of Yahweh. This blessing ultimately leads to Solomon's establishment of the temple. The Chronicler then begins to develop this major concern, which is the centralization of Israel's religion in Jerusalem in chapter 21–22:1. The place of the altar is chosen by Yahweh (21:18) and this choice sets in motion the finalization of the cultic officials and the beginning of the building of the temple, which from David's viewpoint is revealed by Yahweh to be at the site where Yahweh told him to build the altar (22:1). This is confirmed when fire falls from heaven on the altar (1 Chr 21:26). One caveat needs to be emphasized: the Chronicler is writing after the First Temple was destroyed, and the Second Temple was built. Therefore, his interest is truly not the First Temple but rather it is what the temple represents, namely, the means by which the nation communicates with Yahweh.[10] Thus, while the temple is a major point of emphasis, it seems clear that the theological point that is so tightly connected to the temple is the centralized worship properly orchestrated by the priests and Levites. Furthermore, the temple site also depicts the place where Yahweh acted in mercy toward the nation after David prayed for the people (21:17).[11] Yahweh had every reason to destroy the people and the city, yet he chose not to do so.[12]

Chapters 22:2–29:30 form a new unit of material concerning David and his successor, Solomon. These chapters emphasize two important elements; namely, the succession of Solomon and more importantly the preparations for the building of the temple.[13] Therefore, it is not surprising that the Chronicler spends so much attention on the temple. However, David's prayer clearly indicates that Yahweh is the sovereign who allows the temple to be constructed and grants Solomon success (22:11). This picture of David helps explain his instruction to Solomon to follow Yahweh's law (22:12–13).

The Chronicler then explains David's reorganization of the priests and Levites in chapters 23–26. The building of the temple would take away a major duty of the Levites, the carrying of the ark. Thus, the need arises to reorganize the Levites for duties of the temple proper. This final organization of the cultic officials is based on the duties that they were given already in the ark narrative. The careful attention to this matter stresses that there is a need for proper ritual procedures in the worship of Yahweh. This is further emphasized with the establishment of the priests, who are essential for proper worship.[14]

The fact that the Chronicler consistently notes that the priests and Levites were chosen by lot also emphasizes Yahweh's sovereignty. The attention to music (25:1–31) indicates that music was essential for praising Yahweh, and that Yahweh could speak through it to his people. Thus, the Chronicler is portraying the Levitical singers as both proclaimers of Yahweh to the nation and as intermediaries between Yahweh and Israel.[15] The Chronicler as a rule does not address the gatekeepers in as much detail as he addresses other Levitical roles. He does address them here (26:1–19), and theologically speaking he addresses the complete care of the things of Yahweh.[16] This is further emphasized in 26:20–32 with the appointment of Levitical supervision over the treasuries and public affairs. Chapter 27 addresses the military officers and other national officials who had responsibilities outside of the temple complex.

The remaining two chapters, 28–29, return to the same setting as that of chapter 22. They resume David's speeches and are theologically rich. The Chronicler makes clear that Yahweh's choice of David to strengthen completely Israel's borders and of Solomon to build the temple shows Yahweh's authority. The Chronicler also describes David's calling "all Israel" to this occasion which continues that major theme in this narrative as well. Further, throughout these chapters the Chronicler shows continuity with the First Temple and the traditions that surround the tabernacle and the ark. The people's willingness to give to the temple project indicates the proper attitude that one should have regarding the things of Yahweh. Proper attitude leads to Yahweh's being able to bless his people.[17] Yahweh is able to bless because he is a great God. The temple is glorious because it is representative of Yahweh's glory (29:10–13). McKenzie again raises a valid point, "David encourages the people to give...but not because God needs the gifts. God already owns everything, especially the kingdom...The people need to give as a symbol of their devotion to God...and finally for the benefit that it brings them in fostering joy and community."[18] Thus, for the Chronicler all other emphases in his work are merely illustrations pointing to Yahweh as the ultimate hope for the nation.

The ark narrative's function within the Davidic narrative as a whole then appears to be one of organizing central theological themes that drive the narrative as a whole. For example, themes of blessing, sovereignty of Yahweh, care for the sacred, the holiness of Yahweh, the legitimation and organization of the cult, the narrowing of legitimate cultic sites to two sanctuaries as a necessary step toward centralization, and the legitimation of the Davidic dynasty all appear within the ark narrative. The chapters that surround this narrative also address these same themes. Some of these themes do of course appear earlier in the work, even in the genealogies. However, all major themes are tied together for the first time in the ark narrative. Thus, the Davidic section of the Chronicler's work seems to leave a lasting theological impression. Yahweh is the true king who, being absolutely sovereign, chooses to make Jerusalem the place where his presence dwells. This choice brings about David's own desire to build Yahweh a house and centralize both the political and cultic aspects of the nation in Jerusalem. Although this centralization is temporally denied by Yahweh, David is able to organize the cult around two legitimate sanctuaries and then subsequently reorganize the cultic officials for the temple and the military and political officers there as well.

Function of the Narrative within the Book

The ark narrative highlights the significance of Jerusalem. Jerusalem is the place where the centrality of worship occurs after the temple has been built. Kegler thinks that David's organization of the temple services supplanted the exodus as the central saving event in Israel's history.[19] This seems unlikely, but his premise is stimulating. David's organization of the cult is an important element within Israel's history. The ark narrative shows David's first organization of the clergy and emphasizes the significance of worship in Chronicles.[20]

The genealogies also provide vital information about Israel's history. They hint of theological insights by the Chronicler and provide the reader with important background information for the narrative that follows. The genealogies leave the reader with the impression that Yahweh is moving the nation of Israel in a predetermined direction. They also serve the important role of linking the postexilic nation to its glorious past.[21] It also introduces major themes that take place throughout the entire work; for example, twelve tribes are represented in the genealogical material, hence the theme of "all Israel."[22]

The genealogies can be broken down into three smaller units: (1) from Adam to Israel (1 Chr 1); (2) the tribes of Israel (1 Chr 2–8); and (3) names of the residents of Jerusalem. In the genealogies, the Levitical genealogy is one of the most detailed and is placed at the very center of that section of material.[23] Along with the Levites, the tribes of Judah and Benjamin are also given pride of place. Thus, two of the central emphases are found within the central section of the genealogies. The first is the Levites and their various roles within the worship service. The second is the tribe of Judah, which is the line of David and his dynasty. These two major emphases are evident throughout the remainder of the book.

The ark narrative also addresses these major themes. In fact, one could make a case that the ark narrative contains the majority of the twenty-eight themes of the Chronicler, as listed by Pratt.[24] The ark narrative functions at the heart of the Davidic narrative, illustrating proper worship for the nation of

Israel. This theme of proper worship is carried on in the third and final section of the work.

The Chronicler's theology as it pertains to the narratives of the various kings can now be broadly summarized. It is a theologically arranged account of Judah's kings, something that becomes clear in the narratives themselves (2 Chr 10–36). The Chronicler attributes to Judah's righteous kings the building of major structures, their conscientious care and maintenance for the temple and its cult, and their ability to amass large defenses on behalf of the nation. These kings are also able to regain lost territory and authorize the reorganization of the cult, even demand tribute, and they are portrayed as wisely ruling their people. Kings who failed to care for Yahweh and his temple were weak. Their reigns are portrayed as exactly the opposite of those of their righteous counterparts. They did not build, they neglected the temple and its cult, and they could not defend the nation from opposing military threats. In keeping with the paradigm, these kings lose territory, encourage idolatry by ignoring the temple and supporting pagan sanctuaries, and are ultimately exiled from their throne and the land. But there is hope, as the Chronicler ends his work with the decree of Cyrus, thus providing his own readers with hope that the nation could one day return to its glorious status among the nations.

Indeed, the Chronicler holds out hope for a Davidic king and grounds it in an eschatological hope for the nation and the world.[25] This hope is not set in defiance against the Persian Empire but is founded in the Davidic covenant. This hope is clearly illustrated in Solomon's reign. Solomon, like his father, is closely linked to the temple, but neither are merely servants designed to carry out the task of building the temple. They function as cultic founders and as strong monarchs who are given legitimation by Yahweh. All subsequent kings are evaluated by their care for the cult and their ability to maintain proper worship at the temple. Throughout the Chronicler's work he indicates the continuing significance of the Davidic covenant and the temple as the center of cultic worship. Furthermore, in his emphasis on cultic worship, Yahweh's universal kingship comes to the fore (for example, see 1 Chr 16:23–34). These elements were meant for the postexilic reader and are present to give hope for the future. Yahweh, the king of all the earth, will once again act on behalf of the nation and there will once again be a Davidic ruler on the throne of Israel. For the time being, the nation is to maintain proper covenant relations with the great king through the cult.

Major Themes within the Ark Narrative

The Chronicler consistently addresses a number of major themes. McKenzie, among others, has identified four major theological emphases. "They are: Davidic–Solomonic kingship, the temple, 'all Israel,' and divine retribution and reward."[26] While these elements are certainly present in the ark narrative, the narrative itself suggests three major themes that are developed within it and found throughout the work. These three major themes need to be addressed. The issues to be introduced in this section include: (1) the ark, (2) Jerusalem, and (3) worship. Each of these will be treated separately.

The Ark

The ark has several elements that are significant. One element, often overlooked, is the fact that once the Levites were appointed to carry the ark in 1 Chr 15, the ark is frequently called "the ark of the covenant." This phrase does not occur before the Levites are specifically appointed to carry the ark. The Chronicler may be using this phrase as a way of linking the Levites' role in cultic worship directly to the Mosaic covenant.[27] Just as Moses was the covenant mediator, so also the priests and the Levites are now responsible for the maintenance of that covenant through proper worship. The Levites' activities in leading the nation in worship allow the nation once again to maintain covenant relations with Yahweh. Thus, the Chronicler might have used the phrase "the ark of the covenant" in order to support the cultic officials as they are the ones who are now responsible for proper worship and they are in a sense mediators of the covenant.[28] Without their ability to function in the Second Temple, there would be a breakdown in the ritual purity of the people; thus the nation would be hindered from receiving Yahweh's complete blessings.

Furthermore, unlike several scholars, this writer does not see the ark as merely legitimating the temple.[29] It certainly did that, but more is involved than just legitimacy. As the symbol of Yahweh's presence, the ark represented his being with his people. Although the Chronicler may have hope for the ark's being restored to the temple, it also appears that he is showing that the lack of the symbol does not necessarily mean there is a lack of presence.[30]

In many ways the ark, the tent of meeting, and also the temple function in a similar way as other ancient Near Eastern temples and statues of gods. Yet, there are some significant differences as well. For example, the ark is not an anthropomorphic likeness of a god. Thus, unlike these images which are so common among other ancient Near Eastern cultures, Yahweh is not present in a statue. His presence is found above the ark. Yet there is much that could be clearer in the way that Yahweh is present above the ark. For example, Num

10:33–35 may suggest that when the ark is in transit Yahweh rises from his resting place and returns to it when the ark reaches a new site.[31] Furthermore, the idea of Yahweh dwelling between the cherubim (1 Chr 13:6; Ps 80:2; 1 Sam 4:4; 2 Sam 6:2; 2 Kgs 19:15; Isa 37:16) does not reveal any specific location for Yahweh's dwelling as the preposition is missing in all occurrences.[32] At other times the ark is called "Yahweh's footstool" (for example, Ps 99:5; 132:7; 1 Chr 28:2).[33] Finally, it is important to note that Yahweh's presence is, at least temporarily, found in contexts outside of a sanctuary. Fretheim has indicated that there are a number of places in Deuteronomy that suggest this.[34]

There are numerous places where Yahweh could come and be present for one to offer sacrifice and to worship him; however, it seems clear that the ark is basically the place of Yahweh's permanent presence.[35] Thus, when David brings the ark into Jerusalem, he is bringing Yahweh's presence in a permanent sense into his royal city. This could be the reason for David's referring to the temple as a "house of rest" (1 Chr 28:2). Yet, the Chronicler has more in mind than just Yahweh's presence being a permanent fixture in Jerusalem. He identifies several aspects of his presentation of the ark that play a role throughout the work. Begg has identified "a series of key associations for the ark that will be developed in his [the Chronicler's] subsequent references to it: 'rest', the Levites, their musical activities, the two great patrons of the ark, Kings David and Solomon, and its temporary (the 'tent') and permanent (the temple) residences."[36] Thus, the climax for the ark is its installation in the temple. However, the Chronicler continues to address the ark throughout the narrative, until it finally finds rest in the temple.[37] The first mention of the ark comes immediately following the ark narrative in 1 Chr 17:1, where David indicates his desire to provide the ark with a house since he himself has a house made of cedar.[38]

Begg argues that "the climax of the Chronicler's story of the ark comes in 2 Chr 5–7, when on the occasion of the dedication of the temple the ark is installed within it."[39] This does not end the story of the ark, however, as Josiah speaks of it at the end of his reign (2 Chr 35:3). There he tells the Levites that there is no longer a need for them to carry the ark.[40]

Literarily speaking, the ark narrative does much for the legitimating of the Davidic dynasty, the temple, and the rights of the Levites in serving in the temple before the ark. Theologically speaking, it is significant for a number of reasons. The Chronicler devotes a significant amount of space to the ark, but never argues for its return to the Second Temple.[41] Begg, however, argues that the Chronicler had hope in eventually having an ark in the Second Temple.[42] Although Begg raises six issues that support the eventual return of the ark to the temple, they do not demand that the Chronicler believed an ark was necessary for the temple to function properly. It may be better to argue that while the

Chronicler held out hope for the return of the ark to its rightful place in the temple, the ark in itself does not legitimate the temple.[43] The ark narrative clearly indicates that Yahweh allowed the symbol of his presence to be brought into Jerusalem. Yahweh also sanctions Solomon to build the temple (1 Chr 17:12). This would be done at the site where he commanded David to build an altar to stop the plague (1 Chr 21:18). Thus, Yahweh chose the specific site of the future temple, as well as the one who would build it, and in essence gave the only legitimation necessary for the temple. Furthermore, while the ark itself does not legitimate the Levites in their various cultic roles within the temple, David's establishment of the various Levitical and priestly orders within his role as a cult founder and as Yahweh's vice regent legitimates their services. Additionally, their orders were determined not solely by David's appointments nor by appointment from within the Levites themselves but by lot (1 Chr 24:5, 7, 31; 25:8, 9; 26:13, 14, 16) and hence by Yahweh.

The ark certainly helped to legitimate the temple; however, it was not the only source of legitimation. Thus, in the judgment of this writer the ark is an important sacred object that is needed within the temple; however, it is Yahweh himself who sanctions the legitimacy of the temple, the Levites, and the Davidic dynasty. This legitimation certainly allows for the Chronicler to hold out hope for the presence of the ark in the Second Temple, but it does not indicate that the Second Temple is any less legitimate than the first. In fact, one could argue that Yahweh has also legitimated the Second Temple by his prophets. For example, when the people lamented that the Second Temple would be only a shadow of the former one (Hag 2:3; Zech 4:10), Haggai answered the people. Hag 2:4–9, 18–19 indicates that Yahweh has sanctioned the building of his temple and his glory would fill this new temple as well (Hag 2:7).

The ark is an important element for carrying out specific forms of cultic ritual; however, it is not essential for worship. The key example is the fact that according to Leviticus 16:14–15 the blood for the atonement was to be placed on the covering of the ark. This act of sprinkling the blood upon the mercy seat is an often overlooked issue within the debate about what the ark meant to the First Temple and if it is necessary to legitimate the Second Temple. This small point, in the estimation of this writer, is significant because it indicates that while atonement took place in the postexilic period and on into the Roman occupation of Palestine it was done without the sprinkling of blood upon the covering of the ark. Thus, the place of the ark is one of importance because it represents the presence of Yahweh, but it is not essential within the worship system. The concept of presence is more important than the symbol itself.[44] This naturally leads one to look at the city of Jerusalem within the theology of the Chronicler.

Jerusalem

The city of Jerusalem is regarded as holy. The Chronicler emphasizes the fact that this is the place Yahweh has chosen as his capital. Since the temple is present again in Jerusalem in the Chronicler's own day, he is also making a case for it still to be the place that Yahweh has chosen. Yet, there seem to be differences between the way the Chronicler has presented Jerusalem and the way it is presented in Samuel–Kings. The Chronicler seems to be interested in it more as the capital of Yahweh. This means that, unlike the prophets of his time, he did not idealize a future temple. There was no need to do so since the city is the place where Yahweh chose to cause his presence to dwell, and that is sufficient.[45] Kalimi supports this as well when he states, "Jerusalem is depicted by the Chronicler, therefore, as an absolutely theocratic city, 'the City of God / the Lord' in the full sense of the word, more so than any other biblical work."[46]

The Chronicler does not treat the city in light of its eschatological significance. He portrays the city as it is in his own day.[47] It is readily acknowledged that Jerusalem is a focal point mainly because that is where the temple is located, and the Chronicler concentrates on the things in the temple and their continuity between the preexilic and postexilic periods. However, there must be more to Jerusalem's prominent position in the Chronicler's work. For instance, tying Jerusalem's place to the temple leaves one wondering where Yahweh's presence was during the time when Jerusalem had no temple.[48] Has he completely removed himself from the nation of Israel? It would seem that this is not the case: Yahweh still worked on behalf of his people in numerous ways during the exile.[49] Further, Kalimi notes that there is an omission in the Chronicler's use of 2 Kgs 8:16, which suggests that "the concept of Jerusalem as an elected city by the Lord is *unconditional* and permanent. It means that Jerusalem continued to be the Lord's chosen city even in the time of the Chronicler himself."[50]

The Chronicler also spent much time throughout his work building the theme of continuity with the past. In his description of Jerusalem, he also mentions that the temple mount is Mount Moriah (2 Chr 3:1).[51] Thus, there is a connection with the past which indicates that Yahweh's presence was manifest at this site in a special way long before it was even a city.[52] Therefore, the Chronicler may be using the various associations and the different synonyms for Jerusalem in a way that suggests that Yahweh had chosen Jerusalem and as a result of this he allows the temple to be built there.[53] Pruess asserts, "The temple became therefore the 'house of YHWH,' not because he dwelt there, but rather because he may be encountered there."[54] When the temple was destroyed, Jerusalem still continued to be the premier cultic center (Jer 41:5). Additionally, Ezek 11:16 indicates that the exile was not a complete abandonment by Yahweh from the people nor does it appear that the exiles believed that he had abandoned Jerusalem as Daniel prayed toward the city (Dan 6:11).[55] Thus, the city itself is central and placed in continuity with the past.

In the postexilic period, the temple's significance grew because the nation was under the control of the Persian government. However, the Chronicler makes clear that Yahweh has chosen the place of worship, not the Persians.[56] The Chronicler is emphasizing that while the Persians allow the temple to be rebuilt and in fact support its rebuilding, Yahweh is the one who legitimates the temple and the priests and Levites also being properly legitimated serve there. Thus, the Persians have nothing to do with the functions of temple or its worship.

The Chronicler then emphasizes Jerusalem because it is both the political and cultic center of the nation.[57] The temple becomes the central focus because Jerusalem is the place where the people gathered to meet with Yahweh. This happened before a temple was ever built (for example, 1 Chr 13:1–6; 15:3; 16:1–3, 43). It also clearly happened after the temple was built (2 Chr 5:2–3; 15:10–15; 2 Chr 20:5; 23:1–3; 30:1; and 34:29-33). Thus, Jerusalem is central for the Chronicler because it is Yahweh's city from which he rules the nations and all nations will come to him there (1 Chr 16:31).

The centralization of Jerusalem becomes more prevalent in light of the postexilic political situation in Yehud. Persia did authorize and give some aid in rebuilding the temple.[58] The Persians were also relatively tolerant of other national religions.[59] Further, the ark narrative brings these elements to the forefront when David brings the ark into Jerusalem. Dennerlein indicates that the ark is a prerequisite for the temple cult and as such the ark narrative plays a major role in establishing the centrality of Jerusalem for the Chronicler and the worship system in the temple. It now becomes important to investigate the Chronicler's theology of worship.[60]

Worship

The beginning of the worship system and what proper worship entails is clearly introduced by the Chronicler with the entrance of the ark into Jerusalem and David's organization of the cult. There are several places throughout the book where the Chronicler describes public worship. The Chronicler is tying his theology to the worship system in the various life settings that he depicts.[61] Worship for the Chronicler includes joy, the people's appreciation for Yahweh's kindness toward them, singing, and prayer.[62] The Chronicler uses these forms of worship to show his audience that this same pattern of worship is valid in his own day and that it will reflect the people's true identity as the people of Yahweh.

Worship in Israel is to take place at a centralized location (Deut 12:5). After the completion of the temple, Yahweh's name enters the temple proper through the ark.[63] Schniedewind makes the important point that the Chronicler has made some additions to his narrative. The significance of this "is (1) to emphasize the temple site as the place where God comes down to earth and (2) to justify the selection of this site for Yahweh's home on earth."[64] Thus, the temple worship stands at the heart of the Chronicler's theology, and the activities of the Levites, including those of the priests play an important role in that worship.[65] Thus, the way the Chronicler develops his theology of worship plays a significant role in the way he structures the book.

The Chronicler's theology of worship is all encompassing. It addresses nearly every conceivable life situation in the postexilic period. However, in order to address worship adequately it is necessary to limit the discussion to that of public worship that falls outside of the festival theme of the Chronicler.[66] Endres notes that the first of these communal worship settings is found in the ark narrative; thus, it is this narrative that will be used to investigate the Chronicler's theology of worship.[67]

Proper worship must be carried out by the priests and the Levites who were properly set apart for ministry to Yahweh. These cultic ministers were responsible for all aspects of worship in the temple. Just as the Levites were to carry the ark with poles on their shoulders (15:2), proper worship depended on authorized individuals following correct procedures. The Chronicler is narrating the events that took place during the first ascent of the ark to Jerusalem, thereby connecting both temples which results in placing the worship system of the postexilic period equal to the worship system of the preexilic period.

The duties of the Levites are important to the Chronicler. They were to carry the ark and they were also intimately involved in the singing and music of the cult. The song that the Chronicler uses is a representative of the type of worship that took place in his own day. It seems clear that the Psalms were employed and used not only as individual songs in their own right, but also in various combinations. This obviously means that worship entailed songs of thanksgiving and praise.[68] Therefore, the two major emphases in the ark narrative are calling the people to remembrance of what Yahweh has done in the past and that Yahweh is able to deliver in the present situation as well.[69]

The theology of worship in the psalm in particular is anything but simple. Endres rightly notes that this type of "praise for remembrance and salvation seems [to be] part of the theology of laments, which Chronicles inserts in its version of David's installation of the ark."[70] Yet, Jerusalem is not the only place where worship takes place in this period of transition. Gibeon is for the moment the official cultic site for sacrifice, at least until David builds the altar on the site of the future temple (1 Chr 21:26). This is the reason that Solomon went there to sacrifice. As a result of the two legitimate cultic sites, the combination of sacrifice and song is first clearly seen here.

The ark narrative then indicates several cultic activities. This procession takes place with singing, David dances before Yahweh in accordance with the music and song that accompanied the movement of the ark, there are sacrifices, and David blesses the people and provides food for those present. These are illustrations of the joy that should be present in worship. The Chronicler is emphasizing the uniqueness of worship. Although the Chronicler is portraying a corporate worship setting, the people as individuals have some measure of freedom in expressing their own joy in Yahweh. In this respect the idea of remembering is taken as a prayer for Yahweh's intervention.[71] Thus, it seems that the Chronicler has basic goals in his description of worship. There is great joy found in praising and giving thanks to Yahweh, but there also appears to be an element of prayer for Yahweh's intervention on behalf of the nation as well.

The Chronicler continues to develop his theology of worship throughout his work, both from corporate worship and from the various annual festivals in Israel.[72] The ark narrative introduces a new place of worship closely tied to the ark itself. The Chronicler's treatment of the worship here flows through the book in every instance of national worship.[73] Endre's analysis of these other worship settings is helpful. He argues that worship is a joyous occasion accompanied by music and song. These songs all incorporate phrases that reflect Yahweh as merciful and/or full of grace and compassion.[74] These are all repeated aspects of worship for the Chronicler.

One other element should be noted which appears in each occurrence of worship. Worship always reflects the worshipers' tremendous reverence toward Yahweh. For example, in the ark narrative the Chronicler mentions that the Levites sacrifice after the initial six steps because Yahweh helped them in moving the ark (1 Chr 15:26). This suggests, along with the detailed account of the priests and Levites' preparations for moving the ark that while there was joy, music, and singing, there was also fear of not performing according to cultic standards.[75] This fear of Yahweh would have also permeated the procession. Worship does have specific prescribed means that must be performed ritually according to the prescribed method. While this limits the activities of specific aspects of worship—here illustrated by the movement of the ark and more importantly directly by the various sacrifices—there are other elements wherein the people have freedom of expression within the services.

The Chronicler consistently demands strict adherence to cultic procedures on the part of the priests and Levites. In the other national worship settings, such as in the priests' sanctification for the dedication of the temple (2 Chr

6:11), reverence is also evident in the people's action of falling down before Yahweh (2 Chr 7:3). This same reverence is found in 2 Chr 20, where the nation is facing an impending battle. The king and the people bow to the ground before Yahweh (2 Chr 20:18). Although this humility takes place before the joyous victory ceremony, it nevertheless points to the fact that while there was freedom of expression in joyous worship, it is always expressed in humility toward Yahweh. Finally, Hezekiah's national worship ceremonies also substantiate the concept of reverence and proper care for the holy. First, Hezekiah restores proper cultic rituals and has the temple cleansed from impurity (2 Chr 29:5). Then there is a worship ceremony that the king and princes of the city take part in for "all Israel" (2 Chr 29:20–36).

The care the Chronicler takes in indicating that the musicians were placed according to David's command, based on Yahweh's words through his prophets (29:25–27), supports the emphasis on proper procedures. This reverence is implemented in the humbling of the king and all present before Yahweh (29:29–30). Second, Hezekiah orders a Passover feast in 2 Chr 30. The Chronicler indicates that some of the men from the northern tribes "humbled" themselves and went up to Jerusalem (30:11). Further, it is here that the Chronicler makes the intriguing statement that many of the people had not consecrated themselves (v. 18); however, Hezekiah prayed and asked Yahweh to pardon those who prepared their hearts to seek God (v. 19). The implication is that proper worship takes place in the heart (something Jesus will later point out as well [John 4:24]).[76] True, there are some prescribed forms that must be properly observed, but ritual purification only illustrates the proper attitude that is involved in worshiping Yahweh.[77] This same nuance is also found in one of the festival texts (2 Chr 15:15). There the people rejoiced and earnestly sought Yahweh with their whole heart.

Thus, the Chronicler credits David with the organization of worship when he orders the Levites for the movement of the ark, organizes the priests and Levites after the ark arrives in Jerusalem, and orders the twenty-four Levitical courses.[78] The Chronicler sets up the worship pattern that was already given to Moses by the commandment of Yahweh. Even in the institution of the music and singing David acts in accordance with Num 10:10 for the priests and Deut 10:8 and 18:5 for the Levites to stand before Yahweh and minister in his name. Finally, Yahweh himself gives his own approval of David's finalization of worship in Israel when he stops the plague and David builds an altar on the site and more specifically when fire from heaven falls on the altar of burnt offerings during the temple dedication. Throughout his work the Chronicler explains how worship was initially developed during the monarchy and who was to perform cultic functions. The Chronicler also indicates that part of worship involved the announcement of Yahweh's presence among the people.[79] Sacrifices for the Chronicler were not carried out in silence but were accompanied with music and song.[80] While the Chronicler is selective in his choice of public worship, it is clear that worship also took place daily with the morning and evening offerings, which were originally offered at Gibeon but later in the temple on the altar of burnt offerings.

The Chronicler, writing much later than all of these events, has included them in his narrative to show that proper worship was instituted by Moses and David and that it was continued by the monarchy down to the point of exile. The reorganization of the clergy, especially by Hezekiah and Josiah, indicates that while they had the authority to reorganize the cult, they did so in accordance with David's original plans for the worship setting, especially in regard to the music and singing that David instituted.[81] Thus, the Chronicler places his own postexilic traditions in line with the preexilic past.[82] Worship for the Chronicler is necessary because it is the means by which the nation communicates with Yahweh. Proper worship will allow Yahweh once again to act on behalf of the nation because the nation is coming to Yahweh with a pure heart. This worship is to be carried out in the only legitimate place of worship, the Second Temple. Yet other places were needed to be used for worship out of the necessity of distance from this temple. This did not affect proper worship, but the people were not to sacrifice anywhere other than in the temple in Jerusalem.[83] This rule allows for all other aspects of worship to be legitimately carried out elsewhere. However, sacrifice was still the primary means by which worship was carried out, meaning that the temple in the postexilic period is of the utmost importance for the nation and its identity.

Synthetic Analysis

Evidence from the analysis above suggests that a single concept or idea is not enough to portray fully the Chronicler's theology. It may be summed up in a single sentence, however. Yahweh is completely holy and has chosen to reveal himself to Israel in such a way that he may bring glory to himself through an intimate relationship with Israel maintained by proper adherence to cultic regulations which results in his blessing the nation. At the risk of superimposing artificial categories on the text, there are two major generic theological points that can be derived directly from the ark narrative.[84] Taking the standard categories of God and kingdom it is possible to understand the broader theological impressions that the Chronicler develops in the ark narrative.

God

The overwhelming impression that the ark narrative leaves the reader with is that God is a holy God who demands that people approach him properly (1 Chr 13:9–10). Yahweh is also merciful because he did not remove his blessing from David (chapter 14) or from those who cared for the symbol of his presence (13:14). The ark narrative also shows Yahweh's sovereignty. Nothing can be done without Yahweh's consent. This is an especially important concept for the Chronicler's readers because even though they have returned from exile, Persia still maintains political control over the nation. God allows for this situation and he is able to work within in it on behalf of his people. One clear indication of this is that God's name is connected closely with the ark of the covenant (1 Chr 13:6) and therefore his presence is established in the royal city. This emphasizes the fact that God desires to have a close relationship with his people. Such a relationship needs mediation between a holy God and imperfect man. This is often seen in the Mosaic covenant; however, this covenant is not as developed in Chronicles as it is in Samuel—Kings. Rather, the focus is on the Davidic covenant, which is an outgrowth of the Abrahamic and Mosaic covenants. This Davidic covenant was a direct result of David showing concern for the things of Yahweh and desiring to bring the ark into his royal city.

Kingdom

The ark narrative is the first place where David organizes the nation both politically and religiously. It appears that the Chronicler is keenly aware that David is responsible to some degree for Israel's covenant traditions. These traditions are present in the ark narrative in the Chronicler's psalm (1 Chr 16:14–18). The psalm also draws attention to God's sovereignty over the entire earth (v. 31). This may link the sovereignty of God with the fact that God chose David to be king, thus making David his vice-regent.

The covenants call Israel to demonstrate God's salvation to mankind. Such expression is seen in the kingdom of Israel as a model for other nations. One could argue that this is first expressed clearly in the building of the temple. However, one may also state that when David moved the ark into Jerusalem, his royal city, that the presence of God is finally uniquely tied to the political and religious framework which is developed initially in the ark narrative.

The ark narrative's primary interest is the cultic formation of the nation. Proper worship is the central theological thrust of the passage. This emphasis is important for the Chronicler because worship is the means by which the nation can maintain its covenant relationship with God. The initial development of the localization of God to his people takes place in David's bringing the ark to Jerusalem. The procession that is pictured by the Chronicler shows the way proper worship was to be carried out. David furthermore develops some basic elements within the cult by organizing the priests and Levites. David further defines the Levites' ministry as commemorating, giving thanks, and praising God (1 Chr 16:4–6). Thus, for the Chronicler the Levites maintain the covenant between God and Israel.

Summary

The Chronicler has carefully developed the theology of the ark narrative in a way that moves from the very earliest stages of the cult during David's time and shows how those cultic institutions developed within Israel's religious history. Theologically speaking, the ark narrative leaves the reader with the overwhelming impression that Yahweh is a holy God who demands that people approach him properly. The ark, the symbol of Yahweh's presence, was to be brought to Jerusalem because it was the place that Yahweh chose for his name to dwell. Moreover, it could be brought only by proper observance to Mosaic tradition.

The Chronicler also is careful to point out that David is the one who seeks after Yahweh (13:3). David's care for the things of Yahweh will ultimately result in the Davidic covenant (chapter 17). However, the theological richness of the ark narrative is based on its attention to proper worship. This attention to worship places stress on reverence and humility before Yahweh.

The fear of Yahweh is utilized by the Chronicler to address the largest theological problem within the narrative, the death of Uzzah. Uzzah's well intentioned but misdirected protection of the ark makes it completely clear that Yahweh's holiness is not to be approached as commonly as one would approach menial tasks. The role of the priests and Levites is extremely crucial, because they keep the cultic objects and come into close contact with the objects that have been set apart for the worship of Yahweh. In order not to provoke Yahweh to anger, David took measures to ensure proper observations of cultic activities were in compliance with Mosaic standards.

David also took steps to bring the music and singing present in worship into the fore of the cultic activities. This inclusion of music and song allows for some freedom of expression in worship. Such freedom flows out of joy and thanksgiving and reflects an attitude of obedience that comes from the heart. Such heartfelt worship indicates that the following of rules and standards, although important, are not enough in and of themselves to please God. Thus, in Chronicles true worship is joyful and while some ritual elements are fixed, other elements are open and fluid.

The ark narrative plays a major role in the centrality of Jerusalem. Yahweh's choice of Jerusalem as the cultic center is now clear. The city itself has links to the past (Gen 22) and is now firmly established as Yahweh's city before the

First Temple is built. Thus, Yahweh's presence is now no longer just associated with the ark but is also uniquely tied to the city. The Chronicler's readers would have understood the connection between the Sinai traditions and the Davidic institutions as a continuation of legitimate worship. It is this worship that the Chronicler is arguing for in his own day. The worship that is carried out in the Second Temple is also legitimate worship. Just as Yahweh acted on behalf of the patriarchs, Moses, and David, so too will Yahweh act on behalf of those who maintain a proper relationship with him.

Notes

1. There is a surprising number of theological treatments that examine the exilic and postexilic periods but do not address the ark narrative. Nevertheless, some of these treatments have helped shape this writer's thinking. These include: Rainer Albertz, *Geschichte und Theologie: Studien zur Exegese des Alten Testaments und zur Religionsgeschichte Israels*, ed. Ingo Kottsieper and Jakob Wöhrle, BZAW 326 (New York: de Gruyter, 2003), 187–208; 321–58; Othmar Keel and Silvia Schroer, *Schöpfung: Biblische Theologien im Kontext altorientalischer Religionen* (Göttingen: Vandenhoeck and Ruprecht, 2002), 37–91; Othmar Keel and Erich Zenger, eds. *Gottesstadt und Gottesgarten: Zu Geschichte und Theologie des Jerusalemer Tempels*, Quaestiones Desputatae, ed. Peter Hünermann and Thomas Söding 191 (Freiburg im Breisgau: Herder, 2000), 9–68, 207–58; Walter Brueggemann, *Theology of the Old Testament: Testimony, Dispute, Advocacy* (Minneapolis, Fortress, 1997), 567–704; and Ingeborg Gabriel, *Friede über Israel: Eine Untersuchung zur Friedenstheologie in Chronik 1 10–2 36*, ÖBS 10 (Klosterneuburg: Österreichisches Katholisches Bibelwerk, 1990).

2. McKenzie notes that in Chronicles retribution is often immediate and usually resulted in military defeat. See Steven L. McKenzie, *1–2 Chronicles*, AOTC (Nashville, Tenn.: Abingdon, 2004), 120.

3. See Rudolf Mosis, *Untersuchungen zur Theologie des chronistischen Geschichtswerkes*, FTS 92 (Freiburg: Herder, 1973), 51–52. McKenzie makes a valid observation in that the military leaders (12:23–37) included all tribes and there is a particular emphasis on the northern tribes. He further states, "Thus, the three main ideological themes of 1 Chronicles—David, the temple, and all Israel—come together in a unique and forceful way in chapters 11–12. The tribes are united and enthusiastic in their support of David and in their conquest of Jerusalem. As just mentioned, the Chronicler's usual emphasis on ritual worship is lacking because Jerusalem has not yet become a sanctuary. But the Chronicler is obviously laying the groundwork for that eventuality, and the Levites are included among the tribes that endorse David" (McKenzie, *1 and 2 Chronicles*, 130).

4. McKenzie's statement regarding the theology of the ark narrative is quite in line with this writer's purposes. He states, "Because so much of 1 Chr 13–16 consists of lists, and what is not list seems simply taken from Samuel, it is easy to overlook the extraordinary theological richness of this section (13:1–16:43). To begin with, this section stresses the importance of proper worship and ritual activity" (Ibid., 150–51).

5. It should be noted that very little attention is given to individual worship in Chronicles. Here the Chronicler illustrates public worship. Thus, the focus of worship in this work will remain

on worship in community. This is not intended to indicate a lack of need for private worship only that the Chronicler's main concern is the public nature of worship.

6. John W. Kleinig, *The LORD's Song: The Basis, Function and Significance of Choral Music in Chronicles*, JSOTSup 156 (Sheffield: JSOT Press, 1993), 145–48; H. H. Rowley, *Worship in Israel: Its Forms and Meaning* (Philadelphia: Fortress, 1978), 246–47.

7. Gary N. Knoppers, *1 Chronicles, 10–29: A New Translation with Introduction and Commentary*, AB 12A (New York: Doubleday, 2004), 659.

8. McKenzie, *1 and 2 Chronicles*, 158–60.

9. Knoppers, *1 Chronicles 10–29*, 687–88.

10. McKenzie also makes this connection. He states, "For the Chronicler, it is not the temple as a building that is important but the temple as a conduit to God" (McKenzie, *1 and 2 Chronicles*, 177).

11. Ibid. Others such as Selman seem to argue that Yahweh stopped out of obligation to his covenant that he made with David (Martin J. Selman, *1 Chronicles: An Introduction and Commentary*, TOTC 10a [Downers Grove, Ill.: Inter-Varsity, 1994], 46). The text does indicate that Yahweh stopped because of his covenant obligation. The plague was after all among the people. Furthermore, there are instances where divine intervention occurs because of the covenant (e.g., 2 Chr 21:7).

12. This ends the first part of the Davidic narrative. The various themes that have been touched on seem to suggest an overarching structure. (1) Under Saul, the nation was in geopolitical and religious turmoil (chap. 10). (2) David is Yahweh's chosen king who captures Yahweh's chosen city and stabilizes the geopolitical situation (chaps. 11–12). (3) David turns his attention to the cult (chaps. 13–14). (4) David achieves some religious stabilization by bringing the ark to Jerusalem and instituting the cult in Jerusalem and Gibeon (chaps. 15–16). (5) David wishes to finalize this stabilization by building a temple (17). (6) David experiences blessing for following Yahweh's commands through military victory. (7) Yahweh reveals the future site of the temple to David (chaps. 21–22:1).

13. McKenzie, *1 and 2 Chronicles*, 178.

14. Ibid., 193. See also Thomas Willi, "Leviten, Priester, und Kult in vorhellenistischer Zeit: Die chronistische Optik in ihrem geschichtlichen Kontext," in *Gemeinde ohne Temple: Zur Substituierung und Transformation des Jerusalemer Tempels und seines Kults im Alten Testament, antiken Judentums und frühen Christentum*, ed. Armin Lange Beate Ego and Peter Pilhofer, WUNT 118 (Tübingen: Mohr, 1999), 75–96.

15. So Kleinig, *The LORD's Song*, 190–91. See also Roddy Braun, *1 Chronicles*, WBC 14 (Waco, Tex.: Word, 1986), 245.

16. Knoppers, *1 Chronicles 10–29*, 873.

17. McKenzie makes an interesting connection with the exodus tradition here. Israel is presented as a kingdom of priests in their willingness to help with the building of the temple. See McKenzie, *1 and 2 Chronicles*, 223. The exile serves as a good illustration to show that he is more inclined to bless those who love him and seek his will than those who are indifferent toward him. Willingness seems to be the key in the Chronicler's presentation of cultic matters. McKenzie's statement not only speaks to the Chronicler's readers but also to any reader of the book. He states, "The goal of human beings before God, as David articulates it, is the knowledge of God. Such knowledge is not merely intellectual assent or memorization but personal acquaintance fostered by prayer and contemplation of the divine law and will" (Ibid., 224).

18. Ibid.

19. Jürgen Kegler, "Das Zurücktreten der Exodustradition in den Chronibüchern," in *Schöpfung und Befreiung: Für Claus Westermann zum 80. Geburtstag*, ed. Rainer Albertz, Friedemann W. Golka, and Jürgen Kegler (Stuttgart: Calwer, 1989), 54–66.

20. See John C. Endres, "Joyful Worship in Second Temple Judaism," in *Passion, Vitality, and Foment: The Dynamics of Second Temple Judaism*, ed. Lamontte M. Luker (Harrisburg, Pa.: Trinity, 2001), 155–88; John C. Endres, "Theology of Worship in Chronicles," in *The Chronicler as Theologian: Essays in Honor of Ralph W. Klein*, ed. M. Patrick Graham, Steven L. McKenzie, and Gary Knoppers, JSOTSup 371 (New York: T & T Clark, 2003), 165–88.

21. McKenzie, *1 and 2 Chronicles*, 60.

22. While Dan and Zebulun are not given their own representative genealogies, they are mentioned in the list of the sons of Israel (2:1–2).

23. Gary N. Knoppers, *1 Chronicles, 1–9: A New Translation with Introduction and Commentary*, AB 12 (New York: Doubleday, 2003), 261.

24. The list of themes that may be found explicitly in the ark narrative include: (1) all Israel (13:2, 15:3); (2) royal and Levitical families (14:4–7; 15:4–24); (3) royal observance of worship (16:7); (4) religious gatherings (13:2, 15:3); (5) divine kingship (16:14, 31); (6) music (15:16–24; 16:8–36); (7) divine activity (13:10; 15:26); (8) name of God (13:6; 16:2, 8, 10, 29, 35); (9) presence and help (the ark is the very symbol of Yahweh's presence, 15:26 specially states he helped the Levites); (10) covenant (16:15–16); (11) standards (15:15; 16:40); (12) motivations (David longs to seek after Yahweh 13:3); (13) Prayer (14:10); (14) seeking (13:3; 15:13); (15) victory/defeat (14:8–17); (16) building/destruction (14:1; 15:1); (17) increase/decline of offspring (14:3–7); (18) prosperity/poverty (13:14; 14; 16:2–3); (19) celebration/disappointment (both occur, disappointment 13:11–13, and celebration 15:26–16:36); (20) Israel's relations with other nations (14:17). The remaining themes of (21) northern Israel; (22) temple contributions; (23) prophets; (24) humility; (25) abandoning/forsaking; (26) unfaithfulness; (27) repentance; (28) healing and life/ sickness and death are not clearly present. (All themes are taken from Richard L. Pratt, *1 and 2 Chronicles* [Fearn: Mentor, 1998], 14–55.) However, northern Israel is certainly included in "all Israel" and is a sub-theme that should be included within "all Israel." The temple is yet to be built in the narrative; hence, such a theme would be out of place. The theme of "prophets" is in 1 Chr 17, which some (e.g., Japhet) have included in the same literary unit as the ark narrative. Humility is seen in the ark narrative because the narrative makes clear that David is submissive to Yahweh's will. He is a good vice-regent serving the great king. The theme of abandoning and forsaking is also implied in 13:3 in the statement that Saul did not seek the ark, meaning that he forsook his responsibilities toward the sacred object and hence Yahweh himself. The antithesis of the theme unfaithfulness is clearly implied in the ark narrative. David is faithful to Yahweh and as a result he is blessed by Yahweh (1 Chr 14). The two remaining themes, however, seem to be outside of the ark narrative and are primarily reserved for the narratives of the kings (2 Chr 10–36).

25. See Brian E. Kelly, *Retribution and Eschatology in Chronicles*, JSOTSup 211 (Sheffield: Sheffield Academic Press, 1996), especially 148–85.

26. McKenzie, *1 and 2 Chronicles*, 47.

27. Eskenazi also notes this observation but does not pursue it. Tamara C. Eskenazi, "A Literary Approach to the Chronicler's Ark Narrative in 1 Chronicles 13–16," in *Fortunate the Eyes That See: Essays in Honor of David Noel Freedman in Celebration of His Seventieth Birthday* (Grand Rapids: Eerdmans, 1995), 270–71.

28. Kleinig argues that one of the ways that the cult was able to accomplish bringing Yahweh to remembrance of the people and to invoke Yahweh's presence was through the use of song in the temple (Kleinig, *The LORD's Song*, 190).

29. For example, Norbert Dennerlein, *Die Bedeutung Jerusalems in den Chronikbüchern*, BEATAJ 46 (Frankfurt am Main: Lang, 1999), 44; Mosis, *Untersuchungen*, 54; and Peter Welten, "Lade-Temple-Jerusalem: Zur Theologie der Chronikbücher," in *Textgemäss. Aufätze und Beiträge zur Hermeneutik des Alten Testaments: Festschrift Ernst Würthwein zum 70. Geburtstag*, ed. A. H. J. Gunneweg and Otto Kaiser (Göttingen: Vandenhoeck & Ruprecht, 1979), 183.

30. Begg has a helpful general discussion on the ark. See Christopher T. Begg, "The Ark in Chronicles," in *The Chronicler as Theologian: Essays in Honor of Ralph W. Klein*, ed. M. Patrick Graham, Steven L. McKenzie, and Gary Knoppers, JSOTSup 371 (New York: T & T Clark, 2003), 133–45. He notes that Jer 3:16 indicates that the ark will no longer hold a major role in Israelite worship. One should also note that Jer 3:17 indicates that Yahweh's presence is still in Jerusalem.

31. The story of the ark in 1 Samuel may also suggest this because Yahweh's presence is with the ark. The movement of the ark suggests that Yahweh is no longer resting above the ark but also actively on the move and will protect the people. Thus, the reason for the Philistines' fear (1 Sam 4:7–8).

32. The lack of a preposition seems to leave the phrase a little ambiguous as to where the cherubim formed a throne for Yahweh. See Tryggve N. D. Mettinger, *The Dethronement of Sebaoth: Studies in the Shem and Kabod Theologies*, ConBOT, vol. 18 (Lund: Gleerup, 1982), 21–22.

33. One could argue that these references refer to the temple, not the ark; however, the ark would still be viewed as the primary place for Yahweh's presence; hence, it would be the place of his feet. Thus Yahweh dwells in heaven but places his feet elsewhere (Isa 66:1; Lam 2:1). Further complicating matters, Ezek 43:7 states that the temple is both Yahweh's throne and the place of his feet. It is possible and even likely that the idea of footstool is tied to the covering of the ark (ibid., 87–88). Thus, the picture would be one of Yahweh sitting enthroned above the ark with his feet on the covering. This aspect also seems to satisfy the issues involved with the idea that atonement was made by sprinkling the blood on the covering of the ark (Lev 16:13–16 and note also Exod 25:21–22).

34. He argues that Deut 1:30, 33; 2:7; 4:7, 37; 7:21; 9:3; 20:4; 23:14; 31:3, 6, and 8 indicate that presence does not have to be associated with a cultic sanctuary (See Terence E. Fretheim, "The Ark in Deuteronomy," *CBQ* 30 [1968]: 7).

35. The temple also is of course a place where Yahweh's presence dwells. However, it seems clear that prior to the temple Yahweh's presence is associated with the ark. Thus, when the ark moves to Jerusalem so does the presence of Yahweh for the Chronicler. Later, when the ark is placed in the temple, one finds Yahweh's presence there as well (2 Chr 5:13–14).

36. Begg, "The Ark in Chronicles," 134–35.

37. Ibid., 138.

38. One is reminded of Haggai 1:4, where Yahweh declares to the people that they are dwelling in paneled houses but the temple is still in ruins. He then directs them to rebuild it. The connection would most likely be made by the original audience as well. The implication is that David had great concern for the things of Yahweh and although the Second Temple was completed, the people too needed to think of the things of Yahweh first in order to receive the full benefits of his presence (Hag 1:13). Furthermore, Haggai and Zechariah both indicate that the people's failure to put the things of Yahweh first resulted in drought, plagues, famine, and political instability (Hag 1:5, 9–11; 2:15–19; Zech 8:9–10).

39. Begg, "The Ark in Chronicles," 139. On the comparison between the Kings and Chronicles accounts see Dennerlein, *Die Bedeutung Jerusalems*, 180–95.
40. Mosis rightly indicates that Saul's treatment of the ark is a foreshadowing of the exile (see Mosis, *Untersuchungen*, 17–43). However, one should not press this foreshadowing into the Josiah narrative as some have tried to do (see Begg, "The Ark in Chronicles,"142).
41. Several scholars argue that the ark is dispensable and that after it legitimated the temple there was no need for its presence (so Dennerlein, *Die Bedeutung Jerusalems*, 42–45; Mosis, *Untersuchungen*, 50–54; and Welten, "Lade-Temple-Jerusalem," 182–83). Von Rad argues similarly, but that the ark legitimated the Levites not the temple (Gerhard von Rad, *Das Geschichtsbild des chronistischen Werkes*, BWA(N)T 54 [Stuttgart: Kohlhammer, 1930], 100–1).
42. Begg, "The Ark in Chronicles," 143–45.
43. This is against the view of most scholars, including Begg, who argues that "he [the Chronicler] would have found in that tradition (2 Macc 1:10–2:18) a basis for denying full legitimacy to the current temple, as well as for the hope that that temple could someday come into possession of the missing ark, which would confer on the temple a status equal to that of its predecessor" (Begg, "The Ark in Chronicles," 145). Braun, on the other hand, argues that the Chronicler has purposely structured his narrative as a polemic for rebuilding the temple (see Roddy L. Braun, "The Message of Chronicles: Rally Round the Temple," *CTM* 42 [1971]: 502–14).
44. Note the movement of the concept of presence from the ark to Jerusalem in the exilic and postexilic period. In Jer 3:16-17, the ark is no longer the center of cultic attention, but Yahweh still dwells in Jerusalem. This becomes more developed in Zechariah 8, where it is not the ark or the temple that Yahweh will return to but Jerusalem (e.g., 8:3). Joel also indicates that the presence of Yahweh will be in Jerusalem and will result in the nation's having abundant produce (Joel 3:16–18).
45. On the city of Jerusalem there are several helpful discussions. For example, Leslie J. Hoppe, *The Holy City: Jerusalem in the Theology of the Old Testament* (Collegeville, Minn.: Liturgical Press, 2000); Isaac Kalimi, "Jerusalem—Divine City: The Representation of Jerusalem in Chronicles Compared with Earlier and Later Jewish Compositions," in *The Chronicler as Theologian: Essays in Honor of Ralph W. Klein*, ed. M. Patrick Graham, Steven L. McKenzie, and Gary N. Knoppers, JSOTSup 371 (New York: T & T Clark, 2003), 189–205; and M. Poorthuis and Ch. Safrai, eds. *The Centrality of Jerusalem* (Kampen: Pharos, 1996).
46. Kalimi, "Jerusalem,"191.
47. Ibid., 198; also see Tae-Soo Im, *Das Davidbild in den Chronikbüchern: David als Idealbild des theokratischen Messianismus für den Chronisten*, EH 263, Theology Series 23 (Frankfurt am Main: Lang, 1985), 178.
48. Kalimi, "Jerusalem," 190–94; 201. It should be noted that Kalimi also sees other ties as well.
49. For example, Yahweh's direct intervention on behalf of individuals is clearly evident in the deliverance of Shadrach, Meshach, and Abednego from Nebuchadnezzar's furnace (Dan 3:8–30). Daniel is also delivered from the mouth of lions (Dan 6:14–28). The clearest example that Yahweh had not abandoned his people is rightly found by the Chronicler in the edict of Cyrus to allow the people to return and rebuild the temple (2 Chr 36:22–23).
50. Kalimi, "Jerusalem,"193.
51. Although the Chronicler does not address his usage here, it occurs only in Gen 22:2.
52. Horst Dietrich Preuss, *Old Testament Theology*, trans. Leo G. Perdue, vol. 2, OTL (Louisville: Westminster/Knox, 1996), 41.

53. The Chronicler uses several terms to refer to Jerusalem. For example, Jerusalem is called "the City of David," "the city of Judah," and "Zion." One should note, however, that the author of Samuel uses these terms to refer to specific areas within Jerusalem.

54. Preuss, *Old Testament Theology*, 43.

55. One should note that Ezek 1 suggests that Yahweh was also with the exiles in Babylonia. Nevertheless, Yahweh's presence with the exiles did not change the fact that the people of Israel continued to believe that Yahweh chose Jerusalem as the place where his name would dwell.

56. Hoppe, *The Holy City*, 120.

57. Selman notes Jerusalem was the royal city established by David and where the ark should be. See Selman, *1 Chronicles*, 48.

58. Dennerlein, *Die Bedeutung Jerusalems*, 249; also see Thomas Willi, *Juda-Jehud-Israel: Studien zum Selbstverständnis des Judentums in persischer Zeit*, FAT 12 (Tübingen: Mohr, 1995), especially 62–75.

59. Dennerlein, *Die Bedeutung Jerusalems*, 251–52.

60. Ibid., 256.

61. For example, the feasts are a consistent theme and play an important role because they occur in Jerusalem. See Simon J. De Vries, "Festival Ideology in Chronicles," in *Problems in Theology: Essays in Honor of Rolf Knierim*, ed. Henry T. C. Sun et al. (Grand Rapids: Eerdmans, 1996), 104–24. For other services excluding the feasts, see Endres, "Theology of Worship in Chronicles," 165–88.

62. Kleinig concludes that, "The Chronicler explains the ritual status, function and significance of sacred song as an important part of the total sacrificial ritual at the temple in Jerusalem. Thus, since the Chronicler holds that sacred song was instituted by the LORD himself to announce his presence with his faithful people and to proclaim his acceptance of his presence with his faithful people and to proclaim his acceptance of them" (Kleinig, *The LORD's Song*, 191). Leithart has recently argued that the Chronicler viewed worship as having redemptive value. However, this may be pressing the argument in Chronicles too far. See Peter J. Leithart, *From Silence to Song: The Davidic Liturgical Revolution* (Moscow, Idaho: Canon, 2003).

63. William M. Schniedewind, "The Evolution of Name Theology," in *The Chronicler as Theologian: Essays in Honor of Ralph W. Klein*, ed. M. Patrick Graham, Steven L. McKenzie, and Gary N. Knoppers, JSOTSup 371 (New York: T & T Clark, 2003), 236.

64. Ibid., 238. Throughout his article Schniedewind emphasizes that Yahweh dwells in heaven, it is his name that dwells in the temple; however, he also notes that "Chronicles apparently underscores the importance of the temple by re-emphasizing the physical presence of Yahweh in the face of the theology of the name, which implied that only God's name dwelt in the temple" (ibid.).

65. Th. C. Vriezen, *An Outline of Old Testament Theology*, 2d ed. (Newton, Mass.: Charles T. Branford, 1970), 238.

66. The reason for the exclusion of festival worship is such festivals would have a large degree of ritual that was focused on the specific festival. Public worship may have fixed forms; however, such worship may also have a degree of openness about it. Hence, it seems logical that in investigating worship it is best to look at worship under normal circumstances, not in special services.

67. One may argue that this too is a festival event within Israel. However, in the initial setting being described by the Chronicler, there is no reason to suspect the Chronicler as trying to

depict an annual festival here. This becomes all the more clear because without an ark in the Second Temple, there would be no such festival.

68. Endres, "Joyful Worship," 166–69.
69. It is important to note that the priestly blowing of the trumpets is often used for joyous worship and also for sounding an alarm to bring the people into remembrance of Yahweh which will allow God to fight on their behalf (Num 10:9-10). The trumpets are apparently an important aspect of remembrance (1 Chr 16:6, 42; 2 Chr 5:12–13; 15:8–15; and 29:27).
70. Ibid., 169.
71. On this see R. Mark Shipp, "'Remember His Covenant Forever:' A Study of the Chronicler's Use of the Psalms," *ResQ* 35 (1993): 30–32.
72. Regading corporate worship see Endres, "Theology of Worship," 172–86. Regarding the festivals see De Vries, "Festival Ideology,"104–24.
73. It should be noted that the following discussion will incorporate both aspects of worship, corporate and festival. For this purpose little distinction will be made as the setting does not change the various points of emphasis made by the Chronicler. Hence, this aspect of worship transcends all types of cultic meetings.
74. Endres, "Theology of Worship," 186–87.
75. The term itself is absent in the text; however, it would be an expected outgrowth based on the previous failed attempt to move the ark. On fear, see Preuss, *Old Testament Theology*, 155–59.
76. Rowley picks up on this issue as well in the final chapter of his work (see Rowley, *Worship in Israel*, 246–72).
77. It should be noted that this exemption from purification is not among those who are ministering during the sacrifices (v. 17), it is only among the people.
78. Also see Kleinig, *The LORD's Song*, 186.
79. Ibid., 187.
80. Edward Lewis Curtis and Albert Alonzo Madsen, *A Critical and Exegetical Commentary on the Books of Chronicles*, ICC (Edinburgh: T & T Clark, 1910), 221.
81. Riley makes a similar point regarding Hezekiah's reform of, "the cultic personnel [which] are organized at the king's behest according to the Davidic arrangements" (William Riley, *King and Cultus in Chronicles: Worship and the Reinterpretation of History*, JSOTSup 160 [Sheffield: JSOT Press, 1993], 132). One should also note that Solomon also organized the cult and is credited alone with David as a cult founder by the Chronicler (2 Chr 35:3-4).
82. Ibid., 201.
83. This becomes clear in the correspondence between the Jewish leaders at Elephantine and Jerusalem. The Jerusalem leaders allowed the reconstruction of the Elephantine Temple. However, they also made clear that no animal sacrifice was to take place on the altar, only cereal offerings, drink offerings, and incense (see A. E. Cowley, *Aramaic Papyri of the Fifth Century B.C.* [Oxford: Clarendon Press, 1923], §§33.10–11).
84. It is also possible to see another typical theological category of "the people of God" here as well. However, that category is closely connected to the kingdom and since the kingdom is clearly dominate the people will be addressed within that section.

CHAPTER SIX

Conclusion

Summary of Findings

Chapter one indicated the ark narrative played an important role in the way the Chronicler structured his work. It also indicated that the Chronicler is responsible for the ark narrative in its entirety. The implications for a single author's writing both the narrative and the various lists present within it is significant. The arrangement of the priests and Levites has a more central role within the work of the Chronicler than many scholars have previously thought. Worship, for the Chronicler is planned by David and carried out under the authority of the Levites and priests.

Chapter two developed through several lines of argument that it is possible for a single author to have written the material found in 1 Chr 15–16. Gese's analysis of the development of the musical singers is not the best way of looking at the text. The text itself suggests that a single hand was responsible for developing it. The literary structure of each unit was examined and evidence was found that supports the view that a single author with a clear purpose wrote the narrative. Further, the ark narrative (13–16) has tight literary connections to the narratives around it. These narratives were also briefly examined; the conclusion was that they too were from the same hand that wrote the ark narrative proper.

Chapter three served two purposes. First, the major literary hypotheses were reconsidered and it was shown that there were methodological problems within each one based on the literary analysis of chapter three. Further evidence was given from the genealogies and David's final organization of the cult to demonstrate that both of those major sections should be considered original to the Chronicler as well. Thus, all places where major objections to the possibility of single authorship are debated support the possibility that a single author hypothesis is reasonable for the entire work. Second, the ark narrative clearly functions with major themes that are found throughout the book. The purpose of the Chronicler's work was discussed and the findings there supported the general idea of continuity. Yet, that theme is far too broad; therefore, it became necessary to see one specific emphasis that carries that theme through. This emphasis is found in the role of David in three areas: (1) his dynasty, (2) his making Jerusalem his capital city, and (3) his instructions given for the institution and organization of the cult. This emphasis becomes quite apparent in the narratives of the kings and the parallels with ancient Near Eastern royal inscriptions. The ark narrative shows that David was a cult founder who had charged his successors to care for the cult.

Chapter four developed the exegetical analysis and revealed the Chronicler's purposes for this narrative. The Chronicler portrays David as a cultic authority on the same level as that of other ancient Near Eastern kings. He organizes the cultic officials so that the movement of the ark will be executed according to proper Mosaic procedures. The ultimate desire of the Chronicler is for the postexilic nation to take pains to protect proper worship. This worship takes place with the aid of the musicians and singers, who are to play and sing during the various sacrifices, as well as accompany the many other rituals of the cult. The actual movement of the ark into Jerusalem brings into focus the meaning of worship. Joy and praise are major parts of worship, but the Chronicler also emphasizes that proper procedure alone is not enough to please Yahweh. The cultic officials are then given their respective roles (16:4–6). It is necessary that these activities be outlined here because it assures the Levites a role in the temple that is both important and necessary. David appoints them, thus arguing for their proper legitimation. The Chronicler wrote the psalm to illustrate the type of worship that was proper in David's day and also in his own, and it reflects the same terms found in David's command to Asaph to sing (16:4). The inclusion of Gibeon suggests that it was the main cultic site at the time because the larger group of cultic officials were appointed there. These appointments to two functional cultic sites heighten his theme of continuity with the past. The Chronicler is leading his readers to the understanding that the Second Temple is to function in exactly the same manner as that of its predecessor.

Chapter five addressed the theology of the ark narrative and the manner in which the various themes are addressed throughout the work. Theologically speaking, the overwhelming picture that the ark narrative leaves with the reader is that Yahweh is a completely sovereign, holy, and just God. Yet he is also merciful and blesses those who are concerned about his will. David's care for the things of Yahweh will ultimately result in the Davidic covenant (chapter 17). The theology of the ark narrative comes directly out of its attention to proper worship. Thus, the roles of the priests and Levites are essential because they maintain the cultic objects and come into close contact with these sacred objects that have been set apart for the worship of Yahweh. But worship is not just silent, unemotional, and sacrificial. David also takes steps to bring the music and singing present in worship into the fore of the cultic activities. True worship is joyful and while some ritual elements are fixed and solemn, other elements are open and fluid and filled with praise and thanksgiving. The ark narrative also plays a major role in the centrality of Jerusalem. The choice of Jerusalem as the cultic center by Yahweh is now clear. Furthermore, Jerusalem is linked to the past (Gen 22) and is now firmly established before the temple is built. Thus, Yahweh's presence is now tied to the city.

The Chronicler's readers would have seen the connection between Mosaic traditions and the Davidic institutions as a continuation of legitimate worship. It is this worship that the Chronicler is arguing for in his own day. Worship in the Second Temple is just as legitimate as the worship that took place in David's and Moses' day. The Chronicler is full of hope that just as Yahweh acted on behalf of the patriarchs, Moses, and David, he will one day act on behalf of those who maintain proper covenant relations with him. In the Chronicler's day maintaining a proper covenant relationship with Yahweh can only be achieved through the cult and the proper sacrificial worship in the temple.

Implications for Reading Chronicles

The ark narrative reveals that proper worship is at the heart of the Chronicler's purpose. This worship was instituted by David. The Chronicler came to the same history as that found in the books of Samuel and Kings. However, his selectivity and emphases are clearly different. These differences suggest that he wanted the nation of Israel to understand who they were as the people of God.

In order to accomplish this, the Chronicler has uniquely concentrated on the Davidic covenant throughout his work, yet he does not neglect the Mosaic covenant. The Chronicler desires his readers to understand that Israel's relationship with Yahweh is more important than their present political situation. Yahweh acts on behalf of the nation and on behalf of people who are in a covenant-centered relationship with him. The First Temple is gone; the Second Temple now stands, and there are some differences between the two. The Chronicler wants his readers to understand that worship is still legitimate there. The temple is the place Yahweh has chosen for Israel to worship him in contrast to any high place where pagan ritual takes place.

Most important, the Chronicler himself is responsible for including the lists that make up the temple personnel in his work. The main purpose now seems to be the dominating emphasis that the cultic personnel add to the work; namely, worship is to have both praise and sacrifice. The Levites' contribution to the worship system is a major emphasis through the Chronicler's work. The ordering of the Levites by David allows the Levites to enable the people to take part in the worship services. While ritual forms are fixed, the attitude of the worshiper is what is most important. The Levites are charged with the responsibility of leading the public in this attitude of worship. Thus, the Chronicler's hope for the nation is bound in worship.

Implications for Further Study

This work has argued that there is no need to see multiple redactors in the book of Chronicles. Only one author is responsible for the work. Following this conclusion, an exegetical and theological analysis of the ark narrative brought out the point that the Chronicler's primary interest is in proper worship for his own day. Although this work has examined the theme of worship as it developed from the ark narrative, it has not exhausted the subject. Also outside of the thesis, but certainly within the realm of the worship in the postexilic period, is how such worship developed in the synagogue and how it further changed as the political atmosphere of the postexilic period changed. Finally, an examination of how these changes play out in the Gospels may also lead to a more complete understanding of Jewish worship in the first century C.E.

Select Bibliography

I list here only works that have been frequently used or significant to the formation of my ideas in the making of this book. The bibliography is not a complete record of all the works and sources I have consulted. To further condense the size of the bibliography I have separated the books and commentaries from the various articles. In the event that more than one article from the same book is used, I list only the book itself. Additionally, all reference material that is found in the abbreviations in the front matter has also been excluded. Finally, all unpublished material is absent as well; however, the notes will guide the reader to significant sources of this material.

Books and Commentaries

Ackroyd, Peter R. *The Chronicler in His Age.* Journal for the Study of the Old Testament: Supplement Series 101. Sheffield: JSOT Press, 1991.

———. *1 and 2 Chronicles, Ezra, Nehemiah: Introduction and Commentary.* Torch Bible Commentaries. London: SCM, 1973.

———. *Exile and Restoration: A Study of Hebrew Thought of the Sixth Century B.C.* Old Testament Library. Philadelphia: Westminster, 1968.

———. *Studies in the Religious Tradition of the Old Testament.* London: SCM, 1987.

Ahlström, Gösta W. *Royal Administration and National Religion in Ancient Palestine.* Studies in the History of the Ancient Near East 1. Leiden: Brill, 1982.

Albertz, Rainer. *Die Exilszeit 6. Jahrhundet v. Chr.* Biblische Enzyklopädie 7. Berlin: Kohlhammer, 2001.

———. *Geschichte und Theologie: Studien zur Exegese des Alten Testaments und zur Religionsgeschichte Israels.* Edited by Ingo Kottsieper and Jakob Wöhrle. Beihefte zur Zeitschrift für die alttestamentliche Wissenschaft 326. New York: de Gruyter, 2003.

———. *A History of Religion in the Old Testament Period.* Vol. 2, *From the Exile to the Maccabees.* Translated by John Bowden. Old Testament Library. Louisville, Ky.: Westminster/Knox, 1994.

———. *Israel in the Exile: The History and Literature of the Sixth Century B.C.E.* Translated by David Green. Studies in Biblical Literature 3. Altanta: Society of Biblical Literature, 2003.

Albertz, Rainer and Bob Becking, eds. *Yahwism after the Exile: Perspectives on Israelite Religion in the Persian Era. Papers Read at the First Meeting of the European Association for Biblical Studies, Utrecht, 6–9 August, 2000.* Society of Biblical Literature 5. Assen, The Netherlands: Van Gorcum, 2003.

Allen, Leslie C. *1, 2 Chronicles.* Communicator's Commentary Series 10. Waco, Tex.: Word, 1987.

———. *The Greek Chronicles: The Relation of the Septuagint of 1 and 2 Chronicles to the Massoretic Text.* Vol. 2, *Textual Criticism.* Supplements to Vetus Testamentum 27. Leiden: Brill, 1974.

———. *Psalms 101–150.* Word Biblical Commentary 21. Waco, Tex.: Word, 1983.

Alter, Robert, and Frank Kermode, eds. *The Literary Guide to the Bible.* Cambridge: Belknap, 1987.

Andersen, A. A. *2 Samuel.* Word Biblical Commentary 11. Waco, Tex: Word, 1989.

Anderson, Gary A. *Sacrifices and Offerings in Ancient Israel: Studies in Their Social and Political Importance.* Harvard Semitic Monographs 41. Atlanta: Scholars Press, 1987.

————. *A Time to Mourn, a Time to Dance: The Expression of Grief and Joy in Israelite Religion.* University Park, Pa.: Pennsylvania State University Press, 1991.

Anderson, Gary A., and Saul M. Olyan, eds. *Priesthood and Cult in Ancient Israel.* Journal for the Study of the Old Testament: Supplement Series 125. Sheffield: JSOT Press, 1991.

Argall, Randal A. et al., eds. *For a Later Generation: The Transformation of Tradition in Israel, Early Judaism, and Early Christianity.* Harrisburg, Pa.: Trinity, 2000.

Auffret, Pierre. *Merveilles à nos yeux: Étude structurelle de vingt psaumes dont celui de 1Ch 16,8-36.* Beihefte zur Zeitschrift für die alttestamentliche Wissenschaft 235. Berlin: de Gruyter, 1995.

Auld, A. Graeme. *Kings without Privilege: David and Moses in the Story of the Bible's Kings.* Edinburgh: T&T Clark, 1994.

Barthélemy, Dominique. *Les devanciers d'Aquila: Première publication intégrale du texte des fragments du dodécaprophéton: Trouvés dans le désert de Juda, précédée d'une étude sur les traductions et recensions grecques de la bible réalisées au premier siècle de notre ère sous l'influence du rabbinat Palestinien.* Vetus Testamentum Supplements 10. Leiden: Brill, 1963.

Beck, Astrid B. et al., eds. *Fortunate the Eyes That See: Essays in Honor of David Noel Freedman in Celebration of His Seventhieth Birthday.* Grand Rapids: Eerdmans, 1995.

Becker, Joachim. *1 Chronik.* Neue Echter Bible Altes Testament. Würzburg: Echter, 1986.

Becking, Bob, and Marjo C. A. Korpel, eds. *The Crisis of Israelite Religion: Transformation of Religious Tradition in Exilic and Post-Exilic Times.* Oudtestamentische Studiën 42. Leiden: Brill, 1999.

Benzinger, Immanuel. *Die Bücher der Chronik.* Tübingen: Mohr, 1901. Microfiche.

Berquist, Jon L. *Judaism in Persia's Shadow: A Social and Historical Approach.* Minneapolis: Fortress, 1995.

Biran, Avraham, ed. *Temple and High Places in Biblical Times.* Proceedings of the Colloquium in Honor of the Centennial of Hebrew Union College–Jewish Institute of Religion. Jerusalem: Glueck, 1981.

Blenkinsopp, Joseph. *Ezra–Nehemiah: A Commentary.* Old Testament Library. Philadelphia: Westminster, 1988.

Blenkinsopp, Joseph. *Gibeon and Israel: The Role of Gibeon and the Gibeonites in the Political and Religious History of Early Israel.* Society for Old Testament Study Monograph Series 2. Cambridge: Cambridge University Press, 1972.

Braun, Joachim. *Music in Ancient Israel/Palestine: Archaeological, Written, and Comparative Sources.* Translated by Douglas W. Stott. The Bible in Its World. Grand Rapids: Eerdmans, 2002.

Braun, Roddy. *1 Chronicles.* Word Biblical Commentary 14. Waco, Tex.: Word, 1986.

————. *Understanding the Basic Themes of 1,2 Chronicles.* Dallas, Tex.: Word, 1991.

Briant, Pierre. *From Cyrus to Alexander: A History of the Persian Empire.* Translated by Peter T. Daniels. Winona Lake, Ind.: Eisenbrauns, 2002.

Brock, Sebastian P. *The Recensions of the Septuagint Version of 1Samuel.* Quaderni di Henoch 9. Torino: Zamorani, 1996.

Brosius, Maria, and Amélie Kuhrt, eds. *Studies in Persian History: Essays in Memory of David M. Lewis.* Achaemenid History 11. Leiden: Nederlands Instituut voor het Nabije Oosten, 1998.

Brueggemann, Walter. *David's Truth in Israel's Imagination and Memory.* 2d ed. Philadelphia: Fortress, 2002.

————. *Theology of the Old Testament: Testimony, Dispute, Advocacy.* Minneapolis, Fortress, 1997.

Bückers, Hermann. *Die Bücher der Chronik.* Freiburg: Herder, 1952.

Campbell, Antony F. *The Ark Narrative (1 Sam 4–6; 2 Sam 6): A Form-Critical and Traditio-Historical Study.* Missoula, Mont.: Scholars Press, 1975.

Carter, Charles E. *The Emergence of Yehud in the Persian Period: A Social and Demographic Study.* Journal for the Study of the Old Testament: Supplement Series 294. Sheffield: Sheffield Academic Press, 1999.

Clements, Ronald E. *God and Temple.* Philadelphia: Fortress, 1965.

Cody, Aelred. *A History of the Old Testament Priesthood.* Analecta biblica 35. Rome: Pontifical Biblical Institute, 1965.

Cogan, Mordecai and Israel Eph'al, eds. *Ah, Assyria: Studies in Assyrian History and Ancient Near Eastern Historiography Presented to Hayim Tadmor.* Scripta hierosolymitana 33. Jerusalem: Magnes, 1991.

Coggins, R. J. *The First and Second Books of the Chronicles.* Cambridge Bible Commentary. Cambridge: Cambridge University Press, 1976.

Cohen, Shaye J. D. *The Beginnings of Jewishness: Boundaries, Varieties, Uncertainties.* Berkeley: University of California Press, 1999.

Craigie, Peter C. *Psalms 1–50.* Word Biblical Commentary 19. Waco, Tex.: Word, 1983.

Cross, Frank Moore. *From Epic to Canon: History and Literature in Ancient Israel.* Baltimore: Johns Hopkins, 1998.

Curtis, Edward Lewis, and Albert Alonzo Madsen. *A Critical and Exegetical Commentary on the Books of Chronicles.* International Critical Commentary. Edinburgh: T & T Clark, 1910.

Dahm, Ulrike. *Opferkult und Priestertum in Alt-Israel: Ein Kultur-und religionswissenschaft-licher Beitrag.* Beihefte zur Zeitschrift für die alttestamentliche Wissenschaft 327. Berlin: de Gruyter, 2003.

Davies, Philip R., ed. *Second Temple Studies,* vol. 1, *The Persian Period.* Journal for the Study of the Old Testament: Supplement Series 117. Sheffield: JSOT Press, 1991.

Davies, Philip R., and John M. Halligan, eds. *Second Temple Studies,* vol. 3, *Studies in Politics, Class and Material Culture.* Journal for the Study of the Old Testament: Supplement Series 340. Sheffield: Sheffield Academic Press, 2002.

Day, John, ed. *King and Messiah in Israel and the Ancient Near East: Proceedings of the Oxford Old Testament Seminar.* Journal for the Study of the Old Testament: Supplement Series 270. Sheffield: Sheffield Academic Press, 1998.

Desrousseaux, Louis and Jacques Vermeylen, eds. *Figures de David à travers la Bible: XVIIe Congrès de l'ACFEB.* Lectio divina 177. Paris: Cerf, 1999.

De Vries, Simon J. *1 and 2 Chronicles.* Forms of the Old Testament Literature 11. Grand Rapids: Eerdmans, 1989.

Dearman, John Andrew, and Matt Patrick Graham, eds. *The Land That I Will Show You: Essays on the History and Archaeology of the Ancient Near East in Honor of J. Maxwell Miller.* Journal for the Study of the Old Testament: Supplement Series 343. Sheffield: Sheffield Academic Press, 2001.

Dennerlein, Norbert. *Die Bedeutung Jerusalems in den Chronikbüchern.* Beiträge zur Er-forschung des Alten Testaments und des antiken Judentums 46. Frankfurt am Main: Lang, 1999.

Dietrich, Walter. *David, Saul, und die Propheten: Das Verhältnis von Religion und Politik nach den prophetischen Überlieferungen vom frühesten Königtum in Israel.* 2d ed. Beiträge zur Wissenschaft vom Alten und Neuen Testament 122. Stuttgart: Kohlhammer, 1992.

Dietrich, Walter, and Thomas Nauman. *Die Samuelbücher.* Erträge der Forschung 287. Darmstadt: Buchgesellschaft, 1995.

Dillard, Raymond B. *2 Chronicles.* Word Biblical Commentary 15. Waco, Tex.: Word, 1987.

Dörrfuß, Ernst Michael. *Mose in den Chronikbüchern: Garant theokratischer Zukunftser-wartung.* Beihefte zur Zeitschrift für die alttestamentliche Wissenschaft 219. Berlin: de Gruyter, 1994.

Dorsey, David A. *The Literary Structure of the Old Testament: A Commentary on Genesis–Malachi.* Grand Rapids: Baker, 1999.

Duke, Rodney K. *The Persuasive Appeal of the Chronicler: A Rhetorical Analysis.* Journal for the Study of the Old Testament: Supplement Series 88. Sheffield: Almond Press, 1990.

Dyck, Jonathan E. *The Theocratic Ideology of the Chronicler.* Biblical Interpretation Series, ed. R. Alan Culpepper and Rolf Rendtorff, vol. 33. Leiden: Brill, 1998.

Edelman, Diane Vikander, ed. *The Triumph of Elohim: From Yahwisms to Judaisms.* Grand Rapids: Eerdmans, 1995.

Ego, Beate, Armin Lange, and Peter Pilhofer, eds. *Gemeinde ohne Tempel: Zur Substituierung und Transformation des Jerusalemer Tempels und seines Kults im Alten Testament, antiken Judentums und frühen Christentum.* Wissenschaftliche Untersuchungen zum Neuen Testament 118. Tübingen: Mohr—Siebeck, 1999.

Eissfeldt, Otto. *The Old Testament: An Introduction Including the Apocrypha and Pseudepigrapha, and Also the Works of Similar Type from Qumran.* Translated by Peter R. Ackroyd. New York: Harper and Row, 1965.

Endres, John C. et al., eds. *Chronicles and Its Synoptic Parallels in Samuel, Kings, and Related Biblical Texts.* Collegeville, Minn.: Liturgical Press, 1998.

Engnell, Ivan. *Studies in Divine Kingship in the Ancient Near East: Inaugural Dissertation.* Uppsala: Boktryckeri, 1943.

Eskenazi, Tamara C., and Kent H. Richards, eds. *Second Temple Studies,* vol. 2, *Temple and Community in the Persian Period.* Journal for the Study of the Old Testament: Supplement Series 175. Sheffield: JSOT Press, 1994.

Fishbane, Michael A. *Biblical Interpretation in Ancient Israel.* Oxford: Clarendon, 1985.

Fox, Michael V. et al., eds. *Texts, Temples, and Traditions: A Tribute to Menahem Haran.* Winona Lake, Ind.: Eisenbrauns, 1996.

Frankfort, Henri. *Kingship and the Gods: A Study of Ancient Near Eastern Kingship as the Integration of Society and Nature.* Chicago: University of Chicago Press, 1948.

Fried, Lisbeth S. *The Priest and the Great King: Temple-Palace Relations in the Persian Empire.* Biblical and Judaic Studies from the University of California, San Diego 10. Winona Lake, Ind.: Eisenbrauns, 2004.

Fries, Joachim. *'Im Dienst am Hause des Herrn:' Literaturwissenschaftliche Untersuchungen zu 2 Chr 29–31: Zur Hiskijatradition in Chronik.* Arbeiten zu Text und Sprache im Alten Testament. St. Ottilien: EOS, 1998.

Gabriel, Ingeborg. *Friede über Israel: Eine Untersuchung zur Friedenstheologie in Chronik 1 10–2 36.* Österreichische Biblische Studien 10. Klosterneuburg: Österreichisches Katholisches Bibelwerk, 1990.

Galling, Kurt. *Die Bücher der Chronik, Esra, Nehemia.* Das Alte Testament Deutsch 12. Berlin: Evangelische, 1958.

Garbini, Giovanni. *History and Ideology in Ancient Israel.* Translated by John Bowden. London: SCM, 1988.

Goettsberger, Johann. *Die Bücher der Chronik oder Paralipomenon.* Die Heilige Schrift Des Alten Testaments 4. Bonn: Hanstein, 1939.

Görg, Manfred. *Das Zelt der Begegnung: Untersuchung zur Gestalt der sakralen Zelttraditionen Altisraels.* Bonner biblische Beiträge 27. Bonn: Hanstein, 1967.

Grabbe, Lester, L. *A History of the Jews and Judaism in the Second Temple Period.* Vol. 1, *Yehud: A History of the Persian Province of Judah.* Library of Second Temple Studies 47. Sheffield: T & T Clark, 2004.

———. *Judaism from Cyrus to Hadrian.* Vol. 1, *The Persian and Greek Periods.* Minneapolis: Fortress, 1992.

————. *Priests, Prophets, Diviners, Sages: A Socio-Historical Study of Religious Specialists in Ancient Israel.* Philadelphia: Trinity, 1995.

Graf, Karl Heinrich. *Die geschichtlichen Bücher des Alten Testaments.* Leipzig: Weigel,1866. Microfiche.

Graham, Matt Patrick. *The Utilization of 1 and 2 Chronicles in the Reconstruction of Israelite History in the Nineteeth Century.* Society of Biblical Literature Dissertation Series 116. Atlanta: Scholars Press, 1990.

Graham, Matt Patrick, Kenneth G. Hoglund, and Steven L. McKenzie, eds. *The Chronicler as Historian.* Journal for the Study of the Old Testament: Supplement Series 238. Sheffield: Sheffield Academic Press, 1997.

Graham, Matt Patrick, and Steven L. McKenzie, eds. *The Chronicler as Author: Studies in Text and Texture.* Journal for the Study of the Old Testament: Supplement Series 263. Sheffield: Sheffield Academic Press, 1999.

Graham, M. Patrick, Steven L. McKenzie, and Gary N. Knoppers, eds. *The Chronicler as Theologian: Essays in Honor of Ralph W. Klein.* Journal for the Study of the Old Testament: Supplements Series 371. New York: T & T Clark, 2003.

Gunkel, Hermann. *Die Psalmen.* 4th ed. Göttinger Handkommentar zum Alten Testament 2. Göttingen: Vandenhoeck & Ruprecht, 1926.

Gunneweg, Antonius H. J. *Leviten und Priester: Hauptlinien der Tradionsbildung und Geschichte des israelisch-jüdischen Kultpersonals.* Forschungen zur Religion und Literatur des Alten und Neuen Testaments 89. Göttingen: Vandenhoeck & Ruprecht, 1965.

Hanson, Paul D. *The Dawn of Apocalyptic: The Historical and Social Roots of Jewish Apocalytic Eschatology.* Philadelphia: Fortress, 1975.

Haran, Menahem. *Temples and Temple-Service in Ancient Israel: An Inquiry into the Character of Cult Phenomena and the Historical Setting of the Priestly School.* Oxford: Clarendon, 1978.

Harrison, R. K. *Introduction to the Old Testament.* Grand Rapids: Eerdmans, 1969.

Hausmann, Jutta. *Israels Rest: Studien zum Selbstverständnis der nachexilschen.* Beiträge zur Wissenschaft vom Alten und Neuen Testament 124. Stuttgart: Kohlhammer, 1987.

Hayward, C. T. R., ed. *The Jewish Temple: A Non-Biblical Sourcebook.* New York: Routledge, 1996.

Hess, Richard S., and Gordon J. Wenham, eds. *Zion, City of Our God.* Grand Rapids: Eerdmans, 1999.

Hjelm, Ingrid. *Jerusalem's Rise to Sovereignty: Zion and Gerizim in Competition.* Journal for the Study of the Old Testament: Supplement Series 404. London: T & T Clark, 2004.

Hoppe, Leslie J. *The Holy City: Jerusalem in the Theology of the Old Testament.* Collegeville, Minn.: Liturgical Press, 2000.

House, Paul R. *Old Testament Theology.* Downers Grove, Ill.: InterVarsity, 1998.

Hughes-Games, A. *The First and Second Books of Chronicles.* N.p.: Dent, 1902. Microfiche.

Hurowitz, Victor A. *I Have Built You an Exalted House: Temple Building in the Bible in Light of Mesopotamian and Northwest Semitic Writings.* Journal for the Study of the Old Testament: Supplement Series 115. Sheffield: Sheffield Academic Press, 1992.

Hutter, Manfred. *Hiskija, König von Juda: Ein Beitrag zur judäischen Geschichte in assyrischer Zeit.* Grazer theologische Studien 6. Graz: Universität Graz, 1982.

Im, Tae-Soo. *Das Davidbild in den Chronikbüchern: David als Idealbild des theokratischen Messianismus für den Chronisten.* Europäische Hochschulschriften 263. Theology Series 23. Frankfurt am Main: Lang, 1985.

Ishida, Tomoo. *History and Historical Writing in Ancient Israel: Studies in Biblical Historiography.* Studies in the History and Culture of the Ancient Near East. Leiden: Brill, 1999.

————. *The Royal Dynasties in Ancient Israel: A Study on the Formation and Development of Royal-Dynastic Ideology.* Beihefte zur Zeitschrift für die alttestamentliche Wissenschaft 142. Berlin: de Gruyter, 1977.

Janzen, David. *The Social Meanings of Sacrifice in the Hebrew Bible: A Study of Four Writings.* Beihefte zur Zeitschrift für die alttestamentliche Wissenschaft 344. Berlin: de Gruyter, 2004.

Japhet, Sara. *1 and 2 Chronicles: A Commentary.* Old Testament Library. London: SCM, 1993.

————. *1 Chronik.* Herders Theologischer Kommentar zum Alten Testament. Freiburg: Herder, 2002.

————. *The Ideology of the Book of Chronicles and Its Place in Biblical Thought.* Translated by Anna Barber. 2d ed. Beiträge zur Erforschung des Alten Testaments und des antiken Judentums 9. Frankfurt am Main: Lang, 1997.

Johnson, Aubrey R. *Sacral Kingship in Ancient Israel.* 2d ed. Cardiff: University of Wales Press, 1967.

Johnson, Marshall D. *The Purpose of the Biblical Genealogies: With Special Reference to the Setting of the Genealogies of Jesus.* 2d ed. Society for New Testament: Studies Monograph Series 8. Cambridge: Cambridge University Press, 1988.

Johnstone, William *Chronicles and Exodus: An Analogy and Its Application.* Journal for the Study of the Old Testament: Supplement Series 275. Sheffield: Sheffield Academic, 1998.

————. *1 and 2 Chronicles.* Vol. 1, *1 Chronicles 1–2 Chronicles 9: Israel's Place among the Nations.* Journal for the Study of the Old Testament: Supplement Series 253. Sheffield: Sheffield Academic Press, 1997.

————. *1 and 2 Chronicles.* Vol. 2, *2 Chronicles 10–36: Guilt and Atonement.* Journal for the Study of the Old Testament: Supplement Series 254. Sheffield: Sheffield Academic Press, 1997.

Jones, Gwilym H. *1 and 2 Chronicles.* Old Testament Guides. Sheffield: JSOT Press, 1993.

Kalimi, Isaac. *The Books of Chronicles: A Classified Bibliography.* Jerusalem: Simor, 1990.

————. *Zur Geschichtsschreibung des Chronisten: Literarisch-historiographische Abweichungen der Chronik von ihren Paralleltexten in den Samuel-und Königsbüchern.* Beihefte zur Zeitschrift für die alttestamentliche Wissenschaft 226. Berlin: de Gruyter, 1995.

————. *The Reshaping of Ancient Israelite History in Chronicles.* Winona Lake, Ind.: Eisenbrauns, 2005.

Kartveit, Magnar. *Motive und Schichten der Landtheologie in 1 Chronik 1–9.* Coniectanea biblica: Old Testament: Series 28. Stockholm, Sweden: Almqvist & Wiksell, 1989.

Keel, Othmar. *Symbolism of the Biblical World: Ancient Near Eastern Iconography and the Book of Psalms.* Translated by Timothy J. Hallett. New York: Seabury, 1978.

Keel, Othmar, and Silvia Schroer. *Schöpfung: Biblische Theologien im Kontext altorientalischer Religionen.* Göttingen: Vandenhoeck and Ruprecht, 2002.

Keel, Othmar, and Erich Zenger, eds. *Gottesstadt und Gottesgarten: Zu Geschichte und Theologie des Jerusalemer Temples.* Quaestiones Disputatae 191. Freiburg im Breisgau: Herder, 2000.

Keil, Carl Friedrich. *The Books of the Chronicles.* Translated by Andrew Harper. Biblical Commentary on the Old Testament. 2d ed. Leipzig: Dörffling and Franke, 1875. Reprint. Grand Rapids: Eerdmans, 1950.

————. *Commentary on the Books of Kings.* Translated by James Martin. Biblical Commentary on the Old Testament. 2d ed. Leipzig: Dörffling and Franke, 1875. Reprint. Grand Rapids: Eerdmans, 1950.

Kelly, Brian E. *Retribution and Eschatology in Chronicles.* Journal for the Study of the Old Testament: Supplement Series 211. Sheffield: Sheffield Academic Press, 1996.

Kirkpatrick, A. F. *The Book of Psalms.* Cambridge: Cambridge University Press, 1902. Reprint. Grand Rapids: Baker, 1982.

Kittel, Rudolf. *Die Bücher der Chronik.* Göttingen: Vandenhoeck & Ruprecht, 1902. Microfiche. Originally published as *Die Bücher der Chronik und Esra, Nehemia und Esther.*

Kleinig, John W. *The LORD's Song: The Basis, Function and Significance of Choral Music in Chronicles.* Journal for the Study for the Old Testament: Supplement Series 156. Sheffield: JSOT Press, 1993.

Knoppers, Gary N. *1 Chronicles, 1–9: A New Translation with Introduction and Commentary.* Anchor Bible 12. New York: Doubleday, 2003.

———. *1 Chronicles, 10–29: A New Translation with Introduction and Commentary.* Anchor Bible 12A. New York: Doubleday, 2004.

Koester, Craig R. *The Dwelling of God: The Tabernacle in the Old Testament, Intertestamental Jewish Literature, and the New Testament.* Catholic Biblical Quarterly Monograph Series 22. Washington D.C.: Catholic Biblical Association of America, 1989.

Kraus, Hans-Joachim. *Psalms 60–150.* Translated by Hilton C. Oswald. Continental Commentary. Minneapolis: Fortress, 1993.

———. *Worship in Israel: A Cultic History of the Old Testament.* Translated by Geoffrey Buswell. Richmond, Va.: Knox, 1966.

Leithart, Peter J. *From Silence to Song: The Davidic Liturgical Revolution.* Moscow, Idaho: Canon, 2003.

Levine, Baruch A. *Numbers 1–20: A New Translation with Introduction and Commentary.* Anchor Bible 4A. New York: Doubleday, 1993.

Levine, Lee I. *Jerusalem: Portait of the City in the Second Temple Period (538 B.C.E.–70 C.E.).* Philadelphia: Jewish Publication Society, 2002.

Lichtheim, Miriam. *Ancient Egyptian Literature: A Book of Readings.* Vol. 3, *The Late Period.* Berkeley: University of California, 1980.

Long, V. Philips, ed. *Israel's Past in Present Research.* Sources for Biblical and Theological Study 7. Winona Lake, Ind.: Eisenbraun, 1999.

Long, V. Philips, Gordon J. Wenham, and David W. Baker, eds. *Windows into Old Testament History: Evidence, Argument, and the Crisis of "Biblical Israel."* Grand Rapids: Eerdmans, 2002.

Lowery, R. H. *The Reforming Kings: Cult and Society in First Temple Judah.* Journal for the Study of the Old Testament: Supplement Series 120. Sheffield: JSOT Press, 1991.

Maillot, Alphonse, and André Lelièvre. *Les Psaumes: Traduction nouvelle et commentaire. Triosième partie: Psaumes 101 à 150 avec, en appendice, des Psaumes de Qumran.* Paris: Labor et Fides, 1969.

Mark, Alfred. *Les systèmes sacrificiels de l'Ancien Testament: Formes et fonctions du culte sacrificiel à Yhwh.* Supplements to Vetus Testamentum 105 Leiden: Brill, 2005.

Mays, James Luther, David L. Petersen, and Kent Harold Richards, eds. *Old Testament Interpretation: Past, Present, and Future: Essays in Honor of Gene M. Tucker.* Nashville: Abingdon, 1995.

McCarter, P. Kyle. *2 Samuel.* Anchor Bible 9. Garden City, N.Y.: Doubleday, 1984.

McEntire, Mark Harold. *The Function of Sacrifice in Chronicles, Ezra, and Nehemiah.* Lewiston: Mellen, 1993.

McEwan, Gilbert J. P. *Priest and Temple in Hellenistic Babylonia.* Freiburger Altorientalische Studien 4. Wiesbaden: Steiner, 1981.

McKenzie, Steven L. *The Chronicler's Use of the Deuteronomistic History.* Harvard Semitic Monographs 33. Atlanta: Scholars Press, 1985.

———. *1–2 Chronicles.* Abingdon Old Testament Commentaries. Nashville, Tenn.: Abingdon, 2004.

McKenzie, Steven L., and Thomas Römer, eds. *Rethinking the Foundations: Historiography in the Ancient World and in the Bible: Essays in Honour of John Van Seters.* Beihefte zur Zeitschrift für die alttestamentliche Wissenschaft 294. Berlin: de Gruyter, 2000.

Mettinger, Tryggve N. D. *The Dethronement of Sebaoth: Studies in the Shem and Kabod Theologies.* Coniectanea biblica: Old Testament: Series 18. Lund: Gleerup, 1982.

————. *King and Messiah: The Civil and Sacral Legitimation of the Israelite Kings.* Coniectanea biblica: Old Testament: Series 8. Lund: Gleerup, 1976.

Michaeli, Frank. *Les Livres des Chroniques, d'Esdras et de Néhémie.* Commentaire de l'Ancien Testament 16. Neuchâtel: Delachaux & Niestlé, 1967.

Micheel, Rosemarie. *Die Seher- und Prophetenüberlieferungen in der Chronik.* Beiträge zur biblischen Exegese und Theologie 18. Frankfurt am Main: Lang, 1983.

Milgrom, Jacob. *Studies in Cultic Theology and Terminology.* Leiden: Brill, 1983.

Milgrom, Jacob. *Studies in Levitical Terminology.* Vol. 1. Berkeley: University of California Press, 1970.

Millard, Alan, J. K. Hoffmeier, and D. W. Baker, eds. *Faith, Tradition, and History: Old Testament Historiography in Its Near Eastern Context.* Winona Lake, Ind.: Eisenbrauns, 1994.

Miller, J. Maxwell. *The Old Testament and the Historian.* Philadelphia: Fortress, 1976.

Miller, J. Maxwell, and John H. Hayes. *A History of Ancient Israel and Judah.* Philadelphia: Westminster, 1986.

Miller, Patrick D., ed. *The Religion of Ancient Israel.* Library of Ancient Israel. Louisville, Ky.: Westminster/Knox, 2000.

Miller, Patrick D., and J. J. M. Roberts. *The Hand of the Lord: A Reassessment of the "Ark Narrative" of 1 Samuel.* Johns Hopkins Near Eastern Studies. Baltimore: Johns Hopkins University Press, 1977.

Mills, Watson E. *Bibliographies for Biblical Research: Periodical Literature for the Study of the Old Testament.* Lewiston, N.Y.: Mellen, 2002.

Moor, Johannes Cornelis de, ed. *Crises and Perspectives: Studies in Ancient Near Eastern Polytheism, Biblical Theology, Palestinian Archaeology, and Intertestamental Literature: Papers Read at the Joint British–Dutch Old Testament Conference, Held at Cambridge, U.K., 1985.* Oudtestamentische Studiën 24. Leiden: Brill, 1986.

Mosis, Rudolf. *Untersuchungen zur theologie des chronistischen Geschichtswerkes.* Freiburger theologische Studien 92. Freiburg: Herder, 1973.

Movers, F. K. *Kritische Untersuchungen über die biblische Chronik: Ein Beitrag zur Einleitung in das Alte Testament.* Bonn: Habicht, 1834.

Mowinckel, Sigmund. *The Psalms in Israel's Worship.* Translated by D. R. Ap-Thomas. New York: Abingdon, 1962. Reprint, Biblical Resource Series. Grand Rapids: Eerdmans, 2004.

Myers, Jacob Martin. *1 Chronicles.* 2d ed. Anchor Bible 12. Garden City, N.Y.: Doubleday, 1965.

————. *2 Chronicles.* Anchor Bible 13. Garden City, N.Y.: Doubleday, 1965.

Neteler, Bernhard. *Die Bücher der Chronik der Vulgata und des hebräischen Textes.* Müster: Theissing, 1899. Microfiche.

Newsome, James D., Jr., ed. *A Synoptic Harmony of Samuel, Kings, and Chronicles: With Related Passages from Psalms, Isaiah, Jeremiah, and Ezra.* Grand Rapids: Baker, 1986.

Noth, Martin. *The Chronicler's History.* Translated by H. G. M. Williamson. Journal for the Study of the Old Testament: Supplement Series 50. Sheffield: JSOT Press, 1987.

————. *The History of Israel.* Translated by Stanley Godman. Edinburgh: T & T Clark, 1958.

Nurmela, Risto. *The Levites: Their Emergence as a Second-Class Priesthood.* University of Southern Florida Studies in the History of Judaism 193. Atlanta: Scholars Press, 1998.

Oeming, Manfred. *Das wahre Israel: Die "genealogische Vorhalle" 1 Chronik 1–9.* Beiträge zur Wissenschaft vom Alten und Neuen Testament 128. Stuttgart: Kohlhammer, 1990.

Ollenburger, Ben C. *Zion the City of the Great King: A Theological Symbol of the Jerusalem Cult.* Journal for the Study of the Old Testament: Supplement Series 41. Sheffield: JSOT Press, 1987.

Pate, Don. *The Judean Chronicles: Stories from between the Lines of Scripture.* Hagerstown, Md.: Review and Herald, 1997.

Peltonen, Kai. *History Debated: The Historical Reliability of Chronicles in Pre-Critical and Critical Research.* 2 vols. Publications of the Finnish Exegetical Society 64. Helsinki: Finnish Exegetical Society, 1996.

Plöger, Otto. *Theocracy and Eschatology.* Translated by S. Rudman. Richmond, Va.: Knox, 1968.

Pomykala, Kenneth E. *The Davidic Dynasty Tradition in Early Judaism: Its History and Significance for Messianism.* Society of Biblical Literature: Early Judaism and Its Literature 7. Atlanta: Scholars Press, 1995.

Poorthuis, M., and Ch. Safrai, eds. *The Centrality of Jerusalem.* Kampen: Pharos, 1996.

Pratt, Richard L. *1 and 2 Chronicles.* Fearn: Mentor, 1998.

Preuss, Horst Dietrich. *Old Testament Theology.* Translated by Leo G. Perdue. 2 vols. Old Testament Library. Louisville: Westminster/Knox, 1996.

Provan, Iain, V. Philips Long, and Tremper Longman III, eds. *A Biblical History of Israel.* Louisville: Westminster/Knox, 2003.

von Rad, Gerhard. *Das Geschichtsbild des chronistischen Werkes.* Beiträge zur Wissenchaft vom Alten und Neuen Testament 54. Stuttgart: Kohlhammer, 1930.

————. *Old Testament Theology.* Translated by D. M. G. Stalker. 2 vols. Old Testament Library. Louisville: Westminster/Knox, 2001.

Raney, Donald C. *History as Narrative in the Deuteronomistic History and Chronicles.* Studies in the Bible and Early Christianity 56. Lewiston, N.Y.: Mellen, 2003.

Rehm, Martin. *Die Bücher der Chronik.* Die Heiligeschrift in deutscher Übersetzung 5a. Würzburg: Echter, 1949.

Rendtorff, Rolf. *The Old Testament: An Introduction.* Translated by John Bowden. Philadelphia: Fortress, 1986.

Riley, William. *King and Cultus in Chronicles: Worship and the Reinterpretation of History.* Journal for the Study of the Old Testament: Supplement Series 160. Sheffield: JSOT Press, 1993.

Rooke, Deborah W. *Zadok's Heirs: The Role and Development of the High Priesthood in Ancient Israel.* Oxford Theological Monographs. Oxford: Oxford University Press, 2000.

Rothstein, Johann Wilhelm. *Die Genealogie des Königs Jojachin und seiner Nachkommen (1 Chron. 3, 17-24): Eine kritische Studie zur jüdischen Geschichte und Litteratur.* Berlin: Reuther & Reichard, 1902.

Rothstein, Johann Wilhelm, and Johannes Hänel. *Kommentar zum ersten Buch der Chronik.* Kommentar zum Alten Testament 18. 2 vols. Leipzig: Deichertsche, 1927.

Rowley, H. H. *Worship in Israel: Its Forms and Meaning.* Philadelphia: Fortress, 1978.

Rudolph, Wilhelm. *Chronikbücher.* Handbuch zum Alten Testament 21. Tübingen: Mohr-Siebeck, 1955.

Sacchi, Paolo. *The History of the Second Temple Period.* Journal for the Study of the Old Testament Series 285. Sheffield: Sheffield Academic Press, 2000.

Schams, Christine. *Jewish Scribes in the Second Temple Period.* Journal for the Study of the Old Testament: Supplement Series 291. Sheffield: Sheffield Academic Press, 1998.

Schaper, Joachim. *Priester und Leviten im achämenidischen Juda: Studien zur Kult-und Sozialgeschichte Israels in Persischer Zeit.* Forschungen zum Alten Testament 31. Tübingen: Mohr—Siebeck, 2000.

Schipper, Bernd Ulrich. *Israel und Ägypten in der Königszeit: Die Kulturellen Kontakte von Salomo bis zum Fall Jerusalems.* Orbis biblicus et orientalis 170. Göttingen: Vandenhoeck and Ruprecht, 1999.

Schmidt, Francis. *How the Temple Thinks: Identity and Social Cohesion in Ancient Judaism.* Translated by J. Edward Crowley. Biblical Seminar 78. Sheffield: Sheffield Academic Press, 2001.

Schniedewind, William M. *The Word of God in Transition: From Prophet to Exegete in the Second Temple Period.* Journal for the Study of the Old Testament: Supplement Series 197. Sheffield: Sheffield Academic Press, 1995.

Seitz, Christopher R. *Theology of Conflict.* Beihefte zur Zeitschrift für die alttestamentliche Wissenschaft 176. Berlin: de Gruyter, 1989.

Selman, Martin J. *1 Chronicles: An Introduction and Commentary.* Tyndale Old Testament Commentaries 10a. Downers Grove, Ill.: Inter-Varsity, 1994.

————. *2 Chronicles: A Commentary.* Tyndale Old Testament Commentaries 10b. Downers Grove, Ill.: Inter-Varsity, 1994.

Seow, C. L. *Myth, Drama, and the Politics of David's Dance.* Harvard Semitic Monographs 44. Atlanta: Scholars Press, 1989.

Seybold, Klaus. *Studien zur Psalmenauslegung.* Stuttgart: Kohlhammer, 1998.

Shaver, Judson Rayford. *Torah and the Chronicler's History Work: An Inquiry into the Chronicler's References to Laws, Festivals, and Cultic Institutions in Relationship to Pentateuchal Legislation.* Brown Judaic Studies 196. Atlanta: Scholars Press, 1989.

Smith, Daniel L. *The Religion of the Landless: The Social Context of the Babylonian Exile.* Bloomington, Ind.: Stone, 1989.

Smith-Christopher, Daniel L. *A Biblical Theology of Exile.* Overtures to Biblical Theology. Minneapolis: Fortress, 2002.

Soggin, J. Alberto. *An Introduction to the History of Israel and Judah.* 3d ed. London: SCM, 1999.

————. *Joshua: A Commentary.* Translated by R. A. Wilson. Old Testament Library. Philadelphia: Westminster, 1972.

Steins, Georg. *Die Chronik als kanonisches Abschlussphänomen: Studien zur Entstehung und Theologie von 1/2 Chronik.* Bonner biblische Beiträge 93. Weinheim: Athenäum, 1995.

Steussy, Marti J. *David: Biblical Portraits of Power.* Columbia, S.C.: University of South Carolina Press, 1999.

Stone, Michael E., ed. *Jewish Writings of the Second Temple Period: Apocrypha, Pseudepigrapha, Qumran Sectarian Writings, Philo, Josephus.* Compendia rerum iudaicarum ad Novum Testamentum 2. Philadelphia: Fortress, 1984.

Stone, Michael Edward. *Scriptures, Sects, and Visions: A Profile of Judaism from Ezra to the Jewish Revolts.* New York: Collins, 1980.

Strübind, Kim. *Tradition als Interpretation in der Chronik: König Josaphat als Paradigma chronistischer Hermeneutik und Theologie.* Beihefte zur Zeitschrift für die alttestamentliche Wissenschaft 201. Berlin: de Gruyter, 1991.

Swanson, Dwight D. *The Temple Scroll and the Bible: The Methodology of 11QT.* Studies on the Texts of the Desert of Judah 14. Leiden: Brill, 1995.

Tate, Marvin E. *Psalms 51–100.* Word Biblical Commentary 20. Waco, Tex.: Word, 1990.

Tadmor, Hayim, and Moshe Weinfeld, eds. *History, Historiography, and Interpretation.* Jerusalem: Magnes, 1983.

Tertel, Hans Jürgen. *Text and Transmission: An Empirical Model for the Literary Development of Old Testament Narratives.* Beihefte zur Zeitschrift für die alttestamentliche Wissenschaft 221. Berlin: de Gruyter, 1994.

Thompson, J. A. *1, 2 Chronicles.* New American Commentary. Nashville, Tenn.: Broadman & Holman, 1994.

Tilly, Michael. *Jerusalem—Nabel der Welt: Überlieferung und Funktionen von Heiligtums-traditionen im antiken Judentum.* Stuttgart: Kohlhammer, 2002.

van der Toorn, Karel. *Family Religion in Babylonia, Syria, and Israel: Continuity and Change in the Forms of Religious Life.* Studies in the History and Culture of the Ancient Near East 7. Leiden: Brill, 1996.

————, ed. *The Image and the Book: Iconic Cults, Aniconism, and the Rise of Book Religion in Isreal and the Ancient Near East.* Contributions to Biblical Exegesis and Theology 21. Leuven: Peeters, 1997.

Torrey, Charles C. *The Chronicler's History of Israel: Chronicles–Ezra–Nehemiah Restored to Its Original Form.* New Haven, Conn.: Yale University Press, 1954.

Tournay, Raymond J. *Seeing and Hearing God with the Psalms: The Prophetic Liturgy of the Second Temple in Jerusalem.* Journal for the Study of the Old Testament: Supplement Series 118. Atlanta: JSOTS Press, 1991.

Traylor, John H. *1 & 2 Kings, 2 Chronicles.* Nashville, Tenn.: Broadman Press, 1981.

Throntveit, Mark A. *When Kings Speak: Royal Speech and Royal Prayer in Chronicles.* Society of Biblical Literature Dissertation Series 93. Atlanta: Scholars Press, 1987.

Tuell, Steven S. *First and Second Chronicles.* Interpretation. Louisville, Ky.: Knox, 2001.

Ulrich, Eugene C. *The Qumran Text of Samuel and Josephus.* Harvard Semitic Monographs 19. Missoula, Mont.: Scholars Press, 1978.

Ulrich, Eugene C. et al., eds. *Priests, Prophets, and Scribes: Essays on the Formation and Heritage of Second Temple Judaism in Honour of Joseph Blenkinsopp.* Journal for the Study of the Old Testament: Supplement Series 149. Sheffield: JSOT Press, 1992.

Van Seters, John. *In Search of History: Historiography in the Ancient World and the Origins of Biblical History.* New Haven, Conn.: Yale University Press, 1983.

Vaughn, Andrew G. *Theology, History, and Archaeology in the Chronicler's Account of Hezekiah.* Archaeology and Biblical Studies 4. Atlanta: Scholars Press, 1999.

Vink, J. G., et al., eds. *The Priestly Code.* Oudestamentische Studiën 15. Leiden: Brill, 1969.

Vriezen, Th. C. *An Outline of Old Testament Theology.* 2d ed. Newton, Mass.: Charles T. Branford, 1970.

————. *The Religion of Ancient Israel.* Translated by Hubert Hoskins. Philadelphia: Westminster, 1967.

Watson, Wilfred G. E. *Classical Hebrew Poetry: A Guide to Its Techniques.* Journal for the Study of the Old Testament: Supplement Series 26. Sheffield: JSOT Press, 1984.

Watts, James W. *Psalm and Story: Inset Hymns in Hebrew Narrative.* Journal for the Study of the Old Testament: Supplement Series 139. Sheffield: JSOT Press, 1992.

Weinberg, Joel. *The Citizen-Temple Community* Translated by Daniel L. Smith-Christopher. Journal for the Study of the Old Testament: Supplement Series 151. Sheffield: JSOT Press, 1992.

Weinberg, Joel P. *Der Chronist in seiner Mitwelt.* Beihefte zur Zeitschrift für die alttestamentliche Wissenschaft, ed. Otto Kaiser, vol. 239. Berlin: de Gruyter, 1996.

Welch, Adam C. *The Work of the Chronicler: Its Purpose and Date.* The Schweich Lectures on Biblical Archaeology. London: Oxford University Press, 1939.

Wellhausen, Julius. *Prolegomena to the History of Ancient Israel.* Translated by J. Sutherland Black and Allan Enzies. Edinburgh: A & C Black, 1885. Reprint, Reprints and Translations Series. Atlanta: Scholars Press, 1994.

Welten, Peter. *Geschichte und Geschichtsdarstellung in den Chronikbüchern.* Wissenschaftliche Monographien zum Alten und Neuen Testament 42. Neukirchen-Vluyn: Neukirchener, 1973.

de Wette, Wilhelm Martin Leberecht. *Beiträge zur Einleitung in das Alte Testament.* 2 vols. Halle: Schimmelpfennig, 1807. Reprint, New York: Olms, 1971.

————. *Kritischer Versuch über…Bücher der Chronik.* Halle: Schimmelpfennig, 1806. Microfiche. Originally published as *Kritischer Versuch über die Glaubwürdigkeit der Bücher der Chronik mit Hinsicht auf die Geschichte der Mosaischen Bücher und Gesetzgebung: Ein Nachtrag zu den Vaterschen Untersuchungen über den Pentateuch.*

Whitcomb, John Clement. *Solomon to the Exile: Studies in Kings and Chronicles*. Grand Rapids: Baker, 1971.

Willi, Thomas. *Chronik*. Biblischer Kommentar Altes Testament 24. Neukirchen-Vluyn: Neukirchener, 1991.

—. *Die Chronik als Auslegung: Untersuchungen zur literarischen Gestaltung der historischen Überlieferung Israels*. Forschungen zur Religion und Literatur des Alten und Neuen Testaments 106. Göttingen: Vandenhoeck & Ruprecht, 1972.

—. *Juda-Jehud-Israel: Studien zum Selbstverständnis des Judentums in persischer Zeit*. Forschungen zum Alten Testament 12. Tübingen: Mohr, 1995.

Williamson, H. G. M. *1 and 2 Chronicles*. New Century Bible Commentary. Grand Rapids: Eerdmans, 1982.

—. *Israel in the Books of Chronicles*. Cambridge: Cambridge University Press, 1977.

—. *Studies in Persian Period History and Historiography*. Forschungen zum Alten Testament 38. Tübingen: Mohr—Siebeck, 2004.

Wilson, Robert R. *Genealogy and History in the Biblical World*. Yale Near Eastern Researches 7. New Haven, Conn.: Yale University Press, 1977.

Woudstra, Marten H. *The Ark of the Covenant from Conquest to Kingship*. Philadelphia: Presbyterian and Reformed, 1965.

Xeravits, Géza G. *King, Priest, Prophet: Positive Eschatological Protagonists of the Qumran Library*. Studies on the Texts of the Desert of Judah 47. Leiden: Brill, 2003.

Yamauchi, Edwin M. *Persia and the Bible*. Grand Rapids: Baker, 1990.

Articles

Abadie, Philippe. "Le fonctionnement symbolique de la figure de David dans l'oeuvre du Chroniste." *Transeuphratène* 7 (1994): 143–51.

Albright, W. F. "The Date and Personality of the Chronicler." *Journal of Biblical Literature* 40 (1921): 104–24.

Alexander, Philip S. "Retelling the Old Testament." In *It Is Written: Scripture Citing Scripture: Essays in Honour of Barnabas Lindars*, ed. D. A. Carson and H. G. M. Williamson, 99–121. Cambridge: Cambridge University Press, 1988.

Allan, Nigel. "The Identity of the Jerusalem Priesthood During the Exile." *Heythrop Journal* 23 (1982): 259–69.

Allen, Leslie C. "Kerygmatic Units in 1 and 2 Chronicles." *Journal for the Study of the Old Testament* 41 (1988): 21–36.

Altink, Willem. "Theological Motives for the Use of 1 Chronicles 16:8-36 as Background for Revelation 14:16-17." *Andrews University Seminary Studies* 24 (1986): 211–21.

Amit, Yairah. "A New Outlook on the the Book of Chronicles." *Immanuel* 13 (1981): 20–29.

Auld, A. Graeme. "The Former Prophets (Joshua, Judges, 1–2 Samuel, 1–2 Kings)." In *The Hebrew Bible Today: An Introduction to Critical Issues*, ed. Steven L. McKenzie and M. Patrick Graham, 53–68. Louisville, Ky.: Westminster/Knox, 1998.

Bar, Shaul. "A Better Image for Solomon." *The Bible Today* 36 (1998): 221–26.

Barrick, W. Boyd. "Genealogical Notes on the 'House of David' and the 'House of Zadock.'" *Journal for the Study of the Old Testament* 96 (2001): 29–58.

Barstad, Hans M. "On the History and Archaeology of Judah During the Exilic Period." *Orientalia lovaniensia periodica* 19 (1988): 25–36.

Beentjes, Pancratius C. "Identity and Community in the Book of Chronicles: The Role and Meaning of the Verb *Jāḥaś*." *Zeitschrift für Althebräistik* 12 (1999): 233–37.

———. "Inverted Quotations in the Bible: A Neglected Stylistic Pattern." *Biblica* 63 (1982): 506–23.

Begg, Christopher. "The Death of Josiah in Chronicles: Another View." *Vetus Testamentum* 37 (1987): 1–8.

Begg, Christopher T. "'Seeking Yahweh' and the Purpose of Chronicles." *Louvain Studies* 9 (1982–83): 128–41.

Bentzen, Aage. "The Cultic Use of the Story of the Ark in Samuel." *Journal of Biblical Literature* 67 (1948): 37–53.

Ben Zvi, Ehud. "The Authority of 1–2 Chronicles in the Late Second Temple Period." *Journal for the Study of the Pseudepigrapha* 3 (1987–88): 59–88.

———. "A Gateway to the Chronicler's Teaching: The Account of the Reign of Ahaz in 2 Chr 28,1-27." *Scandinavian Journal of the Old Testament* 7 (1993): 216–49.

———. "A Sense of Proportion: An Aspect of the Theology of the Chronicler." *Scandinavian Journal of the Old Testament* 9 (1995): 37–51.

Berg, Sandra Beth. "After the Exile: God and History in the Books of Chronicles and Esther." In *The Divine Helmsman: Studies on God's Control of Human Events. Presented to Lou H. Silberman*, ed. James L. Crenshaw and Samuel Sandmel, 107–27. New York: Ktav, 1980.

Blenkinsopp, Joseph. "The Judaean Priesthood During the Neo-Babylonian and Achaemenid Periods: A Hypothetical Reconstruction." *Catholic Biblical Quarterly* 60 (1998): 25–43.

Blenkinsopp, Joseph. "The Mission of Udjahorresnet and Those of Ezra and Nehemiah." *Journal of Biblical Literature* 106 (1987): 409–21.

Botterweck, G. Johannes. "Zur Eigenart der chronistischen Davidgeschichte." *Theologische Quartalschrift* 136 (1956): 402–35.

Braun, Roddy. "Chronicles, Ezra and Nehemiah: Theology and Literary History." In *Studies in the Historical Books of the Old Testament*, ed. J. A. Emerton. Vetus Testamentum Supplements 30, 52–64. Leiden: Brill, 1979.

———. "Solomon, the Chosen Temple Builder: The Significance of 1 Chronicles 22, 28, and 29 for the Theology of Chronicles." *Journal of Biblical Literature* 95 (1976): 581–90.

Braun, Roddy L. "The Message of Chronicles: Rally Round the Temple." *Concordia Theological Monthly* 42 (1971): 503–16.

———. "A Reconsideration of the Chronicler's Attitude toward the North." *Journal of Biblical Literature* 96 (1977): 59–62.

———. "Solomonic Apologetic in Chronicles." *Journal of Biblical Literature* 92 (1973): 503–15.

Bretschneider, Joachim. "Götter in Schreinen: Eine Untersuchung zu den syrischen und levantinischen Tempelmodellen, ihrer Bauplastik und ihren Götterbildern." *Ugarit-Forschungen* 23 (1991): 13–32.

Brueggemann, Walter. "David and His Theologian." *Catholic Biblical Quarterly* 30 (1968): 156–81.

Brunet, Adrien M. "Le chroniste et ses sources." *Revue biblique* 60 (1953): 481–508.

———. "Le chroniste et ses sources." *Revue biblique* 61 (1954): 349–86.

———. "La théologie du chroniste: Théocratie et messianise." In *Sacra pagina: Miscellanea biblica congressus internationalis catholici de re biblica*, ed. J. Coppens, A. Descamps, and E. Massaux, vol. 1, 384–97. Gembloux: Ducuot, 1959.

Buss, Martin J. "The Psalms of Asaph and Korah." *Journal of Biblical Literature* 82 (1963): 382–92.

Butler, Trent C. "A Forgotten Passage from a Forgotten Era (1 Chr. 16:8-36)." *Vetus Testamentum* 28 (1978): 142–50.

Campbell, Antony F. "Yahweh and the Ark: A Case Study in Narrative." *Journal of Biblical Literature* 98 (1979): 31–44.

Cancik, Hubert. "Das jüdische Fest: Ein Versuch zu Form und Religion des chronistischen Geschichtswerkes." *Theologische Quartalschrift* 150 (1970): 335–48.

Caquot, André. "Peut-on parler de messianisme dans l'oeuvre du Chroniste?" *Revue de théologie et de philosophie* 99 (1966): 110–20.

Cargill, Jack. "David in History: A Secular Approach." *Judaism* 35 (1986): 211–22.

Cazelles, Henri. "Review of H. G. M. Willamson, *Israel in the Book of Chronicles*," *Vetus Testamentum* 29 (1979): 375–80.

Ceresco, A. R. "The Chiastic Word Pattern in Hebrew." *Catholic Biblical Quarterly* 38 (1976): 303–11.

Ceresco, A. R. "The Function of Chiasmus in Hebrew Poetry." *Catholic Biblical Quarterly* 40 (1978): 1–10.

Chong, Joong Ho. "Were There Yahwistic Sanctuaries in Babylon?" *American Journal of Theology* 10 (1996): 198–217.

Cody, Aelred. "Priesthood in the Old Testament." *Studia Missionalia* 22 (1973): 309–29.

Cowley, A. "The Meaning of *Māqōm* in Hebrew." *Journal of Theological Studies* 17 (1916): 174–76.

Cross, Frank Moore. "A New Qumran Biblical Fragment Related to the Original Hebrew Underlying the Septuagint." *Bulletin of the American Schools of Oriental Research* 132 (1953): 15–26.

———. "A Reconstruction of the Judean Restoration." *Journal of Biblical Literature* 94 (1975): 4–18.

Dandamaev, M. A. "Babylonian Popular Assemblies in the First Millennium B.C." *Bulletin of the Canadian Society for Mesopotamian Studies* 30 (1995): 23–29.

De Vries, Simon J. "Festival Ideology in Chronicles." In *Problems in Theology: Essays in Honor of Rolf Knierim*, ed. Henry T. C. Sun et al., 104–24. Grand Rapids: Eerdmans, 1996.

———. "Moses and David as Cult Founders in Chronicles." *Journal of Biblical Literature* 107 (1988): 619–39.

———. "The Schema of Dynastic Endangerment in Chronicles." *Proceedings, Eastern Great Lakes and Midwest Biblical Societies* 7 (1987): 59–78.

Dempsey, Deirdre Ann. "The Ark and the Temple in 1 and 2 Chronicles." *The Bible Today* 36 (1998): 233–39.

Demsky, Aaron. "The Genealogy of Gibeon (1 Chronicles 9:35-44): Biblical and Epigraphic Considerations." *Bulletin of the American Schools of Oriental Research* 202 (1971): 16–23.

Dick, Michael B. "Prophetic Parodies of Making the Cult Image." In *Born in Heaven, Made on Earth: The Making of the Cult Image in the Ancient Near East*, ed. Michael B. Dick, 1–53. Winona Lake, Ind.: Eisenbrauns, 1999.

Dillard, Raymond B. "The Literary Structure of the Chronicler's Solomon Narrative." *Journal for the Study of the Old Testament* 30 (1984): 85–93.

———. "The Reign of Asa (2 Chr 14–16): An Example of the Chronicler's Theological Method." *Journal of the Evangelical Theological Society* 23 (1980): 207–18.

- ———. "Reward and Punishment in Chronicles: The Theology of Immediate Retribution." *Westminster Theological Journal* 46 (1984): 164–72.

Dion, Paul E. "The Civic-and-Temple Community of Persian Period Judaea: Neglected Insights from Eastern Europe." *Journal of Near Eastern Studies* 50 (1991): 281–87.

Dirksen, P. B. "1 Chronicles 16:38: Its Background and Growth." *Journal of Northwest Semitic Languages* 22 (1996): 85–90.

———. "1 Chronicles 28:11-18: Its Textual Development." *Vetus Testamentum* 46 (1996): 429–38.

———. "The Future in the Book of Chronicles." In *New Heaven and New Earth Prophecy and the Millennium: Essays in Honour of Anthony Gelston*, ed. P. J. Harland and C. T. R. Hayward. Vetus Testamentum Supplements 77, 37–51. Leiden: Brill, 1996.

Dirksen, Piet. "The Development of the Text of 1 Chronicles, 15:1-24." *Henoch* 17 (1995): 267–77.

Dombrowski, D. W. W. "Socio-Religious Implications of Foreign Impact on Palestinian Jewry under Achaemenid Rule." *Transeuphratène* 13 (1997): 65–89.

Duchesne-Guillemin, Jacques. "La Religion des Achéménides." In *Beiträge zur Achämenidengeschichte*, ed. Gerold Walser. Historia 18, 59–82. Wiesbaden: Steiner, 1972.

Duchesne-Guillemin, Marcelle. "Music in Ancient Mesopotamia and Egypt." *World Archaeology* 12 (1981): 287–97.

Dumbrell, William J. "The Purpose of the Books of Chronicles." *Journal of the Evangelical Theological Society* 27 (1984): 257–66.

Dyck, Jonathan. "Dating Chronicles and the Purpose of Chronicles." *Didaskalia* 8 (1996–97): 16–29.

Dyck, Jonathan E. "The Ideology of Identity in Chronicles." In *Ethnicity and the Bible*, ed. Mark G. Brett, 89–116. Leiden: Brill, 1996.

Emerton, J. A. "Priests and Levites in Deuteronomy." *Vetus Testamentum* 12 (1962): 129–38.

Finkelstein, Israel. "The Rise of Jerusalem and Judah: The Missing Link." *Levant* 33 (2001): 105–15.

Flanagan, James W. "Succession and Genealogy in the Davidic Dynasty." In *The Quest for the Kingdom of God: Studies in Honor of George E. Mendenhall*, ed. H. B. Huffmon, F. A. Spina, and A. R. W. Green. Winona Lake, Ind.: Eisenbrauns, 1983.

Freedman, David Noel. "The Chronicler's Purpose." *Catholic Biblical Quarterly* 23 (1961): 436–42.

Fretheim, Terence E. "The Ark in Deuteronomy." *Catholic Biblical Quarterly* 30 (1968): 1–14.

———. "The Priestly Document: Anti-Temple?" *Vetus Testamentum* 18 (1968): 313–29.

Fritz, Volkmar. "The 'List of Rehoboam's Fortresses' in 2 Chr 11:5-12—a Document from the Time of Josiah." *Eretz-Israel* 15 (1981): 46–53.

Gese, Hartmut. "Zur Geschichte der Kultsänger am zweiten Tempel." In *Abraham unser Vater: Juden und Christen im Gespräch über die Bibel: Festschrift für Otto Michel zum 60. Geburtstag*, ed. Otto Betz, Martin Hengel, and Peter Schmidt, 222–34. Leiden: Brill, 1963.

Glatt-Gilad, David. "Regnal Formulae as a Historiographic Device in the Book of Chronicles." *Revue biblique* 108 (2001): 184–209.

Goldingay, John. "The Chronicler as a Theologian." *Biblical Theology Bulletin* 5 (1975): 99–126.

Gosse, B. "L'Alliance avec Abraham et les relectures de l'histoire d'Israël en Ne 9, Pss 105–106, 135–136 et 1 Ch 16." *Transeuphratène* 15 (1998): 123–35.

Gosse, Bernard. "Les citations de Psaumes en 1 Ch 16:8-36 et la conception des relations entre Yahvé et son peuple dans la rédaction des livres des Chroniques." *Église et théologie* 27 (1996): 313–33.

Grabbe, Lester L. "Review of E. Yamauchi, *Persia and the Bible*." *Journal for the Study of Judaism in the Persian, Hellenistic and Roman Period* 22 (1991): 295–98.

Halpern, Baruch. "The Construction of the Davidic State: An Exercise in Historiography." In *The Origins of the Israelite States*, ed. Volkmar Fritz and Philip R. Davies. Journal for the Study of the Old Testament: Supplement Series 228, 44–75. Sheffield: JSOT Press, 1996.

———. "Sacred History and Ideology: Chronicles' Thematic Structure—Indications of an Earlier Source." In *The Creation of Sacred Literature, Composition and Redaction of the Biblical Text*, ed. Richard E. Friedman. Near Eastern Studies, 35–54. Berkeley: University of California Press, 1981.

Hanks, Thomas D. "The Chronicler: Theologian of Grace." *Evangelical Quarterly* 53 (1981): 16–28.

Hauer, Chris Jr. "David and the Levites." *Journal for the Study of the Old Testament* 23 (1982): 33–54.

Hauer, Christian E. "Who Was Zadok?" *Journal of Biblical Literature* 82 (1963): 89–94.

Hertzberg, H. W. "Mizpah," *Zeitschrift für alttestamentliche Wissenschaft.* 47 (1929): 161–196.

Hill, Andrew E. "Patchwork Poetry or Reasoned Verse? Connective Structure in 1 Chron 16." *Vetus Testamentum* 33 (1983): 97–101.

Hurowitz, Victor A. "Temporary Temples." In *Kinattūtu ša dārâti: Raphael Kutscher Memorial Volume,* ed. Anson Rainey, 37–50. Tel Aviv: Institute of Archaeology, 1993.

Japhet, Sara. "Conquest and Settlement in Chronicles." *Journal of Biblical Literature* 98 (1979): 205–18.

———. "The Historical Reliability of Chronicles." *Journal for the Study of the Old Testament* 33 (1985): 83–107.

———. "Postexilic Historiography: How and Why?" In *Israel Constructs Its History: Deuteronomistic Historiography in Recent Research,* ed. Albert de Pury, Thomas Römer, and Jean-Daniel Macchi. Journal for the Study of the Old Testament: Supplement Series 306, 144–73. Sheffield: Sheffield Academic Press, 2000.

———. "The Supposed Common Authorship of Chronicles and Ezra–Nehemiah Investigated Anew." *Vetus Testamentum* 18 (1968): 330–71.

———. "The Temple in the Restoration Period: Reality and Ideology." *Union Seminary Quarterly Review* 44 (1991): 195–251.

Jones, Douglas. "The Cessation of Sacrifice after the Destruction of the Temple in 586 B.C." *Journal of Theological Studies* 14 (1963): 12–31.

Kalimi, Isaac. "Die Abfassungszeit der Chronik: Forschungsstand und Perspectiven." *Zeitschrift für alttestamentliche Wissenschaft* 105 (1993): 223–33.

———. "The Capture of Jerusalem in the Chronistic History." *Vetus Testamentum* 52 (2002): 66–79.

———. "History of Interpretation: The Book of Chronicles in Jewish Tradition from Daniel to Spinoza." *Revue biblique* 105 (1998): 5–41.

———. "The Land of Moriah, and the Site of Solomon's Temple in Biblical Historiography." *Harvard Theological Review* 83 (1990): 345–62.

———. "Literary-Chronological Proximity in the Chronicler's Historiography." *Vetus Testamentum* 43 (1993): 318–38.

———. "The View of Jerusalem in the Ethnographical Introduction of Chronicles (1 Chr 1–9)." *Biblica* 83 (2002): 556–62.

Kapelrud, Arvid S. "Temple Building, a Task for Gods and Kings." *Orientalia* 32 (1963): 56–62.

———. "Tradition and Worship: The Role of the Cult in Tradition Formation and Transmission." In *Tradition and Theology in the Old Testament,* ed. Douglas A. Knight, 101–24. Philadelphia: Fortress, 1977.

Kegler, Jürgen. "Das Zurücktreten der Exodustradition in den Chronikbüchern." In *Schöpfung und Befreiung: Für Claus Westermann zum 80. Geburtstag,* ed. Rainer Albertz, Friedemann W. Golka, and Jürgen Kegler, 54–66. Stuttgart: Calwer, 1989.

King, Philip J. "The Musical Tradition of Ancient Israel." In *Realia Dei: Essays in Archaeology and Biblical Interpretation in Honor of Edward F. Campbell, Jr. at His Retirement,* ed. Prescott H. Williams and Theodore Hiebert, 84–99. Atlanta: Scholars Press, 1999.

Klein, Ralph W. "Abijah's Campaign against the North (2 Chr 13): What Were the Chronicler's Sources?" *Zeitschrift für die alttestamentliche Wissenschaft* 95 (1983): 210–17.

———. "Supplements in the Paralipomena: A Rejoinder." *Harvard Theological Review* 61 (1968): 492–95.

————. "A Theology for Exiles–the Kingship of Yahweh." *Dialog* 17 (1978): 128–34.

————. "Recent Research in Chronicles." *Currents in Research: Biblical Studies* 2 (1994): 43–74.

Knierim, Rolf. "Criticism of Literary Features, Form, Tradition, and Redaction." In *The Hebrew Bible and Its Modern Interpreters*, ed. Douglas A. Knight and Gene M. Tucker. The Bible and Its Modern Interpreters, ed. Douglas A. Knight, vol. 1, 123–66. Philadelphia: Fortress, 1985.

Knoppers, Gary N. "Classical Historiography and the Chronicler's History: A Reexamination of an Alleged Nonrelationship." *Journal of Biblical Literature* 122 (2003): 627–50.

————. "'The God in His Temple:' The Phoenician Text from Pyrgi as a Funerary Inscription." *Journal of Near Eastern Studies* 51 (1992): 105–20.

————. "Hierodules, Priests, or Janitors? The Levites in Chronicles and the History of the Israelite Priesthood." *Journal of Biblical Literature* 118 (1999): 49–72.

————. "Of Kings, Prophets, and Priests in the Books of Chronicles." *The Bible Today* 36 (1998): 214–20.

————. "Review of Ernst Michael Dörrfuss, *Moses in den Chronikbüchern*." *Catholic Biblical Quarterly* 58 (1996): 705–7.

————. "Sources, Revisions, and Editions: The Lists of Jerusalem's Residents in MT and LXX Nehemiah 11 and 1 Chronicles 9." *Textus* 20 (2000): 141–68.

Kugel, James. "Levi's Elevation to the Priesthood in Second Temple Writings." *Harvard Theological Review* 86 (1993): 1–63.

Kuhrt, Amélie. "The Cyrus Cylinder and the Achaemenid Imperial Policy." *Journal for the Study of the Old Testament* 25 (1983): 83–97.

Kuntzmann, Raymond. "Le trône de Dieu dans l'oeuvre du Chroniste." In *Le trône de Dieu*, ed. Marc Philonenko, 19–27. Tübingen: Mohr, 1993.

Laato, Antti. "The Levitical Genealogies in 1 Chronicles 5–6 and the Formation of Levitical Ideology in Post-Exilic Judah." *Journal for the Study of the Old Testament* 62 (1994): 77–99.

Leithart, Peter J. "Attendants of Yahweh's House: Priesthood in the Old Testament." *Journal for the Study of the Old Testament* 85 (1999): 3–24.

Lemke, Werner E. "The Synoptic Problem in the Chronicler's History." *Harvard Theological Review* 58 (1965): 349–63.

Lipschits, Oded. "Judah, Jerusalem, and the Temple 586–539 B.C." *Transeuphratène* 22 (2001): 129–42.

Lloyd, Alan B. "The Inscription of Udjahorresnet: A Collaborator's Testament." *Journal of Egyptian Archaeology* 68 (1982): 166–80.

Loader, J. A. "Redaction and Function of the Chronistic 'Psalm of David.'" In *Studies in the Chronicler*, ed. W. C. van Wyk. Oud-Testamentiese Werkgemeenskap in Suid-Africa: Old Testament Essays, ed. Wouter C. van Wyk 19, 69–75. Johannesburg: Weeshuispers, 1976.

Lohfink, Norbert. "Die deuteronomistische Darstellung des Übergangs der Führung Israels von Moses auf Josue." *Scholastik* 37 (1962): 32–44.

Malamat, Avraham. "King Lists of the Old Babylonian Period and Biblical Genealogies." *Journal of the American Oriental Society* 88 (1968): 168–73.

Mantel, HugoHaim Dov. "The Dichotomy of Judaism During the Second Temple." *Hebrew Union College Annual* 44 (1973): 55–87.

McCarter, P. Kyle. "The Ritual Dedication of the City of David in 2 Samuel 6." In *The Word of the Lord Shall Go Forth: Essays in Honor of David Noel Freedman in Celebration of His Sixtieth Birthday*, ed. Carol L. Meyers and M. O'Connor, 273–77. Winona Lake, Ind.: Eisenbrauns, 1983.

McCarthy, Dennis J. "Covenant and Law in Chronicles–Nehemiah." *Catholic Biblical Quarterly* 44 (1982): 25–44.

————. "An Installation Genre?" *Journal of Biblical Literature* 90 (1971): 31–41.

McKenzie, Steven L. "Why Didn't David Build the Temple?: The History of a Biblical Tradition." In *Worship and the Hebrew Bible: Essays in Honour of John T. Willis*, ed. M. Patrick Graham, Rick R. Marrs, and Steven L. McKenzie. Journal for the Study of the Old Testament: Supplement Series 284, 204–24. Sheffield: JSOT Press, 1999.

Meek, Theophile James. "Aaronites and Zadokites." *American Journal of Semitic Languages and Literature* 45 (1929): 149–66. Microfilm.

Merrill, Eugene H. "The 'Accession Year' and Davidic Chronology." *Journal of the Ancient Near Eastern Society* 19 (1989): 101–12.

———. "A Theology of Chronicles." In *A Biblical Theology of the Old Testament*, ed. Roy B. Zuck, 157–87. Chicago: Moody, 1991.

Meyers, Carol. "David as Temple Builder." In *Ancient Israelite Religion: Essays in Honor of Frank Moore Cross*, ed. Patrick D. Miller Jr., Paul D. Hanson, and S. Dean McBride, 357–76. Philadelphia: Fortress, 1987.

Meyers, Eric M. "The Persian Period and the Judean Restoration from Zerubbabel to Nehemiah." In *Ancient Israelite Religion: Essays in Honor of Frank Moore Cross*, ed. Patrick D. Miller Jr., Paul D. Hanson, and S. Dean McBride, 509–22. Philadelphia: Fortress, 1987.

Miller, J. Maxwell. "The Korahites of Southern Judah." *Catholic Biblical Quarterly* 32 (1970): 58–68.

Moriarty, Frederick L. "The Chronicler's Account of Hezekiah's Reform," *Catholic Biblical Quarterly* 27 (1965): 399–406.

Murray, Donald F. "Dynasty, People, and the Future: The Message of Chronicles." *Journal for the Study of the Old Testament* 58 (1993): 71–92.

Myers, Jacob Martin. "The Kerygma of the Chronicler: History and Theology in the Service of Religion." *Interpretation* 20 (1966): 259–73.

Na'aman, Nadav. "Royal Vassals or Governors? On the Status of Sheshbazzar and Zerubbabel in the Persian Empire." *Henoch* 22 (2000): 35–44.

Newsome, James D., Jr. "Toward an Understanding of the Chronicler and His Purposes." *Journal of Biblical Literature* 94 (1975): 201–17.

Noordtzij, Arie. "Les intentions du Chroniste." *Revue biblique* 49 (1940): 161–68.

North, Robert Grady. "The Chronicler: 1–2 Chronicles, Ezra, Nehemiah." *New Jerome Biblical Commentary*, ed. R. E. Brown, Joseph A. Fitzmyer, and Roland E. Murphy, 362–98. Englewood Cliffs, N.J.: Prentice Hall, 1990.

———. "Does Archaeology Prove Chronicles' Sources?" In *A Light unto My Path: Old Testament Studies in Honor of Jacob M. Myers*, ed. Howard N. Bream, Ralph D. Heim, and Carey A. Moore, 375–401. Philadelphia: Temple University, 1974.

———. "Theology of the Chronicler." *Journal of Biblical Literature* 82 (1963): 369–81.

Noth, Martin. "Eine siedlungsgeographische Liste in 1 Chr. 2 und 4." *Zeitschrift des deutschen Palästina-Vereins* 55 (1932): 97–124.

Olyan, Saul. "Zadok's Origins and the Tribal Politics of David." *Journal of Biblical Literature* 101 (1982): 177–93.

Polk, Timothy. "The Levites in the Davidic-Solomonic Empire." *Studia biblica et theologica* 9 (1979): 3–22.

Puech, Émile. "La Pierre de Sion et l'autel des holocaustes d'après un manuscrit hébreu de la grotte 4 (4Q522)." *Revue biblique* 99 (1992): 676–96.

von Rad, Gerhard. "The Tent and the Ark." In *The Problem of the Hexateuch and other Essays*. Translated by E. W. Trueman Dicken. London: Oliver and Boyd, 1966.

———. "Die Nehemia-Denkschrift." *Zeitschrift für die alttestamentliche Wissenschaft* 76 (1964): 176–87.

Rainey, Anson F. "The Order of Sacrifices in Old Testament Ritual Texts." *Biblica* 51 (1970): 485–98.

Rendsburg, Gary A. "The Internal Consistency and Historical Reliability of the Biblical Genealogies." *Vetus Testamentum* 40 (1990): 185–206.

———. "Late Biblical Hebrew and the Date of P." *Journal of the Ancient Near Eastern Society of Columbia University* 12 (1980): 65–80.

Romerowski, Sylvain. "Les régnes de David et de Salomon dans les Chroniques." *Hokhma* 31 (1986): 1–23.

Rudolph, Wilhelm. "Problems of the Books of Chronicles." *Vetus Testamentum* 4 (1954): 401–9.

Saebø, Magne. "Messianism in Chronicles? Some Remarks to the Old Testament Background of the New Testament Christology." *Horizons in Biblical Theology* 2 (1980): 85–109.

Schniedewind, William M. "King and Priest in the Book of Chronicles and the Duality of Qumran Messianism." *Journal of Semitic Studies* 94 (1994): 71–78.

Schumacher, J. N. "The Chronicler's Theology of History." *The Theologian* 13 (1957): 11–21.

Schweitzer, Steven James. "The High Priest in Chronicles: An Anomaly in a Detailed Description of the Temple Cult." *Biblica* 84 (2003): 388–402.

Sérandour, A. "Les récits bibliques de la construction du second temple: Leurs enjeux." *Transeuphratène* 11 (1996): 9–32.

Shipp, R. Mark. "'Remember His Covenant Forever:' A Study of the Chronicler's Use of the Psalms." *Restoration Quarterly* 35 (1993): 29–39.

Solomon, A. M. "The Structure of the Chronicler's History: A Key to the Organization of the Pentateuch." *Semeia* 46 (1989): 51–64.

Steck, Otto H. "Das Problem theologischer Strömungen in nachexilischer Zeit." *Evangelische Theologie* 28 (1968): 445–58.

Steins, Georg. "Zur Datierung der Chronik: Ein neuer methodischer Ansatz." *Zeitschrift für die alttestamentliche Wissenschaft* 109 (1997): 84–92.

Stern, Ephraim. "The Province of Yehud: The Vision and the Reality." In *The Jerusalem Cathedra: Studies in the History, Archaeology, Geography and Ethnography of the Land of Israel*, ed. Lee I. Levine, vol. 1, 9–21. Jerusalem: Wayne State University Press, 1981.

Sugimoto, Tomotoshi. "The Chronicler's Techniques in Quoting Samuel–Kings." *Annual of the Japanese Biblical Institute* 16 (1990): 30–70.

———. "Chronicles as Independent Literature." *Journal for the Study of the Old Testament* 55 (1992): 61–74.

Tadmor, Hayim. "'The People' and the Kingship in Ancient Israel: The Role of Political Institutions in the Biblical Period." In *Jewish Society through the Ages*, ed. H. H. Ben-Sasson and E. Ettinger, 46–68. New York: Schocken, 1971.

———. "Traditional Institutions and the Monarchy: Social and Political Tensions in the Time of David and Solomon." In *Studies in the Period of David and Solomon and Other Essays*, ed. Tomoo Ishida, 239–57. Winona Lake, Ind.: Eisenbrauns, 1982.

Talmon, Shemaryahu. "Synonymous Readings in the Textual Traditions of the Old Testament." *Scripta hierosolymitana* 8 (1961): 335–83.

Talshir, David. "The References to Ezra and the Books of Chronicles in B. Baba Bathra 15a." *Vetus Testamentum* 38 (1988): 358–59.

———. "A Reinvestigation of the Linguistic Relationship between Chronicles and Ezra–Nehemiah." *Vetus Testamentum* 38 (1988): 165–93.

Throntveit, Mark A. "Linguistic Analysis and the Question of Authorship in Chronicles, Ezra, and Nehemiah." *Vetus Testamentum* 32 (1982): 201–16.

Townsend, Jeffery L. "The Purpose of 1 and 2 Chronicles." *Bibliotheca sacra* 144 (1987): 277–92.

The Significance of the Ark Narrative

Ulrich, Eugene C. "Horizons of Old Testament Textual Research at the Thirtieth Anniversary of Qumran Cave 4." *Catholic Biblical Quarterly* 46 (1984): 631–36.

Van Seters, John. "Creative Imitation in the Hebrew Bible." *Studies in Religion* 29 (2000): 395–409.

———. "Solomon's Temple: Fact and Ideology in Biblical and Ancient Near Eastern Historiography." *Catholic Biblical Quarterly* 59 (1997): 45–57.

Walters, Stanley D. "Saul of Gibeon." *Journal for the Study of the Old Testament* 52 (1991): 61–76.

Weinberg, Joel. "Transmitter and Recipient in the Process of Acculturation: The Experience of the Judean Citizen-Temple Community." *Transeuphratène* 13 (1997): 91–105.

Weinberg, Joel P. "Der Köning im Weltbild des Chronisten." *Vetus Testamentum* 39 (1989): 415–37.

———. "Das Wesen und die funktionelle Bestimmung der Listen in 1 Chr 1–9." *Zeitschrift für die alttestamentliche Wissenschaft* 93 (1981): 91–114.

Weinfield, Moshe. "High Treason in the Temple Scroll and in The Ancient Near Eastern Sources." In *Emanuel: Studies in Hebrew Bible, Septuagint, and Dead Sea Scrolls in Honor of Emanuel Tov*, ed. Shalom M. Paul et al. Supplements to Vetus Testamentum 94, 827–32. Leiden: Brill, 2003.

Weiss, Raphael. "A Peculiar Textual Phenomenon." *Textus* 18 (1995): 27–32.

Welten, Peter. "Lade-Temple-Jerusalem: Zur Theologie der Chronikbücher." In *Textgemäss: Aufätze und Beiträge zur Hermeneutik des Alten Testaments: Festschrift Ernst Würthwein zum 70. Geburtstag*, ed. A. H. J. Gunneweg and Otto Kaiser, 169–83. Göttingen: Vandenhoeck & Ruprecht, 1979.

Whitelam, Keith W. "The Symbols of Power: Aspects of Royal Propaganda in the United Monarchy." *Biblical Archaeologist* 49 (1986): 166–73.

Willi, Thomas. "Thora in den biblischen Chronikbüchern." *Judaica* 36 (1980): 102–5; 48–51.

Williamson, H. G. M. "The Accession of Solomon in the Books of Chronicles." *Vetus Testamentum* 23 (1976): 375–79.

———. "The Composition of Ezra 1–6." *Journal of Theological Studies* 34 (1983): 1–30.

———. "The Death of Josiah and the Continuing Development of the Deuteronomistic History." *Vetus Testamentum* 32 (1982): 242–47.

———. "Eschatology in Chronicles." *Tyndale Bulletin* 28 (1977): 115–54.

———. "The Origins of the Twenty-Four Priestly Courses: A Study of 1 Chronicles 22–27." In *Studies in the Historical Books of the Old Testament*, ed. J. A. Emerton. Vetus Testamentum Supplements, ed. J. A. Emerton et al., vol. 30, 251–68. Leiden: Brill, 1979.

———. "Postexilic Historiography." In *The Future of Biblical Studies: The Hebrew Scriptures*, ed. Richard Elliott Friedman and H. G. M. Williamson, 189–207. Atlanta: Scholars Press, 1987.

———. "Sources and Redaction in the Chronicler's Genealogy of Judah." *Journal of Biblical Literature* 98 (1979): 351–59.

———. "The Temple in the Books of Chronicles." In *Templum Amicitae: Essays on the Second Temple Presented to Ernst Bammel*, ed. W. Horbury. Journal for the Study of the New Testament: Supplement Series 48, 15–31. Sheffield: JSOT Press, 1991.

Williamson, Hugh. "Judah and the Jews." In *Studies in Persian History: Essays in Memory of David M. Lewis*, ed. Maria Brosius and Amélie Kuhrt. Achaemenid History 11, 145–63. Leiden: Nederlands Institut voor het Nabje Oosten, 1998.

Wilson, Robert R. "The Old Testament Genealogies in Recent Research." *Journal of Biblical Literature* 94 (1975): 169–89.

Wright, George E. "Cult and History: A Study of a Current Problem in Old Testament Interpretation." *Interpretation* 16 (1962): 3–20.

Wright, John W. "The Founding Father: The Structure of the Chronicler's David Narrative." *Journal of Biblical Literature* 117 (1998): 45–59.

———. "The Legacy of David in Chronicles: The Narrative Function of 1 Chronicles 23–27." *Journal of Biblical Literature* 110 (1991): 229–42.

Wright, John Wesley. "Guarding the Gates: 1 Chronicles 26:1-19 and the Roles of Gatekeepers in Chronicles." *Journal for the Study of the Old Testament* 48 (1990): 69–81.

Zadok, Ran. "On the Reliability of the Genealogical and Prosopographical Lists of the Israelites in the Old Testament." *Tel Aviv* 25 (1998): 228–54.

Zerafa, P. P. "'Il sacerdozio nell'antico Testamento." *Sacra doctrina* 60 (1970): 621–58.

Zimmerli, Walther. "The History of Israelite Religion." In *Tradition and Interpretation: Essays by Members of the Society for Old Testament Study*, ed. G. W. Anderson, 351–84. Oxford: Oxford University Press, 1979.

Subject Index

A

Aaron, 16, 105
Abiathar, 12, 16, 60, 88, 105
Abrahamic covenant, 98, 128
Ahio, 87, 105
All Israel (theme), 76, 77, 82, 85, 92, 95, 116, 117, 119, 130, 132,
Altar, 27, 68, 87, 100–101, 102, 111, 112, 114, 115, 121, 124, 126–127, 136
Anger, divine, 50, 129
Ark of the Covenant/Yahweh, 18, 85, 119–121, 128,
Asaph, 14, 21, 24, 27, 35, 38, 57, 58, 91, 96–97, 130, 138,
Assurnasirpal II, 67, 82
Atonement, 121, 133
Azitawadda inscription, 68

B

Babylonian exile, 69, 135
Biblical criticism. *See* Form-critical issues; Redaction criticism
Biblical sources, 1, 5, 6, 7, 11, 16, 51, 97
Blessing(s), 6, 31, 32, 43, 67, 68, 69, 70, 78, 82–83, 84, 95, 102, 103, 108, 112, 113, 115, 116, 119, 127, 128, 131
Blood, 93, 121, 133
Building projects, 67–68, 83, 85
Burnt offering, 93, 95, 126–127

C

Casting of lots, 71
Cedar, 64, 81, 120
Central sanctuary. *See* sanctuary
Centrality of Jerusalem, 123, 129, 138
Cereal offering, 93, 136
Chenaniah, 91, 107
Chief priest. See high priest(s)
Civil servants. *See* officials, non-cultic

Cleanliness and uncleanness. *See* purity and impurity
Clothing/clothes, 88, 93–94, 109
Commemorate, 28, 129
Community, 3, 4, 5, 6, 25, 50, 98, 106, 131
Compassion, divine, 125
Composition
    Of Chronicles, 1, 8, 11, 24, 39,
    Of Chronicles and Ezra-Nehemiah, 47–49
    Of the Psalm, 26, 40
Continuity, 2, 7–8, 25, 53–54, 55, 60, 73, 77, 79, 84, 98, 101, 104, 106, 116, 122–123, 137, 138
Covenant, 7, 25, 50, 54–55, 64, 69, 71, 72, 89, 96, 98, 114, 118, 119, 128–129, 138, 139
Cult
    Ark, the. *See* Ark of the Covenant
    Davidic ordering of, 3, 17, 27–29, 49, 60, 71, 73, 95, 96, 99–102, 114, 139
    Jerusalem cultus, 20–22, 24, 25, 27, 29, 51, 53, 56, 58–62, 95–96, 100–102, 103, 114–115, 117,
    Musicians, 15, 36, 50, 89–90, 93, 126, 138
    Officials, 18, 21, 54, 70, 88, 94, 100, 114, 115, 117, 119, 138,

D

Dancing, 37, 64, 94, 125
David–Solomon succession, 8, 61, 63, 80, 115,
Davidic prayer, 68, 72, 115, 131
Davidic promises, 64, 81
Dead Sea Scrolls, 3
Deuteronomistic, 3, 4, 6, 8, 16, 60, 63, 68
Dittography, 33, 34

Studies in Biblical Literature

This series invites manuscripts from scholars in any area of biblical literature. Both established and innovative methodologies, covering general and particular areas in biblical study, are welcome. The series seeks to make available studies that will make a significant contribution to the ongoing biblical discourse. Scholars who have interests in gender and sociocultural hermeneutics are particularly encouraged to consider this series.

For further information about the series and for the submission of manuscripts, contact:

Peter Lang Publishing
Acquisitions Department
P.O. Box 1246
Bel Air, Maryland 21014-1246

To order other books in this series, please contact our Customer Service Department:

(800) 770-LANG (within the U.S.)
(212) 647-7706 (outside the U.S.)
(212) 647-7707 FAX

or browse online by series at:

WWW.PETERLANG.COM